THE AFFORDABLE PORSCHE

PORSCHE

The complete guide to buying and running a low-cost Porsche

THE AFFORDABLE PORSCHE

PORSCHE

The complete guide to buying and running a low-cost Porsche

Iain Ayre

First published in August 2010

A catalogue record for this book is available from the British Library

ISBN 978 1 84425 099 8

Library of Congress catalog
card no 2004104455

Published by Haynes Publishing,
Sparkford, Yeovil, Somerset BA22 7JJ, UK
Tel: 01963 442030 Fax: 01963 440001
Int. tel: +44 1963 442030
Int. fax: +44 1963 440001
E-mail: sales@haynes.co.uk
Website: www.haynes.co.uk

Haynes North America Inc, 861 Lawrence Drive,
Newbury Park, California 91320, USA

Design and layout by James Robertson

Printed in USA

The exchange rate applied to quoted £ Sterling vs. $US prices is that applicable in early 2010.

All photographs copyright of the author unless otherwise stated.

WARNING

Acknowledgements

The names of many people who helped with this book over the last five years were lost due to emigration, a computer change, hard-drive issues and AOL cancelling old emails automatically. I personally appreciate every individual who took the time to help. If you're not mentioned, it's because the geeks and their evil electronic spawn lost your name, not because I wasn't grateful.

The last fact-check was carried out with enthusiasm by Stuart Davidson, who heads up the service department of Weissach Porsche in Vancouver. On my first visit there, a gleaming new Carrera was on the next hoist to a 914, so Weissach are genuinely happy to look after any Porsche, affordable or otherwise. They also sell Lotuses (Loti?) and Lamborghinis, so they're serious about amusing motor cars.

Stuart kindly said that he enjoyed the task of checking through *The Affordable Porsche*, and said it was both entertaining to read and made him want to go and buy an old Porsche just for fun, all of which is music to an author's ears.

Stuart's only major query was in connection with the model years of North American Porsches. The dates I have used are European, in common with other British-published books. Most Porsche models were available in Europe before they were available in North America, and a model year is not a calendar year. Americans also tend to refer more to model years, whereas Europeans prefer actual build dates.

Check out Weissach on www.weissach.com.

Coincidentally, the very last person to cast his eye over this *meisterwerk* before it ambled off to my remarkably patient editor at Haynes was also exactly the kind of reader at whom it's aimed. David Birchall is an ex-pat Brit living in Vancouver whose serious cars are much more upmarket vehicles such as a 1935 Bentley and a 1953 Aston, but he fancied a bit of cheap fun so he went to California to buy a 911. The car he came back with is a 1982 3-litre 911SC with 120,000 miles on it, which cost him $10,500.

The gearchange is agricultural and slow, the expensive stereo has been removed, and the car isn't actually as fast as you would think; but it's rust-free, it's in generally sound condition, it's worn in rather than worn out and he's enjoying charging around in it. He plans to replace the massive rear bumper with a GRP one, which will make a very useful improvement to the weight balance of the car, as well as looking better.

The paperwork for importing cars from the US into Canada is a minor bore: you have to wait for 24 hours after purchase before importing, to allow for theft checks etc. You also need full-time headlight illumination and a tech inspection, and as it's a European-built car you need to pay import tax. However, the hassle level is similar to importing into the UK, and saving $10,000 on the cost was well worth the effort.

▶ **Buying this 911SC in California and shipping it back to the UK would have come in under our ten-grand benchmark.**

Contents

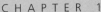

CHAPTER 1

The affordable Porsche

and how to find one

The Affordable Porsche is not an exhaustive library tome for information collectors. It's a practical look at how people with ordinary incomes can get their hands on something special for sensible money, and it takes a wide and shallow approach. Which parallels the increasing width and shallowness of the author, come to think of it.

Haynes have recently published the *Porsche Data Book*, written by Marc Bongers and translated out of the original German. I'd recommend investing in a copy, as it contains much more detailed specification info on all models than there's room for in this book.

Most people who want a Porsche want a 911, and the picture in most people's heads will be a '70s Carrera or a Turbo. To get the most out of this book, read all the 911 chapters and use the information and warnings to confirm or rethink what year is actually best for you. As an example, I have driven what many people would regard as the best possible Porsche, a 1972 Carrera. Very nice, but after researching this book and driving many Porsches the model I fancy most is a 1967/68 911, or a cheaper 912/6 (a 912 fitted with a six-cylinder 911 engine) which is more or less the same thing.

'Backdating' is an increasingly popular idea: take a less attractive but galvanised mid-year 911 and put earlier bumpers and trim on it. You can even forward-date the engine to 3 litres to create your ideal Porsche on a pick'n'mix basis – why not?

When it comes to actually viewing cars for sale, feel free to scan and print the buying advice in Chapter 14 and take it with you when you go to look at them.

It may not be welcome advice for Brits, but it's nonetheless the case that you should probably go to America to get the best value in 911s and 356s. Many of the later galvanised Porsches are quite cheap on both sides of the Atlantic anyway and last quite well in a wet and corrosive British

◀ **Prime Porker possibles – you just have to get your timing right.** [Porsche AG]

▲ California offers the best in 911s, both for choice and value. Like most European sports cars, they were exported to California in huge numbers.

environment, but all Porsches eventually rust, so a Stateside trip to find one with a really solid body makes sound economic sense. You get much better prices and much less rusty cars, so root out your passport and have a chat with your chequebook.

Much of the information in this book comes from real people in the Porsche world, and while I've done all I can to avoid any mistakes, the owners and repairers I've talked to have individual, differing and personal views about their experience of Porsches.

There is much contradictory crap written in books and magazines about Porsches: Haynes make considerable efforts to keep their authors accurate, and have in fact cornered me and beaten me with copies of Paul Frere's *Porsche 911 Story* in order to encourage accuracy. However, many publishers aren't bothered about accuracy, so beware of relying on what you find in some Porsche books. *The Affordable Porsche* has had to be partly rewritten before publication, largely because of inaccurate information in published books at the research stage. I believe you can trust the information in Haynes books, but when buying further books elsewhere on specific Porsche models, bear in mind that just because something has been printed does not mean it's true. That said, I'm pretty confident that any remaining whoopsies in *The Affordable Porsche* are minor and the basic recommendations stand.

Any published engine power figures from anywhere should only ever be taken as a rough overestimate: power figures are inevitably sourced, via books and magazines, from the manufacturers, so that's a Chinese whisper for a start. Even if manufacturers' bhp figures aren't straightforward porky-pies, you can bet that a manufacturer's power test engine, even if it were still standard, would be blueprinted, would be devoid of any

ancillaries, and would run on helpfully low-viscosity oil and at the perfect running temperature and humidity. In the real world, even a hot day is going to lose you several bhp anyway, so it's always wise to treat power figures with exactly the respect they deserve. Having said that, I believe that Porsche may be less prone to fluffing up bhp figures than most.

The Affordable Porsche as an idea was conceived as a result of my usual reaction to saloon bar wisdom. There is always a bloke in a pub who will tell you that buying and running a Porsche is impossible on an average income, and also that a 911 will slide off the road tail-first and kill you, even if you could afford one. Another bloke will also tell you with the same beer-induced air of experience and authority that a Shelby Cobra is unmanageably lethal. The Internet is also almost entirely written by blokes with information researched to saloon bar standards, so bear that in mind too. None of these people have ever driven either a 911 or a Cobra.

There's usually some truth at the bottom of pub wisdom, but when you chase down the rumours the real picture tends to be much less dramatic.

The 911's reputation for rear-end caprice is admittedly to some extent deserved. Volkswagen's People's Car started out with the engine hanging right out behind the rear axle line, but in a Beetle that really doesn't matter. Its handling is certainly poor, but nobody expects a Beetle to handle well, any more than they do a Trabant: that's not what they're for. I don't know whether a Trabant handles well or not, and I don't care. Nor does anybody else: much like the Beetle, the stinky but treasured compressed-fibre Trabi could trundle an East German worker off to his concrete-bicycle factory during the week and out for a picnic on a Sunday, and that would do very nicely.

Even in the later Karmann Ghia versions of the Volkswagen Beetle, the handling and performance are more or less irrelevant. If you ask a Karmann Ghia owner how their car handles on the edge, they will probably just look puzzled – it's likely to be the first time the question has ever come up. Rapid progress is simply not what they are for. They're cute, amusing and stylish, not fast, and if they handle like a shopping trolley it doesn't matter.

The very first Porsches took the Beetle floorpan off in a new direction, though – they were deliberately lightened to go faster. Although politically and financially necessary at the time, that design decision was a really big mistake in the choice of priorities, as the first task should have been to move the engine to a rear-mid position in front of the axle. The next 40 years or so were spent ingeniously bodging this essentially bad design.

And a damn good thing too. There is far too much dull, sensible motor engineering around, and hardly any individuality or eccentricity left. Somebody recently told me that they used some Kia Shuma parts on a Lotus Seven replica, and I don't even know what a Kia Shuma is. I don't need to know, either. I'm sure a Kia Shuma provides cost-effective shopping trips, and I'm also fairly sure that selecting nicely ripe avocados would be the most fulfilling and stimulating part of a shopping trip in a Kia Shuma.

The Porsche company displayed a dogged streak of individualist fun from the '50s up until the mid-'70s, when they decided it was time to replace the odd but characterful 911 with a much more sensible front-engined V8 cruiser, the 928. 'No thanks,' said their customers more or less in unison. 'We want more 911s.'

It was only in the late 1990s that the accountants finally got their way and the 911 was properly tamed. However, whether or not the car has lost its character will be the subject of the 2020 edition of *The Affordable Porsche* rather than the 2010 one.

As to the nasty handling of the older 911s that we can actually afford to buy, the truth is that the placing of a six-cylinder engine right at the back of the car does indeed have a pendulum effect once the tail has stepped properly out of line, and the chance of a big crash is always there. I know people who have crashed 911s without any apparent good reason. On the other hand, several other owners have said that their cars have hung on and stayed on the road when their driving mistakes had richly deserved a crash. One of them lifted off halfway through a corner when all four tyres were already squealing, and just got louder squealing as his early 911 hung on with its fingernails.

The sensible approach is to be aware of the unpredictability of the rear end, and if you are going to drive a 911 hard, take it out regularly on track days and just keep pushing it and pushing it until it spins. When you really know the warning signs well, you're prepared. Again on the bonus side of the 911 equation, if you are going to have a crash, hitting something tail-first is a very good crash to choose. With its strong monocoque, and with the rear-mounted engine hitting first and good seats giving neck support, there's a better chance of walking away from a pranged 911 than there is with most cars. In '70s rallying, it was a preferred option to try to go in tail-first if you were heading irrevocably for a biggie.

On the other hand, if you're just going to drive normally you needn't bother worrying about where the engine is. None of the 911-bashing pub gossips has ever thought deeply enough to realise that even with the handicap of the engine hanging off the back, a Porsche handles very well indeed compared to most cars, and if you can get as far as provoking a 911's tail end out of line, you would already have crashed if you were driving an ordinary car.

For fun and excitement, one does need some raw thrills, and the earlier the 911 the closer you are to the feel of the road. Of the serious 911 enthusiasts I've talked to, many have more than one 911, often from very different periods, and all of them say they enjoy driving the older cars much more. One or two leave their '90s Porsches in the garage and haul out a '60s 911 instead, even for long trips. Five-speed gearboxes are optional on the early cars, and make a huge difference to everyday drivability. You can genuinely use an old five-speed 911 for business. Okay, it's noisier and bumpier than a modern car, but it's not too bad, and it's also usable and reliable enough to use as a rational daily driver unless your entire life is spent on the road.

▼ **$8,750 buys you a solid 1980 911SC with some minor panel damage, but with a one-owner history and servicing by a speed shop rather than a dealer. A recent ring job should keep it going for a long time, and you can check for blue oil smoke and carry out a compression check just to be sure.**

▲ **An earlier 911 offers the purest of Porsche flat-six experience, and the pre-1970 cars can also still be bought for better prices than later more powerful and more popular models.**

With a 911 in particular, you are really still driving old style rather than modern style – you're not being wafted along almost as a passenger, remote from any feel of the road. The soundtrack from a wailing air-cooled flat six is pretty melodic, too. Like much of life, Formula One racing has become monumentally dull of late, not least because of the remarkable lack of danger involved. Barring a freak accident, an F1 driver can expect to hit the Armco at 150mph and walk away. If your life is also becoming too safe and controlled, a 911 will bring back an edge, if only for an hour or so.

What does 'affordable' mean? The rather arbitrary line has been drawn at around £10,000 Sterling or $16,000 American at early-2010 exchange rates. You can get a very usable Porsche for a lot less than that, and indeed some older and less popular models seem to offer spectacularly better value for money than a Ford Focus. If I didn't live in Canada I would have definitely made an offer on a low-miles late-model 924S that was for sale at a Porsche specialist in Manchester. This had 70,000 miles on the clock, it was in generally good condition, it was fast, smooth and stiff on the road, and it was on sale for £1,895. Lots of Porsche snobs will sneer at the 924 as being an Audi GT with a Volkswagen LT van engine, but the later 924s had a pure Porsche engine which had to be detuned because the old 924 was lighter and therefore faster than the new 944. Update the ECU on a Porsche-engined 924 and you've got most of that deleted power back, although the compression ratio on the detuned engine remains lower. The 924/944 is a good-looking 2+2 GT with near 50/50 weight balance, and it handled well enough to

deserve its own budget race series. This is a hell of a lot of car for two grand, and if you want the bonus of Porsche badges as well you've got a few thrown in for free.

You can also sometimes get better value at the other end of the money range by buying a better and later car for more than the 'affordable' budget – getting the best car you can find right from the start can sometimes save you a lot of money further down the line. For example, if you can stretch to a later and cleaner 911, that could be the most economical all-round long-term decision even if you're over budget for the initial purchase.

Porsche's legendary reliability has to be taken to some extent with a pinch of salt, as there's a natural tendency for enthusiasts to get carried away with unjustified praise. The 2.7-litre engine is a case in point. It was made of magnesium in the search for lightness, and the bore size and power may have been too much for the strength of the crankcase material: it doesn't work very well compared to Porsche's aluminium engines. The cylinder heads come loose and the crankcases leak oil, although those problems can be sorted out by respectively engineering new stud threads, by assembling the engine in the right order, and by putting a drip tray under the car. It's not a terminal problem, but it wasn't the pinnacle of Porsche's engineering achievements either.

Very early Porsches are unavoidably ancient now, and are still based on Palaeolithic Beetle engines. Don't expect too much from them in the way of reliability or performance, although they do seem to be pretty good compared with their early '50s contemporaries. Air-cooling gives you the benefit of less to go wrong, but it's not a very good way of cooling a car engine, and you may pay for that in other ways. Air-cooled Beetle enthusiasts, optimists all, are probably the worst for blind, ill-founded optimism, and will preach to you about their cars' utter reliability with fundamentalist fervour even when the spare engine they keep in the garage casts visible doubt on this. My worst few cars ever in terms of reliability have all been VWs – one a charming but temperamental split-screen camper van that blew an engine up annually, another a Golf that started nearly all the time, and the third a Scirocco Storm with random but inevitably disabling electrical faults. The Scirocco at least provided nice comfy leather seats on which to sit while waiting for the AA.

There will undoubtedly be some Porsche snobs who will sneer at this book as much as at the 924 and 914: their views are unimportant, as it's not written for them. When you dig around the Porsche world a little, you will find that some people just want to be seen in a new Porsche as a status statement, which is fine if that's what blows their frocks up. Fortunately, it has now become possible again to drive a Porsche without being pigeonholed as one of these boring brand-junkie fashion victims. The 911 has been fully socially rehabilitated, but there was a time when it was compulsory for every City yobbo with a sharp charcoal suit and white socks to drive from Essex into London EC1 early each morning in a red 911. In the short term, Porsche sold a lot of cars to these boys, but the 911 came to be associated with a fairly dodgy class of people, and by the time the bubble burst and the City bonuses evaporated nobody else would be seen dead in one. A similar fate overtook the Ford Capri, but Ford are far less vulnerable to fashion

than a sports car company. The same is happening to BMW right now: if the people who drive your cars wear baseball caps the wrong way round, you no longer have a premium product.

Porsche went through a hard time in the 1990s, but the Boxster seems to have taken the company back to its roots – simple, fast fun, good handling, and good value. It's not cheap, but then good engineering just isn't cheap. It's often good value, though.

The move to selling a Porsche-branded VW Tuareg/Cayenne pimp jeep is raking in some quick cash, but it may be a bad idea in the long term. Mercedes can get away with flogging vans and Tunisian taxis as well as posh cars, but if you think

▲ If you're not fixated on a 911, you don't even have to fly to SoCal. This sound 924S – with the Porsche rather than the VW van engine – was on a specialist Manchester dealer forecourt for £1,895. I'd have bought it myself, if I didn't live in Canada.

◄ There are four main differences between a 912 and a 911: two fewer cylinders, badging, two fewer dash clocks on early ones, and a 50 per cent discount on the cost. The two cars are otherwise pretty well identical. You do probably have to go to LA for a good one, though.

▲ The 914 is a light, agile, mid-rear-engined, VW-based Porsche convertible that's only let down by serious rust and a weedy engine. Buy a California one to avoid the rust, and then pop a 250bhp Beetle engine or a V8 in to liven up the straight-line performance – job done.

about it there are no Lotus, Maserati, Ferrari or even Alfa Romeo vans, or people carriers, or pimp jeeps. Too much devaluation of the brand could do some serious damage in the middle and long term – we'll have to wait and see. There is a rumour that the VW Tuareg could also be branded as a Lamborghini, which would cripple Cayenne sales to people trying to buy status through car badges. A Lambo Cayenne/Tuareg for the school run…? Go and listen to some Stuttgart graves and you'll hear spinning noises. Whatever, the best of luck to them.

The point of the above digression is that times change, and not always for the worse: if you're of the generation that associates Porsches with cocaine-fuelled Thatcherite vulgarity, that's fading away now and you can drive an older one without embarrassment. If you drive a Porsche in Britain, you may even be let out of a side-road into traffic nowadays – ten years ago you'd have had no chance.

You will definitely be very wise to join a club. Apart from the obvious savings to be made by knowing where to obtain things and to get done, it's the best way to find a good car. There are certainly Porsche snobs in the clubs, but I haven't met any during my research. The Independent Porsche club in the UK seems to cater more for hands-on enthusiasts than the main Porsche GB club, but many people belong to and enjoy both. The people I've met researching this book are primarily petrolheads who enjoy and appreciate the engineering that has gone into Porsches. They have all been friendly and down-to-earth, and I've enjoyed talking to them. If you decide you really fancy a 914 or whatever, the best move you can make is to join a club, find out who are the hard-core 914 people, and tell them you seriously want one. They will take this as a challenge and will

often find you a good and already well-known car from within the club membership, or will happily give up Saturday mornings to help you to hunt down a good one. This is fun for them – they enjoy using their knowledge to investigate potential new club cars, and they are always pleased to welcome another enthusiast.

Sadly, I'm going to upset some Porsche club enthusiasts with this book, because I have no particular loyalty to any specific model or to the Porsche company. My contract is with you, because you have bought this book, and some of my suggested ways to achieve the sort of Porsche you want are definitely not going to appeal to either concours enthusiasts or true Porsche fanatics. I may not be served with a fatwa as such, but I'd say there's a good chance of at least a thinwa.

For example, the 912 section of the Orange Coast area of the Porsche Club of America, nice chaps all, think the 912 is the best thing since Helena Bonham-Carter. They also think that using a 912 as a cheap route to a 911-style car is satanic, because the 912 is a fine car in its own right, and they believe that all 912s should be preserved and respected. In a sense they're right – the lighter four-cylinder engine balances the misplaced weight behind the axle better. However, it doesn't have the wail or the punch of a six, the engine isn't especially powerful or long-lived, and although values are rising there are still 912s being scrapped because they're not worth restoring. So – take a rough 912 that has no future, sort out its rust and other problems, fit a home-rebuilt flat six 911 engine and you have achieved a nice affordable period Porsche 911, more or less. If you've rescued your 912/911 hybrid from being crushed for scrap, nobody can reasonably bitch about what you do with it. The resulting car will never be worth as much as a 'proper' 911, but who cares? It's yours and it was affordable.

It will also cause upset when I recommend plastic replicas of Speedsters as an excellent option. You can't afford a genuine Speedster, or you wouldn't be reading this. You might well seriously fancy a genuine 356 from the 1950s; I certainly do. They offer great kitsch bathtub cuteness, they're a lot more competent than you would think, the thin and spindly steering wheel offers light, sensitive steering to match the rest of the controls, the whole car is simple enough to be relatively reliable for a very old machine, and you can fix them yourself. However, body repairs are hugely expensive, and from an ethical standpoint repairs should be done properly because of the rarity and increasing historic importance of the cars. The prices of genuine second-hand replacement 356 parts are stratospheric, and your budget of ten grand will only get you a fairly rough coupé. An affordable 356 is thus possible, but it's unlikely to be good value.

A Beetle-based Speedster replica, on the other hand, gets you virtually a brand new Speedster for the same sort of money. The bodywork is GRP, so it's light and strong and will never deteriorate. The engine is the Beetle variant of your choice, so you can go for a 912 engine for some sort of authenticity or a 2,500cc injected VW desert buggy engine for serious thrills, or even a turbocharged Subaru flat four. Some replicas use floorpans from genuine old Beetles, so on a budget you can't get much closer to a 356 than that. (Some replicas have a dedicated tubular steel chassis, a marked improvement over original or Beetle-floored cars.) The entire mechanicals are usually overhauled when the cars are built, and the second-hand price for a good UK replica such as a Chesil is between £7,500 and £12,000 depending on the specifications. In Canada you can buy a Speedster replica built to a very high standard by the Intermeccanica company, still run by Frank Reisner's son Henry. Intermeccanica used to build fabulous swoopy Italian-bodied Pininfarina-designed GT cars that used Detroit muscle, went like greased greyhounds and cost a fortune, so the Intermeccanica badge on their Speedsters is seriously exclusive and exotic to those who know.

Affordability doesn't necessarily mean buying cheaply, particularly where running costs over time are concerned. It does mean buying wisely, though. Many of us would be looking for a Porsche purely for personal solo weekend fun, and on

an average income there's a limit to how much you can reasonably spend on a toy or a hobby, particularly if you're married.

The domestic financial politics of buying a serious or seriously silly car is discussed in my last book for Haynes, *The Kit Car Manual*. Kit cars have evolved way beyond nasty Cobra replicas built out of dead Ford Cortinas, and are now concerned with extreme speed and handling. Three seconds to 60, and 160mph (255kph), are now commonplace. Many kit cars are used on the track, some for fun and some for serious racing, and when somebody wants a competitive racing engine they have to get a £5,000 bill past their beloved wife or girlfriend. One domestic-finances manoeuvre that has proved politically successful is to make a very big deal

▲ Even if this were an ordinary Speedster rather than a rare and intriguing roadster, we couldn't afford it. Shame, as it's cute. A 365 coupé is possible, but really good ones are out of reach.

◄ Perhaps we can't afford a real Speedster, but a good quality replica such as an Intermeccanica is within reach, and is stronger, pretty similar in character and astonishingly cheap to run. Financially, it's a Beetle that will never rust, with spares at hobby-car prices.

▲ The 928 has gone straight from supercar to three-grand banger, and apart from the electrics is as dependable as annual snow chaos in England. It's also capable of nearly 170mph and costs a few hundred pounds a year on classic insurance. Get one before everybody else finds out.

out of the First Task of the 911, or the Caterham Seven, or whatever impractical and expensive toy we're talking about. This first task, planned together for ages and in detail, will be to take the wife in question on a trip to Paris/Venice/wherever, during which she will be fed on chocolates and champagne and will be driven around looking cool and rich and being visibly envied by Parisiennes and other women who are not in a very expensive-looking sports car. Most wives will at least think about that one: they know perfectly well what you're up to, but you may well get away with it anyway if you handle the deal with style.

A couple of decades of kit car life have also revealed that the way to increase your car budget and maintain domestic bliss is to add to the global budget the price of a new kitchen. A touch of luxury splurging on, say, granite worktops and a branded fan oven puts you in a top domestic political position when, for example, you need a set of proper Fuchs alloys. Top wheels, but they come at a price which may not initially make complete sense to a wife or girlfriend, until balanced against the cost of her granite worktop. New bathroom tiling is also politically astute – it's cheap, it's quite quick and it gains many Brownie points.

It has to be said that some Original Equipment parts for older Porsches can come with very nasty price tags. Oddly enough the newer cars can be a lot cheaper for parts, as modern production thinking has brought unit manufacturing costs down: a Boxster bonnet is £300 compared to £700 for a 911 one. Bear in mind that Porsche profits have recently reached a billion dollars for the first time, and they didn't achieve that by selling stuff cheap.

However, as one Porsche owner who also runs an Austin-Healey Sprite points out, Porsche-made

parts actually fit. You don't have to spend any time filing them to shape and sanding mating surfaces flat – you just bolt them on and they work. The longevity of Porsche parts is also a very important aspect of the value equation. If something costs three times as much but works three times as long, that's a good deal as long as you're planning to keep the car for a while.

Another creative approach to budgeting is to rearrange your fleet and its finances to incorporate a Porsche into them. Most weekend fun cars require you to own a sensible car as well: you can't go shopping in a Frogeye and you can't shoot off for a romantic long weekend in the mountains in a roofless Lotus Seven either. However, you can both go shopping and cross continents in most types of Porsche – so you don't need to waste money on 15 grands' worth of newish Toyota as well. If your weekend Porsche is genuinely a usable alternative car, there's no reason why you can't sell the newish daily driver and run a relatively worthless middle-aged Corolla or whatever during the week. It will probably be almost as reliable as a new Corolla if you get one that's merely ageing rather than knackered, and you won't have to waste time on washing it or looking after it.

However, creative budgeting is only really needed at the upper end of the affordable budget Porsche market, where you're maybe trying to get the best 911 you can achieve. If you can find the sort of Porsche action you're looking for at the bottom end of the market, the cost can really be astonishingly low and you won't have to sell anything at all.

The 914, for example, has a VW Variant engine and is regarded with contempt by many Porsche enthusiasts. However, it's low, light and genuinely mid-engined, so it's a very capable performer in its own right, and makes the most of its low-powered Beetle-derived engine. Less affordable is the rare and sought-after '914/6', which is a 914 with a mid-rear-mounted 911 flat six and is probably what the 356-911 family should have been all along. One Los Angeles owner bought a 914 new, drove it for a couple of weeks, decided the engine was a joke and crammed a Chevy small-block in it. The resulting monster is still on the road and still provides a top blend of fear and joy for its owner. Another '914/8' discovered in LA has a 600bhp alloy Chevrolet engine fitted as well as a serious semi-hidden rollcage, and now gets some astonishing dragstrip times. A 914 with a more powerful VW engine is also a good cheap and easy option.

Likewise available for pocket money is the 924. Earlier VAG van-engined ones are very much frowned upon by status-conscious Porsche

enthusiasts. However, the VW LT van engine was well developed by Audi and used in several car applications, and is cheap and strong. Still devalued by the uncool van-engine business, the largely forgotten Porsche-engined 924S is also available for peanuts, even though it comes with a pure-bred Porsche 2.5-litre four that has a reasonable claim to being spiritually half of a 928's V8. The 924S still has visibly Audi door handles and so on, but that's a silly reason for boycotting a top bargain Porsche. 944 values also suffer from association with the 924, but the 944 is a supremely competent and very fast car, and even more fun in turbo form.

The 928 offers low-budget fun as well, depending on your approach. These were very expensive new, and remain very complicated. They were never really popular, and they've now gone straight from supercar to banger. Buying a 928 means you can get a superb and gleaming low-miles 150mph supercar if you apply most of your notional ten grand to it, but you can also pick up a rough but usable example for just a few thousand. The electrics may not all work, but they may not have worked when it was new.

Add your few hundred pounds for classic insurance and just drive and enjoy it until something big goes wrong. The bill will undoubtedly be more than the car is worth, so at that point you can scrap it to help out other 928 owners and to boost your 928 fund, and then go out and buy another one.

Even within the world of the 911 there are some bargains to be had. Anybody who is trying to sell a faded left-hand-drive 1975 911 Targa with large and hideous bumpers and a Sportomatic gearbox is going to be very tempted by a relatively small wad of notes waved in front of him, and you can then throw the gearbox away and fit a proper one. Apart from a few tricky mechanical aspects, the

911 is a do-it-yourself mechanic's car – even after all this time the engine is still basically held in by four bolts.

Affordability and availability vary greatly depending on which side of the Atlantic you call home. For the really cheap Porsches, buying in the UK costs more or less the same as in North America, and they're mostly in convenient right-hand drive anyway. If you're going to pay £2,000 for a good 924, there's no point in going to California to buy the same car for the same sort of money. On the other hand, if you want to get the best 356 or 911, you're definitely looking at a trip to the States.

A sideways approach is to check out prices in Germany and Belgium, which can sometimes be a lot cheaper than in the UK, although you still get rust problems. Those and American cars are all left-hand drive, but does that really matter? LHD is actually no big deal in practical terms, but in the UK it can offer you a useful 20–30 per cent price discount. Forty years ago, the UK had lots of A-roads with fairly light traffic, no speed limit and no speed cameras. To make fast progress you simply had to pull halfway out into the other lane, check that there was enough space to overtake, boot it to get past quickly and safely and be on your way. A left-hand-drive car was a nuisance because you had to hang an extra four feet out on the wrong side of the road before you could see what was coming, although staying further back obviously cut the risk because it allowed you to see more.

Those days are over, though – the only real disadvantage of LHD these days is getting tickets out of automatic car park machines. If you're really too lazy to get out of the car, just drive through the ticket gate backwards. Which is top fun anyway.

The few remaining A-roads now carry so much

▲ **Dunkel's annual Los Angeles Porsche swapmeet is a top place for enthusiasts to sell bits and pieces to each other at generally reasonable prices, and there are some good cars on sale as well.**

▲ Having been made by Porsche in the first place, rust-free California body panels, even if slightly wrinkled, will fit a lot better than cheap new ones.

traffic that there's no longer any point in overtaking anything just to gain 20 feet, and if you do see a clear stretch, you can bet there's a camera waiting for you. On motorways it makes no difference at all which side of the car you're sitting on. This doesn't apply to foreign trucks on British motorways, whose drivers can't see much at all behind or to the right even if they're bothering to look: keep your wits about you these days and be ready for exhausted Hungarian truckers lurching out into the overtaking lanes without any warning.

LHD also offers the advantage of being on the correct side of the car when driving in France, where they have lots of empty *Routes Nationales*, and where you can still enjoy some serious driving on smooth and entertaining roads if you plan your journeys well. Weird, incomprehensible French country-road junctions seem to make more sense from an LHD car, which is a small bonus.

The idea of buying a car in the US is initially rather daunting for a Brit, but is not such a big deal in reality: Chapter 14 has the info you need. Like all these things, it's relatively easy when you know how.

For any really old Porsche, whether a 356 derivative or an early 911, your worst problems are availability and rust. In the UK, if you see a Speedster on the road it's a replica. There are a few 356 coupés in Britain, but they're rare and expensive – most good ones will be well over the £10,000 budget. In the Los Angeles area, though, you will see daily-driver 356s in restaurant and mall car parks – California is where many of them were sold to, and the 30 per cent humidity and almost constant sunshine means that a reasonably well looked after car rusts extremely slowly. The same applies to early 911s, which are essentially developed 356 coupés with more modern shell styling and engineering, and six-cylinder engines. An earlier 912 is a 911 fitted with a late 356 engine.

They all do rust eventually, but you have a very good chance of finding early Porsches in California that have no serious rust at all. Even our featured 356, abandoned for 20 years in a Los Angeles garden, just had a few bubbles around the edges of its boot and bonnet – no floor rust and no wing rust at all.

Something that has come as a surprise to me since moving to Vancouver is the lack of vehicle rust there compared to the UK, despite the significantly greater rainfall and high humidity of western Canada. My own 1958 Chevy Delray is lace-edged in places, but the chassis is still rock solid. Looking at cars in Chicago, on the other hand, most older ones have gaping holes where the bodywork has rotted through. There's no MOT in the US or Canada, so a car can just be driven until it collapses. The air in Chicago and the Great Lakes area is filthy because of huge and dirty industry, and it seems that the air in the UK is similar. Acid rain is not a fashionable worry these days, but acid rain falling on old Porsches is bad news with or without media attention. This all means it can be worth looking for a clean-air area to buy your car, and the western states of the USA are going to be top sources for clean bodyshells. The climates in California, Arizona, Nevada, Utah and even up as far as Oregon, Washington and British Columbia seem to protect rather than destroy steel bodywork.

Los Angeles air is now apparently squeaky clean, because factories have for years faced massive fines for emitting any pollutants: the last smog alert was 15 years ago. The Los Angeles area also has about the highest ratio of Porsches per square foot in the world. The cost of a Porsche hunt in the Los Angeles basin can also be re-budgeted as an annual family holiday, and is therefore theoretically free, as you've got to pay for a holiday every year anyway. Disneyland, Knott's Berry Farm, Universal Studios and staying near one of the LA beaches such as Redondo Beach will also usefully occupy a family while you get down to the serious business of a 911 hunt.

The pre-galvanised Porsches are definitely better bought as rust-free as possible, and then protected when they arrive in the UK. The galvanised shells should be fine in the UK, though, shouldn't they? Sadly, no. Galvanising merely delays rust rather than stopping it. In the UK this protection lasts for around 30 years or so, which means that 911s from the '70s are just about ready to crumble. You need to know that partly corroded ex-galvanised steel is something of a bitch to weld, if you're planning any MIG-welding action on your own.

The downside of the California sunshine is

the UV and heat damage to paint and trim. The reason why you get plastic seats and imitation wood trim on even fairly upmarket American cars is that the sun destroys leather and veneer in just a few years. This would be a problem for a serious vintage Porsche enthusiast in the US, as replacing a 356 interior with the correct replica trim is a very expensive prospect. However, as an *affordable* Porsche enthusiast you can use cracked and sun-damaged seats as a lever to knock the price down, and the car can then be retrimmed back in the UK, where good second-hand Porsche trim is relatively plentiful as the occasional day of weak and sporadic British sunshine is much kinder to plastics. Anybody scrapping a rotten UK Porsche may have a good interior going for a reasonable price. More ambitiously, you can buy a second-hand sewing machine, strip the seats to their bones and then retrim them in vinyl or even in leather yourself, based on identical copying of the original seat panels and construction. This is skilled work, but achievable for an amateur with patience and practice – just make a start with the least visible panels.

If the sun has burned the paint right off, some of the cars you're considering buying will look horrible. This will be reflected in the price you have to pay and also in a lower UK import duty and VAT bill, and you will get a better look at the condition of the body the less paint there is on it. Budget £3,000 for a reasonable respray, and knock that off the price you're prepared to pay for the car.

Something useful I've discovered recently is that American car dealers check the compression of everything that comes on to the forecourt. They know very well that a mileage reading is as

worthless as a manifesto promise, and they also know that a highway-cruised 200,000-mile car can be in fine mechanical condition. The compression test reveals bore and piston wear and the condition of the head and valve gear. If there's good compression and there are no unpleasant knocking or rattling noises, the engine is probably in good shape. A compression tester costs about £15.

Shipping to the UK is not a big deal. Ideally the car will be drivable – or pushable if you've bought a project – and can be loaded on a roll-on, roll-off ferry to be shipped to a UK port. You then pay customs duty and VAT, convert the indicators to show yellow, get a UK period-related registration and off you go.

The concept of the affordable Porsche, then, goes from around £1,000 for a rough but functional 924 up to £10,000 plus, which gets you a usable older 911. If you want one you can have one: here's how.

▲ **Anybody for a very fast shopping jeep with a 911 front end bodged on to it? Thanks, but no thanks.**

◀ **The tower block in the middle of this picture is the bridge of a container ship: it seems remarkable that they don't fall over. Consolidated container shipping, where your car waits to go with a batch of others, offers the best transatlantic value.**

CHAPTER 2

911: 1963–70

the prime porkers

Affordability rating ★★★

When most people think of a Porsche, they think of a 911. When they decide they really want a Porsche, what they want is also usually a 911. This is good, in that lots were made and sold and there are lots about, but also bad, in that everybody wants the good ones so they're expensive.

Our budget of £10,000 can potentially get us something quite good, but the first task is to sort out which 911 is best for you as an individual. The 911 was made from 1963 to 1996 (1998 in North America) so it gradually evolved into something quite different, although retaining its integrity throughout. The first 911 was an air-cooled flat six performance sports car with the engine behind the rear axle, and so was the last 911. It shares this integrity of concept with only a few car models: the Chevrolet Corvette has kept its two-seater rear-drive layout, its over-powered V8 and its spirit intact. (If you think a 911 has a frisky tail in the wet, have a play with a 1960s Corvette.) In contrast, Ford's Mustang lost its way horribly in the 1970s, with grotesque styling and feeble engines, and it's now stopped evolving and become a replica of itself – so it's to Porsche's credit that they kept the faith for as long as they did.

Porsche's Targa concept is a semi-convertible with a soft or hard detachable roof section and either a glass or a soft plastic rear window. Targas are cheaper and well worth considering for a pure road car, even if the styling is somewhat clumsy. The centre section of the roof comes off and leaves behind what is effectively a big roll-over bar behind your head. The Targas also have a stronger sill section to compensate to some extent for the missing roof, and the end result is quite stiff, for an open-top. Targas do leak, however, and a replacement seal kit from Porsche costs £500.

◄ **The early 911 is conceptually quite pure and possibly the most rewarding to drive.**
[Porsche AG]

BASICS

Body:	Non-galvanised, later galvanised, steel monocoque coupé and Targa.
Engine:	Rear-mounted light alloy air-cooled flat six.
Gearbox and transmission:	Four- or five-speed all-synchro depending on year and model.
Suspension:	Front, independent MacPherson struts, lower wishbones, longitudinal torsion bars. Later, anti-roll bars. Rear, independent, semi-trailing arms, torsion bars, telescopic shocks.
Steering:	Unassisted rack and pinion.
Brakes:	Discs all round.

Fuller specifications and further detailed technical information can be found in Chapter 15.

Fortunately there are aftermarket alternatives, and quite a lot can be achieved towards a good seal by adjustment.

Whatever 911 period you choose, it would be wise to read and familiarise yourself with the buying and owning advice in all the 911 chapters, as the 911 remains basically the same car throughout and much 1967 advice is just as valid for later cars.

The early cars offer lightness, a revvy engine, a direct feel to the controls and response to the road, good economy and reliability, a shorter and more twitchy wheelbase, simplicity and period good looks. Nowadays, they would also be regarded as more upmarket than the rather leerier later cars.

EVOLUTION

1963	Launched in September.
1965	Targa option introduced.
1967	Wider track, uprated S option with more power, less weight, rear anti-roll bar and Fuchs alloy wheels optional.
1968	911T appears – iron barrels, lower compression, lower price. 911L (lux) has vented discs. Sportomatic gearbox appears.
1969	Wheelbase lengthened by 2.224in, wider track on some models, wider body flares on all, Bosch injection appears on E and S models. Unsuccessful hydropneumatic front suspension introduced on E (can be replaced by torsion bars).

HISTORY

The 911 that originally evolved from the 356 was 5in longer than the Speedster-period cars, and a couple of inches narrower. The suspension was by torsion bar with tubular shocks all round, and the rear axle now had jointed driveshafts rather than a swing axle. The engine was a flat six with an aluminium casing containing seven main bearings lubricated by a dry-sump system, and fuel was provided by two triple-choke Solex carbs. 1967 seems to have been an excellent vintage for 911s, with 130bhp and a light car providing a top blend of power and delicacy.

Way ahead of its time was the optional five-speed box with a dogleg first gear left over from racing. The idea is that in racing you only use first gear once, at the start. It's something of an affectation to retain the dogleg gearchange in a road car, but even if it's irritating at first, you soon get used to it.

The wheels in the early days were 15in steels with 165x15 tyres. Not much rubber on the road, but at least the tyres were radials. The front end was light enough to feel unstable to most people. Large blobs of cast iron were fitted on each side of the front bumper to provide a fairly effective but somewhat low-tech solution. At about the same period, people were loading a layer of bricks into the front luggage compartments of their Hillman Imps for just the same reason.

Early Solex carbs were floatless, and suffered from flat spots and complaints – so they were changed to Zeniths.

The Targa was introduced in 1965.

The 1967 911S offered 160bhp compared to the ordinary 911's 130bhp.

In 1968 the budget 911T appeared, with cheaper detailing and 110bhp. The 911E was then the standard version and the 911S the faster one. The wheelbase was lengthened by a couple of inches in 1969, which improved the rear end's twitchy tendencies.

HANDS ON –
The rally driver's view

Commander Eoin Sloan says buy a pre-'70 911 for value and fun. He's an ex-Navy engineer, and likes the precision and quality of the older Porsches. His own silver rallying car is showing the traditional signs of competition with cracking at the back of the sills, but he'll happily repair it and carry on spanking the car most weekends.

The aim of weekend rallying and classic rallying is to keep the car to precisely the right speed over a timed distance, and for that you need a car that's agile, very competent on wiggly roads, pretty strong and also powerful enough for a burst of speed when you screw up the route and need to catch up big time. You also need a car that makes a nice noise and is fun to drive hard. Fun being the central purpose of weekend motorsport, as well as trying to win.

The cut-off year for the 911 is 1972 as far as Eoin's concerned, as the car then began to get heavier, with big tombstone seats, power steering and so on. He says look at earlier T, L, E and S models and don't bother to differentiate between them – the condition of the individual car you're looking at is much more important. Competition versions of the earlier 911 are about if you look for them, but most of the 'competition' 911s are a matter of delete options, with the interiors and so on stripped out to save weight. Unbolting and removing trim is much easier than paying lots more money for a car on which Porsche did exactly the same job in 1967.

A really clean 1968 911T is going to cost around the £15–16,000 mark in the UK. Eoin reckons that gets you the best of the 911 experience anyway, and he isn't quite clear about why people would pay more for the later heavier and more civilised cars. The early ones give you a shorter, twitchier chassis and a good power-to-weight ratio, and you get to feel everything that's going on through the controls and the seat. Can't argue with that – make sure you try an earlier 911 as well as the usual mid-'70s ones.

HANDS ON – The owner's view

Jeff Jeeves is a British early-911 owner, but also runs a 993 Carrera 4 and a 1985 3.2 as well as his 1967 911, so his views are eminently worth listening to.

He says it's definitely sensible to buy one as early as a 1967, because it's mechanically simple, the parts are relatively cheap and available, and it's more fun than the Carrera. He has had no handling worries, and does drive the car quite hard. Even the first time he backed off the throttle halfway round a corner didn't cause a skid, although he was expecting one: that came as a nice surprise. It's best to take any newly acquired 911 out on a few track days to find out when it's going to let go in hard cornering. A normal non-Porsche 1965 sports car will start skidding early on in a hard corner, but controllably – there's simply not much grip. A 911 will hang on significantly better, but will then let go much more rapidly. The same applies to crossply versus radial tyres.

PRODUCTION 1963–70

Porsche 911/911T/911S
1964–68/1967–68/1966–68

911 Coupé	6,607
911 Targa	236
911T Coupé	1,611
911T Targa	789
911S Coupé	3,573
911S Targa	925

Additionally 82 '901' coupés before name changed to 911

Porsche 911T/911E/911S (2-litre)
1968–69

911T Coupé	1,611
911T Targa	789
911E Coupé	1,968
911E Targa	858
911S Coupé	1,492
911S Targa	614

Porsche 911L
1967–68

Coupé	1,169
Targa	444

Porsche 911T/911E/911S (2.2-litre)
1969–71

911T Coupé	11,019
911T Targa	6,000
911E Coupé	3,028
911E Targa	1,848
911S Coupé	3,154
911S Targa	1,496

You can genuinely maintain an early 911 yourself, according to Jeff. You just have to learn its weird layout and peculiarities. Porsche parts are also easy to deal with – buy a Porsche part and it just bolts on, whereas with his MG Midget, everything has to be filed and fiddled with before it fits.

If you can't stomach the cost of a pro engine rebuild, it can make a lot of sense to collect second-hand bits and work on a spare engine yourself. Jeff's car is in top nick and works beautifully, but he has still collected a spare engine, carbs, bumpers and so on.

Jeff bought his 911 in California for $6,000 eleven years ago, and it would have cost a lot more in the UK: currently he thinks it's worth about £15,000. In some ways it would even now make sense to stretch up to that level to get a really good early 911, because Jeff's initial careful and quite expensive purchase means he can just drive and enjoy his car without having to pay big maintenance and repair bills. His advice to us all is to buy the best you can. Jeff has no problem driving an LHD car, and says it's only a problem if you're tailgating before overtaking, which is stupid anyway. He makes a very good point: if you're far enough back to leave some accelerating room for overtaking, sitting an extra three feet over in the left-hand seat won't make a significant difference to how far ahead you can see. The only problem then is some fool tailgating you because he thinks you're not going to overtake at all. For motorway and urban driving, Jeff doesn't even notice which side of the car he's on.

Another advantage of the older cars is the cost of classic insurance, which offers excellent deals for old performance cars. A newer Porsche would carry a stonking insurance bill, but provided that Jeff keeps another car insured (which could be a disposable Daewoo or something equally insurance-premium-friendly) the insurance on the 911 with unlimited miles, comprehensive with agreed value, costs him £160.

He particularly likes the purity of the early shape, and appreciates the way the 993 and 996 have been cleaned up to return to that simple styling, with even the tea-tray spoiler disappearing back into the bodywork. He thinks the Speedster was way ahead of its time, and highly approves of the modern replicas, which offer people the Speedster experience without getting involved in having to look after an ancient car.

The very earliest 911s ran on Solex carbs, and these can cause grief. Jeff's car runs Webers with a

tunable choke for each cylinder, and he relies on the very experienced Tony at Redline Tuning in Langley, Middlesex, to keep the engine on song. The car retains its advertised 130bhp, it runs beautifully, and Jeff gets 25mpg out of it driving locally, and about 20mpg if he gives it some exercise. This he does as often as he can, because it's so nice to drive. The controls are all light and sensitive, and also very well balanced – the steering, gears, clutch and brake are all as light as each other.

Although Jeff likes his car just the way it is, because it has never been messed about with and he has most of its history going right back, he says it's a very sensible idea to apply some later Porsche upgrades to early 911s, particularly if they've already been altered to some extent or if they don't have much history. In essence, the lighter early shell gets a lot more out of 200bhp than a later and heavier car would.

Problems and warnings? Nothing major. The heater is either on or off, and tends to cook your foot. The clutch release has been a minor nuisance.

WHAT TO LOOK FOR

STRUCTURE
Structurally, there are many potential rust problems with early 911s, which is why it's worth going to California to buy a car. Structural crumblings include sills, floors, inner wings, fuel tank area, and up

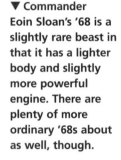

▼ Commander Eoin Sloan's '68 is a slightly rare beast in that it has a lighter body and slightly more powerful engine. There are plenty of more ordinary '68s about as well, though.

into the inner rear wings, and of course the bolt-on front wings and the join between them and the body. The rear wings include the slam panel and door catch mounts, so check them. The areas around the lights at either end of the car are also vulnerable, as water can creep in and rot them out. Screen rubbers front and rear can perish and leak, taking out the front bulkhead and the rear wings. The repair of screen seal leak damage at each end tends to cost around £1,200. This is particularly important for imported California cars, because the rubbers don't last well in hot dry air. That doesn't matter if the cars remain in San Diego. However, import them into the acid rain of Manchester and the cracked rubbers start leaking and rusting out the bodywork as soon as it lands on the dockside.

It's essential to pull out the front boot carpet before buying, to see what's going on in the rust and dirt traps beneath, but once the carpet's out leave it out if you buy the car – you don't need to keep a reservoir for damp in there.

Galvanised cars fare better, but galvanising did not start until 1971 and was only applied to the floorpan. In any case, once galvanic corrosion has eaten the zinc it starts on the steel underneath. Best advice on buying any Porsche is to stretch to the best car structurally that you can afford, unless you like a challenge and enjoy welding.

One thing to point out is that if you can actually see a few visible rust bubbles on a panel, the rust

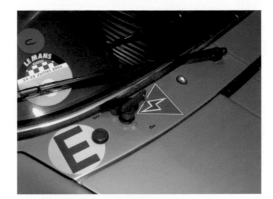

◄ Some competition prep requires an off-switch for the electrics to avoid a fire. This is also a useful anti-theft device, as it isolates the battery completely.

◄ Cars with a competition history quite often develop this crack on the rear end of the sills. It's not a huge problem, but add the repair cost to the budget if you're buying one.

◄ Check also for a crack at this corner of the boot lid aperture where the body flexes under stress.

▲ Jeff Jeeves has three 911s, but his favourite is the old '67. The new cars are faster and smoother but lack the driver involvement provided by the shorter, older cars.

▶ The rear edge of the door should have a perfectly parallel shut line. The rear wing is single-skin: prone to rust, but also relatively easy to repair.

▶ ▶ The front edge of the door and shut line should also look like this. Front wings are detachable, which makes home repair easier.

beneath is always worse than it looks. When the few bubbles are cleaned out back to solid metal, a quarter-inch bubble will turn into a four-inch hole. Whatever interior steel panel is lurking underneath that bubbled exterior panel may have an eight-inch hole in it. In many ways it's better to buy a cheap and horrible car with big visible holes, rather than quite a nice-looking 911 with a few rust bubbles. The latter will obviously cost a lot more to buy, but in reality will finish up in a similarly horrible state once you've cut all the rust out.

The front-end metalwork on an early 911 is single-skin, which is a bonus as you can largely see what's going on there. Many cars have been damaged and repaired at the front, and you should carefully check the symmetry of the inner wings and spare wheel well. If it all looks spot-on, it's either original or has been properly restored, which comes to the same thing.

It's worth taking the sill tread plates off to see what's going on with the sills, as the local air wherever the car drives is passed through the sills

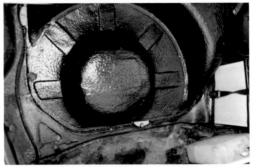

◀ Looking underneath, the front edge of the luggage compartment and bumper support areas are clean and solid. Again, single-skin panels make life easier.

◀ The spare wheel well is a water trap, but is easy to repair if only lightly rusted. Check the whole area for accident damage as well.

◀ After 40 years or so in the California sun, the light lenses have faded. No problem, buy second-hand British ones that haven't seen much sun at all.

◀ The rear lights as well as the front sidelights and headlights frequently conceal nasty rot. Take them off for a look-see if the seller will let you.

to heat the cabin, and that air can be damp, salty and acid in many places. New wings are available, but wings that fit are expensive, so it may be worth having new metal let into old ones if they're only rusted in patches. As well as being single-skin the early cars are not galvanised, which means repair is as easy or as hard as any other old car if you can get the panels at sensible prices. Then protect and paint it and away you go for another few years.

If you are taking on big rust repairs, brace the shell very carefully and comprehensively during repairs. If you replace the sills without bracing the shell, the whole structure will sag out of shape and will be repaired bent, and then the fine Porsche shut lines will mean that the doors won't go back on. Jack the car up on the suspension and leave the doors on. The doors themselves can be reskinned quite easily and cheaply, as much as any other classic, but duplicating the Porsche-quality shut lines will take a bit of time and trouble. Still, that's partly why you want a Porsche, and that's why they originally cost twice as much as an E-Type.

For enthusiastic drivers, it may help to know that a Targa with a glass rear window is a usefully more rigid structure than one with a soft plastic rear window.

ENGINE

Check the compressions and listen carefully for mechanical noises with the engine both cold and warm. If all is well and you change the oil every 3,000 miles, keep the engine in tune and use it as a second car, you can expect to rebuild your 911 engine only once in your life.

▲ There's a fine line between patinated and knackered. Jeff's interior has patina. The sun is more cruel to interiors than rain is, so the UK can be a better hunting ground for scrap 911s with usable interiors.

TRANSMISSION

It has to be worth chasing down a car with a five-speed gearbox, because it changes the whole picture from a weekend funster to a genuinely daily-usable practical classic.

MAINTENANCE AND REPAIRS

STRUCTURE

A complete new interior kit with new skins for the seats, door cards and so on was offered for $300 in the US, while quotes in the UK were £300 for carpets and £1,000 for a retrim in vinyl. Research far and wide before spending any money.

Fuel tank rust in little-used cars can be a problem. Webers in particular are sensitive to any crud in the fuel, so it's worth thinking about having the tank plastic-coated inside and out to make sure that only fuel gets into the carbs, not rust flakes.

ENGINE

Everything is available for a 911. The parts may be cheaper in Germany and the USA, so it's well worth hunting around. The big US market in particular keeps competition up and prices down. A flywheel in the UK, for example, was quoted at £300, while in the US it costs $100, still in a Porsche box. American specialist service standards tend to be efficient and helpful, although High Street US car parts sales people are as hopeless as the British ones: they once took four attempts to provide me with the correct brake hose for a Chevrolet van. Good news is that with only four major bolts holding the 911's engine in, clutch changes are easy.

A complete engine stripdown is a little daunting for an amateur, but taking the engine to a specialist means a bill for several thousand pounds. However, a good rebuild, with regular use and constantly refreshed oil, could last the life of the car, and possibly the owner.

For sparks and fuelling you're looking for a distributor with points and a pair of Weber carbs, not electronic injection and an ECU. It's all very accessible for the amateur, and there's a limit to what can be charged for a set of points, while there's no limit to what can be charged for an ECU – how about a 993 upgrade ECU at £3,250 plus VAT?

If it comes to taking the engine out, you disconnect the electricals and linkages; then there are basically four bolts holding the engine to the gearbox. It takes an experienced enthusiast about an hour and a half to get the engine out of a 911.

TRANSMISSION

For hands-on types: if third gear is worn, you can take it out, turn it the other way round and get another 100,000 miles out of it.

IMPROVEMENTS AND MODIFICATIONS

STRUCTURE

Later cars with ugly big bumpers can be significantly lightened and visually improved by removing the originals and fitting slim '67 bumpers instead.

Don't take out the lumps of iron you'll find at the front of the car unless you're prepared to fit the later chin spoiler that's needed to hold the front end down at speed. The standard bonnet and front bodywork design creates a lot of lift.

ENGINE

It's probably well worth considering an upgrade/update to Weber carbs if you still have a pair of Solexes on your early 911 – you can always put them back on later if a concours enthusiast wants to buy the car.

While you're at it, you can change the spec by specifying bigger barrels and pistons for more capacity, and by fitting hotter cams. Taking a 130bhp 2-litre engine up to 2.4 litres with S cams would get you 160bhp and bigger grunt as well. You can also bolt in bigger engines such as a 3.2.

BRAKES/TYRES

You can upgrade to 911SC brakes, and wider wheels and tyres from later models. The car will happily take more grippy tyres and a lot more power without complaining.

PRICES

At this age, condition oscillates between excellent restos and abandoned projects. You'll probably use up your ten grand and more to achieve a good early Porsche 911, even with a trip to the US to ensure minimal rust. Possibly going well over budget for a better car would be a better investment, or taking the converted-912 route. Alternatively, buying a rotten old shed of a car and a MIG-welder could be a good plan, as the structure is simple and not galvanised, therefore easier to weld. All 911s remain desirable, so bargains will be rare. The cars are simple and easy to maintain, so lowering future running costs could sensibly offset an increase in your initial budget.

Early 911s, for build-date reasons, can be eligible for various classes of classic racing and rallying which can inflate their prices. This becomes progressively less important as eligibility dates are rolled forwards to keep entry numbers viable. UK historic rallying required pre-Ford Escort cars until the grids declined to a TR3 and a couple of Healeys, then they relented and moved the date forwards; which included later 911s and reduced the prices of early ones.

BEST BUYS

After 40 years, the individual condition of each car is much more important than model details. LHD and Targas are cheaper, five-speeds are more expensive. The best plan in general would be to go to California and buy a car with a really clean shell and good mechanicals, flat paint and a bad interior – the British lack of sun means interiors last well in the UK and are available second-hand.

▲ **This is a 1969 911S Targa, for sale at Giordano Classic Cars in Washington. It's much messed about – but it's a California desert car with minimal rust apart from the battery tray. $6,000 takes it away.**

▼ **The rear is riding high because there's no engine: choose from a 1973 2.4-litre or a 1969 911E engine for an additional dollar consideration. It's still way cheaper than a shiny and drivable 911.**

▼ ▼ **The interior looks horrible, but is actually just filthy. A few hours with a damp cloth and some Armor-all and it would look quite respectable.**

CHAPTER 3

911: 1971–80
flares and turbos

Affordability rating ★★★

The most affordable possible 911 is probably a left-hand-drive 1976 Targa with big US-spec impact bumpers, visible rust, flat paint in a dodgy '70s colour and a semi-automatic Sportomatic gearbox. However, even if it's nasty it's still a 911 – so buy it for the right money, fix it up the way you want it and you can finish up with a good car at a good price. The cars were legally required to have those gross bumpers when sold new, but there's nothing stopping us from changing them now.

Backdating in this way is increasing in popularity all the time: check out www.ddk-online.com and www.forums.pelicanparts.com.

As the 1970s grooved on, the 911 changed from a light car with a revvy engine to a heavier car with more grunt, and the wheelbase lengthened, making it less sensitive and twitchy.

Some engines are much better than others – but with only four bolts holding it to the gearbox, you can easily change the power plant. 2.0, 2.2 and 2.4 are popular engine sizes, but the 2.7 is deeply unpopular. The 3.0 and 3.2-litre engines are also good, but the cars bearing them are getting newer and more expensive, which is reflected in the cost of the later engines.

If you're serious about buying a 911 you will need to buy some books about their history and failings, of which there are many. Books, that is, rather than failings. Paul Frere's *Porsche 911 Story*, also from Haynes, is satisfyingly thick and authoritative. Be slightly suspicious about the information given in some Porsche books, though – the publication of this book was significantly delayed by the need to filter out much inaccurate crap that got in at the research stage. Haynes make an effort to ensure their authors are accurate, but some publishers don't bother.

◄ **Big flares, big muscles and matt black trim, and the Bay City Rollers are playing on the stereo radio cassette deck.** [Porsche AG]

BASICS

Body	Non-galvanised, later galvanised, steel monocoque coupé and Targa.
Engine	Rear-mid-mounted air-cooled flat six, normally aspirated and turbocharged.
Gearbox and transmission	Five-speed all-synchro or four-speed Tiptronic depending on year and model.
Suspension	Front, independent MacPherson struts, lower wishbones, longitudinal torsion bars, anti-roll bar. Rear, independent, semi-trailing arms, torsion bars, telescopic shocks, optional anti-roll bar.
Steering	Unassisted rack and pinion.
Brakes	Discs all round.

Fuller specifications and further detailed technical information can be found in Chapter 15.

HISTORY

We can establish some basics of what sort of 911 is going to suit you and your budget with a brief look at the history of the car through the 1970s.

Through 1969–71 the 911 got better brakes, bigger tyres and body flares to cover them, and injection on E and S models. The 2-litre engine went up to 2.2, which gave the base T model 125bhp, the standard E model 155bhp and the S 180bhp.

1972 saw an increase to 2,350cc, with power levels at 140bhp, 165bhp and 190bhp. All 911s were now injected, and a new chin spoiler kept the front end on the deck by reducing aerodynamic lift by 50 per cent, obviating the need for the previous lumps of iron in the front.

In 1973 the Carrera RS lightweight was offered with 210bhp, but that information is slightly surplus to requirements as we can't afford one. If you like the look of the Carrera, it's possible to follow a well-trodden path and create a lookalike with similar performance. The number on the boot lid may originally have said 911T, but only you and a few anal-retentive Porsche fanatics will know that.

In 1974 the poo hit the cooling fan with Porsche's reputation for reliability over the 2.7-litre engine. A new 2,687cc injection engine offered 133bhp for the base 911 (the T classification having been dropped) and 167bhp for the other models, the S and the Carrera. However, the new engine casing was made of cast magnesium, and the cylinder head studs started pulling out of it. The engine also suffered from overheating problems, and leaked oil as the casings warped. We need to get this in perspective, though. The 2.7-litre engine isn't as bad as malicious pub gossip maintains. Lodgesport in Manchester report that even now, their regular 911 repair work consists mostly of failed oil thermostats, seized heater controls and 915 gearbox problems, rather than a continuous string of 2.7 stud replacements. Once properly sorted, the stud problem usually remains sorted. It's a simple engineering fix, and once the block has been machined to replace the stud drilling, then fitted with better head studs and reassembled in the correct order, the engine tends to stay fixed. Even the oil leaks can be minimised, although you'll probably be wise to invest in a drip tray.

The whole 911 range in that year also suffered from a serious styling disaster with huge and heavy new US bumpers front and rear. The cars themselves were improved by a nicer interior and bigger 16mm anti-roll bars at both ends, but that wasn't much of a trade-off for the horrible bumpers.

In 1975 the introduction of the Turbo caused a big sensation, but there was very little fuss made about the telling fact that the engine casings used for the Turbo engine had quietly gone back to being made of aluminium instead of magnesium.

More electrical goodies appeared for 911 models, as well as a new problem with the smog gear. If you pushed the throttle pedal during

EVOLUTION

1972	Bigger capacity at 2,341cc, bigger anti-roll bars, front air dam reduces lift.
1973	Carrera name returns. US 911T gets Bosch K-Jetronic injection and 140bhp.
1974	Bigger capacity at 2,687cc – the much derided magnesium 2.7 engine. Bosch injection on all models, big US bumpers appear. Interior redesign, electric windows.
1975	Turbo gets aluminium crankcase, other models get exploding airbox.
1976	Shells are galvanised. Engine options include 3.0, 2.7 and 2.0.
1977	Dilawar studs partly improve 2.7-litre stud problems, LHD cars get brake servos. 2.7-litre engine abandoned in autumn: engine options are now 3.0 SC and 3.3-litre Turbo.
1978	Bigger bearings, stronger crank, better clutch. SC has improved torque curve, smog gear is improved.
1979	Intercooler appears on Turbo. Sportomatic is deleted. Bigger vented crossdrilled brakes on Turbo.

cold starting rather than using the hand throttle between the seats, the engine would backfire through the air box and blow it up. It wasn't a matter of if it would blow up, but when.

In 1976 the 911 line-up comprised just two models – the 3.0 Turbo, and the 2.7 911S. The economy 912 four-cylinder model had become the 912E with the VW engine from the 914. Same car, different motor and gearing. New detail goodies included heated rear windows.

1977 saw the 2.7 fitted with new cylinder head studs made of Dilawar, with the idea that it expands and contracts at the same rate as magnesium. This was an attempt to stop the studs pulling out. The fix was partly successful and certainly improved matters. However, in this year the magnesium casing was abandoned, and the 911 options became the 3.0SC and the 3.3 Turbo, both with aluminium engine casings for 1978.

In some ways the history and detailed problems of a specific year model are irrelevant, as the condition of each car is by now much more important. A rusty '72 911S could cost lots more than a solid '75, but it's easier to repair a dodgy 2.7-litre engine than a rotten floor.

HANDS ON –
The expert's view

The Autofarm's Josh Sadler has a single piece of advice for anybody buying a 911 for ten grand: don't.

Having said that, he qualifies it. 'I would never recommend anybody to buy a 911 for ten grand. That said, if someone's prepared to travel, to look, to steer away from the popular models, to be happy with LHD, there are some good ones out there.' If you don't know what you're doing around a socket set and will have to get professional help with your Porsche, you would be better to buy a more expensive one in better condition that will need much less work – it will be cheaper every time. If you double your budget, you can get a seriously good car that should run for years with only service and maintenance expenses along the way. In the UK, says Josh, the real starting point is well above £15,000.

Double the budget? That's hardly an affordable Porsche, is it? Yes, it can be. Think carefully about your genuine capabilities and available time. Will you really want to spend weekends on big repairs, buy the tools and so on, or do you just want a Porsche and are vaguely thinking of looking after it yourself? If you're realistically not going to be a regularly hands-on owner/mechanic, a ten-grand 911 may soon become financially pretty

PRODUCTION 1971–80

Porsche 911T/911E/911S (2.4-litre) 1971–73

911T Coupé	10,173
911T Targa	7,147
911E Coupé	2,470
911E Targa	1,896
911S Coupé	3,160
911S Targa	1,894

Porsche 911/911N/911S 1973–75/1975–77/1973–77
(These were British names for selected models on sale in these periods)

911 Coupé	5,232
911 Targa	4,088
911N Coupé	9,904*
911N Targa	8,182*
911S Coupé	4,927
911S Targa	3,051

* Includes 911 Lux

Porsche 911SC 1977–83

Coupé (180bhp)	10,382
Targa (180bhp)	8,108
Coupé (188bhp)	5,010
Targa (188bhp)	3,603
Coupé (204bhp)	16,099
Targa (204bhp)	9,837
Cabriolet (204bhp)	4,096

Porsche 911 Turbo (930) 3-litre/3.3-litre 1974–77/1977–90

3-litre Coupé	2,850
3.3-litre Coupé	14,476
3.3-litre Coupé, slant-nose	948
3.3-litre Targa	193
3.3-litre Cabriolet	918

indigestible, particularly when repairs begin to cost serious money on a regular basis.

Take a longer view. In practical terms, will you still be able to keep your 911 in ten years, or will you have to trade it for some ghastly people-carrier to tote baby buggies and frozen pizzas around? If it's going to be your one special car, and if you'll be able to spread the cost over many years, it could make good economic sense to buy the best right now. You could also pick a top model and thus get a better price if you ever do have to sell: they're not making 911s any more, and good ones are getting harder to find every year.

The cost of a budget Porsche depends on where we are in the boom-bust cycle. In the boom part of the cycle, the absurd inflation of house prices sometimes means you may well be 'earning' more by owning a house than by working. Releasing some of that equity is a pretty cheap source of money, and as long as the housing bubble doesn't completely deflate, the cost of even a nice 911 will soon be absorbed. If the housing market collapses completely, at least you'll be able to drive away from your repossessed house in a nice car. If we're in the bust part of the cycle, prices of luxuries such as Porsches drop dramatically, and if you're still employed you can wave a wad of fivers around and get a bargain.

Josh underlines the idea that you can save some real money or upgrade to a car in better condition by picking unpopular models. Left-hand drive knocks 25–30 per cent off the value of a 911, and for most of us it makes no practical difference. As I've already pointed out in Chapter 1, in cities or on motorways LHD is the same as RHD, but on squirly A-roads it's a nuisance for overtaking, as you have to either hang back for a better view or stick the passenger side of the car right out to see what's coming. Josh finds that LHD cars get up his personal nose because he has a 20-mile A-road commute, but fortunately he can pick which 911 he's going to drive home in, a privilege only open to classic Porsche dealers and people who are too rich to have to read this book.

In the UK, Josh says the cunning plan of buying a UK-purchased 912 and stuffing in a 911 engine isn't a good one. The 912 has always been too cheap to be worth restoring or even properly

maintaining, so the few that remain in Britain tend to be neglected and nasty. 911 engines themselves are no longer ten a penny: according to Josh, 'the available 911 engines that fall out of wrecks are knackered anyway.' He does have time for the 912, though, having raced one 30 years ago – but repairs are as costly as or more costly than for 911 engines, and you'll get better value all round from a 911. Tellingly, his race 912 finished up with a flat six RS engine in it anyway.

He also secretly rather fancies a 911 with an aluminium 5,700cc Chevrolet small-block, which he reckons would go like a rocket, although he's not sure what the terminal oversteer would be like. Certainly the cost of building and fitting a 500bhp V8 or buying an American crate performance motor would stack up very well against a major Porsche flat-six rebuild, although you'd need wheelie bars on the back bumper.

Targas, he says, are indeed cheaper, because they leak and rust at the bottom of the roof bar, and because they're structurally weaker than the roofed cars. (Ever seen one racing?)

Big-bumper cars are also cheaper, and although they had to be loaded down with the huge and nasty bumpers when new, they don't now – so you can simply restore them to what they would have looked like had they remained unburdened by American parking impact regulations.

Josh confirms that the 2.7-litre engine has a bad reputation for pulling head studs out of the block,

▼ The Carrera RS is the 911 that everybody wants: lots of power, handling and charisma, and not too heavy or too soft.

◀ You do have to know what you're doing when you buy a choice model: one of the Carreras in the Autofarm's workshop is a replica. The Autofarm will tell you if this is the case, but others might not.

but his view on this balances it up a little. Firstly, pulled studs are more of a hot-climate problem than a British problem, and secondly it's a routine and once-only repair job for the Autofarm. They drill out the stripped threads and fit an insert with new threads – job done. So don't avoid a 2.7, just moan on for a while about the expensive design mistake when you're buying one, and knock more money off whatever offer you're going to make for it.

The particular year of a 911 has a big impact on its value: early short-wheelbase 1965–8 cars are actually not as expensive as you might expect. They may be a best buy, actually: they used to be sought after because of pre-'65 FIA historic competition rules, but that ruling was extended to 1967 and then to 1974, and people who are serious about classic racing – and they nearly all are – want the faster, better-handling later cars, so early ones may become better value. They're more crude, but big fun, and the 911 purists love them.

The top-selling cars at the Autofarm, which people pay serious money for, are the 2.2 and 2.4 from 1970 to 1973, not the pristine earlier classics as you might have thought.

After 1974, the big-bumper cars are cheaper, but the galvanised bodies came in from 1976, so early big-bumper cars can have horrible rust. Mind you, galvanising only delays rust until about now, as we've noted. So you're mostly looking at restored cars today, and trying to assess the quality of the repairs rather than the car. It's hard to find a good '76–'83 now, expensive or otherwise.

However, if you have the will to get stuck in and learn welding and mechanics, Josh will also encourage you to buy a nasty 911 and restore it

yourself. There's a Targa in at the Autofarm at the moment that is a family heirloom with roughly twice its cash value invested in repairs: that's fine if it's a treasured Dad's old car, but very bad news if the owner had been trying to run it as a cheap Porsche project. On the other hand, as a hands-on DIY project it could still have made lots of sense.

As far as Josh is concerned, 911s are definitely within the amateur weekend mechanic's grasp, and a low-pressure home restoration of a fairly nasty car will not only provide the pleasure of transformation from a wreck to a gleaming winged chariot of fire, but will give you an intimate knowledge of what will become your very personal car.

HANDS ON –
The owner's view

Californian Lee Rice has taken an alternate route. He has been improving and developing his 911 over several decades and 320,000 miles into something completely different. Lee is a retired aircraft engineer who now works on tuning other people's Porsches for performance. He says a good 911 for $15,000 is very possible, with care. He's never been rich, and has always had to run his Porsche as well as a house with a mortgage, a wife, two kids and a dog, but he's still getting a lot of fun out of a car that had surely paid for itself by 1976.

His blue 911 has been with him since 1971, and has changed its personality as many times as the late Michael Jackson's changed his appearance. Lee moved his allegiance to Porsches from Corvettes because of quality control. He originally wanted a faster 911, but couldn't manage the extra cash for a 911S. However, he got a good deal on the car he finally bought, and turned it into something rather faster than a 911S before too long anyway. He had to use the car to get to work, and found it completely reliable and also fast enough to be worth racing at the weekends. There was a local SCCA meeting on a track that is now covered by houses, and even with his commuting mileage adding 30,000 miles per annum Lee found the car went very well indeed on the circuit. The brakes weren't up to hard track use, but the rest of the car was great. He asked other Porsche owners what were the good tweaks for them, but he was told just leave it standard and push it harder, which he found to be top advice. However, he couldn't bring himself to leave the car unmodified for long, and his first mod was to upgrade to 911S brakes, with stainless-braided Teflon brake hoses. That meant he could brake later, but then he was running out of tyre, so he moved up to 185 tyres and American Racing magnesium rims. They cracked after a while, at which point he realised he should just have saved up more money and coughed up for a set of proper Fuchs alloys.

The car was then lowered all round, and that helped a little with high-speed stability. Then on his 80-mile daily commute to LA airport, he was rear-ended fairly hard, which trashed the back of the car. A deal with the repairer saw a wing off a 934 race car being blended into the new rear bodywork, and the crash-damaged engine was replaced with a 2.2-litre S engine, with mechanical fuel injection. The car spent some time screaming round the Riverside track, and more aerodynamics were brought in with an air dam across the

front. That resulted in an astonishing improvement. Previously, Lee had had to accelerate towards his highway offramp, then brake hard to get the front tyres to grip enough to steer off the Interstate. That was the case even with the lumps of iron fitted to the front end. The dam and rear spoiler transformed the car, which was now docile and obedient. There have been several wings on the back over the years, including an RSR street repro one and a small Carrera wing.

As time went on and funds permitted, the car got a good-quality paint job and a set of fat Fuchs alloys, 11in at the back and 9in at the front.

Lee really wanted a 3-litre RS as soon as he saw one, but there was no chance, as only 50 were made and none of them had his name on it. His 911 pretty soon began to look like an RS, though, with the repro wing on the tail.

The flares on Lee's car are actually genuine Carrera steel repair panels from Porsche, welded into his original rear wings. A big project, but achievable and a lot better than messing about with GRP. Also, GRP expands and contracts at different temperatures from steel, and does it in different directions, so GRP arches on steel cars will always crack and come off sooner or later. Just like steel studs in a magnesium crankcase, come to think of it.

Regular home maintenance is obviously no problem for an aircraft engineer, but nobody likes to take an engine out any more often that they have to. However, before long the 2.2-litre engine wasn't fast enough, and was pulled out and sold. Twenty years later and in another car, the bottom end has now covered 225,000 miles with about half that many on the heads, and still runs as well as ever.

Lee's new engine was rather special, and was built from a blown 3-litre Turbo engine. It has SC cylinders, RSR pistons, late-model injection and old-fashioned magnesium air inlet stacks. It wasn't as fast as he expected, but it's all a learning experience. It was still strong enough to break the bar across the top of the engine bay, though, which has now been beefed up with scaffold pole in order to effect a permanent repair. After some fiddling, Lee ported the throttles out a little, and spaced the injectors back out of the airflow, then worked out that for max power the engine needed 42mm throttle butterflies rather than the standard 35mm. He was thinking about a set of very tall intake stacks at $4,000 a set, but then the whole engine concept changed again.

That engine was sold, and a new one was started, based on a good 3-litre Turbo. He'd found

▼ Lee Rice's car started off as a standard early 911. It's not a replica of anything in particular: the front air dam and oil cooler are among many additions.

THE AFFORDABLE PORSCHE

the Turbo cars to be 'a bit of a dog' at the bottom end of the rev range, so he decided to see if he could improve matters. His 911 weighs 2,380lb compared to the Turbo at 2,700, so a spot of turbo puff would help it along even better. Fitting top-drawer Raceware rods and nuts was probably overkill, but Lee knew that the bigger engines had a tendency to throw rods so he didn't want to take the chance. He used an oil pump from the 3.3-litre engine, and a C2 intercooler from 1992. This is perfect, he says – its internal design is beautifully streamlined and gets the maximum possible cooling airflow. Unfortunately this intercooler is the size of a suitcase and wouldn't fit under his engine lid, so a bigger 3.8 wing had to be sourced, fitted and painted. The stock intake manifold was ported and a later K27 turbocharger was fitted. Finally Lee got some new exhaust manifolds made which were short, smooth and fat, and which went through 911SC heat exchangers. 911SC cams were also fitted, and a later model fuel system. The result of all that work was full boost and full power at 3,000rpm, which is exactly what he wanted.

As the car is still the same shell that was registered in 1968, air pumps and other smog gear could be quietly discarded, all of which helps the airflow and power. At this level of performance things can go wrong quickly, so Lee now runs a fuel pressure gauge as well as a Greddy turbo gauge that records vacuum as well as pressure. Low fuel pressure means a lean mix, and combining that with a turbocharged engine at full chat is a Bad Idea, in the same way that pulling the pin on a grenade without throwing it is a bad idea.

Gearboxes have been a problem as Lee's engines have gone beyond 400bhp, and the 915 transmission, even when fitted with oil spray and a transmission cooler, is not up to that sort of abuse. After two 915 transmissions broke, Lee did the necessary engineering and fitted a G50. This needed a short bellhousing, and he used a torque biasing differential. The transmission was built as a custom job with a high fifth gear for cruising. Theoretically, Lee would get 205mph (330kph) at 7,300rpm. First gear is also higher, resulting in less wheelspin off the line. The system is finished off with a RUF-Sachs clutch and a G50 shifter and hydraulic clutch-pedal assembly, and the latest and fattest half-shafts to avoid any more breakages: Lee has yet to find out where the weakest point in the system now lurks.

So should you hunt down a collection of late scrappers and start mixing and matching to get the best engine and transmission? No, says Lee. If he had bought the whole rear end from a crashed G50-equipped car it would have been much easier,

quicker and cheaper than messing about with all the individual bits. With many common conversion projects, it's better to buy a conversion kit from a good supplier. Even if it seems like a big price it will be cheaper than doing it yourself.

The brakes were inadequate again as the engine had got bigger, so a set of big cross-drilled discs went in. Advice on brakes for a developing early car says that you should start looking for 1978/9 Turbo brakes now, as they bolt straight on to early cars. The Brembo replacement kit for those brakes is also good value, and competition has brought Brembo's prices down. Big Red brakes from Brembo are more cheaply available, now that the company has moved on to eight-piston calipers. Yes, I did say

▲ The rear tea-tray spoiler on Lee's car looks pretty extreme, and you might think he was showing off...

▼ ...Then you might look at the engine and see the huge intercooler underneath it. Most engine covers simply won't shut over this monster intercooler.

▲ The interior is mostly still original. Lee says a good comfortable steering wheel the right size for you is very important for fast driving.

▼ This original seat has been broken and mended more times than Lee can remember, and is now braced by adjustable steel rods. He should have coughed up and bought a Recaro race seat 20 years ago, he says.

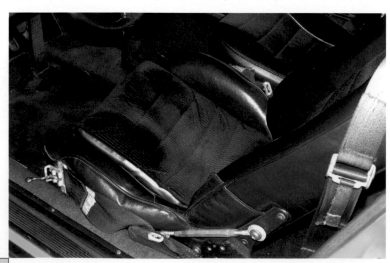

eight. For a lighter earlier Porsche you need less braking anyway.

An air scoop on top of the wing directs cooling air to the oil cooler, which is a Mazda RX3 item adapted to fit. It's bigger than the Porsche one, and is made in Germany by Behr. It works fine, even with the extra turbocharger heat.

Items that have worn out through sheer use include the English OBA steering wheel, which has been re-upholstered, and the seat belts. Lee has now worn out three sets – they don't last anywhere near as long as an engine.

Something worth knowing is that frayed seat belts or seat belt strapping with a nick in the edge can be nearly useless in a crash. If you think about the way you cut just the edge of an old towel to make it easy to rip it up for garage use, seat belt webbing works the same way – so Lee changes his harnesses when they begin to look worn.

Lee could never afford a set of new Recaros, so he's spent 30 years bodging the car's original seats and welding the frames back together when they break. They currently have threaded bar

triangulating the backs to the bottoms, which can be adjusted with a spanner and won't break again. However, rather than 30 years of intermittent work Lee says he should have remortgaged and bought some Recaros, or better still, got a pair out of a scrap Ford RS Turbo. No Porsche badges on Ford-sourced Recaros, but who cares?

A mistake that Lee recommends not making is to grind off the roof gutters to gain 15mph (25kph) in top speed. This works, but it also ruins the structural strength of the roof, so you need to weld in a multi-point rollcage as well to stiffen it back up again.

After all the hassle, would Lee recommend anyone to start with a '68 and follow his path? Too right he would. His total budget has been $30–35,000 including three different engines, and for way less than that he could still build a pre-1970 400bhp 911 turbo conversion that would cream a 993.

He built a nice Porsche for his brother, based on a very clean 1971 911T. It's fitted with a 2.7 engine with RS pistons, cylinders and cams, 911S fuel injection, a rebuilt 915 box, 911S brakes, wing and body mods, and well-made fake Fuchs wheels. He had to poke about for the right parts at the right prices, but the car cost $12,000 and the upgrade parts cost $3,000 – and you can't complain about that. If the studs pull on the 2.7, which they haven't as yet, it only takes Lee half an hour to remove a 911 engine.

Condensed advice from him on specific engines is interesting. 200bhp is reasonably available even from an early 2-litre 130bhp engine. It needs widened ports, bigger carbs or at least jets, S cams and a reworked ignition curve, all of which can be done for a reasonable-sized budget and gets you close to the 200bhp. For more power, a set of high compression pistons and rings is $1,000. $3,500 gets a set of new bigger-bore barrels and pistons.

The 2.7-litre isn't a bad place to start for a higher performance engine, not least because they're cheap – everybody hates them because of their rep for warped casings, oil leaks and stripped head studs. However, if you get them machined properly and don't ask too much of them, you can still get a fairly reliable 250bhp with porting and a cam change. Even if you keep another 2.7 for a spare, that has to be a very cheap way of getting from 130bhp to 250bhp, with a big boost in low-down grunt just from the big capacity rise. The word 'affordable' drifts into view.

911SC engines are also available as people upgrade to 3.2 and 3.4 engines.

The last word from Lee is the same iconoclastic idea that I've mentioned regarding the 912, with a twist. He doesn't like the 912 engine at all, having repaired a few. In his experience they cost almost as much to overhaul as a 911 engine, and they're much weaker and don't last very long. He reckons it's a waste of a good car not to change the mediocre four-pot Porsche engine in the 912 for an excellent six-pot Porsche engine with twice as many bearings. There's a further bonus as well – due to the small power of the 912 four-cylinder engine, the gear ratios are very low. That means when you attach even one of the smaller flat sixes to a 912 gearbox, the acceleration goes from sad to remarkable.

So – by buying the right 911 of the type that nobody much wants, you can acquire for a sensible price an excellent base from which to develop a much better and faster car, and all for the price of a second-hand Ford Focus. What are you waiting for?

WHAT TO LOOK FOR

(See also Chapter 2, as much of its information is equally valid for later cars.)

STRUCTURE

Hard-earned advice about buying a 911 comes from various club members here and in the US, and inevitably starts with rust. There was underseal on the floorpans from 1971, and from 1975 the whole shell was galvanised. However, once the galvanising has been partly or wholly eaten away, 911s still rot like any steel car. Underseal can be a very mixed blessing – if it's chipped or has been allowed to flake off anywhere on the body, the gaps allow damp to creep in and then ensure that the area under the underseal remains damp, which is bad news.

Something nasty on older cars which you may not have thought of is that while the major rust points have probably been restored by now, there is secondary rusting going on – not just new rusting of the fresh panels, but old rusting of the never-repaired areas that take decades longer to rust. For instance, the roof pillar may have been repaired, but the roof itself may be getting thin. Older 911s have had several decades to rust by now, so you need to look everywhere on an earlier car, not just at the expected rusting points.

In general, galvanised cars rust in the front tank support areas, the inner wings, the sills and the B-posts. Earlier non-galvanised cars go in the outer wings, inner wings, front crossmembers, battery box, floor, roof, boot, doors, heater tubes, screen frame, strut tops and the rear axle tubes across the back of the engine bay. Having digested that, are you sure you don't fancy a nice GRP Speedster replica?

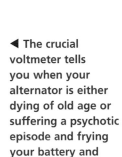

◀ Changing standard 911 mirrors for the little aerodynamic mirrors from a much more upmarket model looks cute and probably makes the car go one per cent faster. However, you only need to win a race by one per cent.

◀ The crucial voltmeter tells you when your alternator is either dying of old age or suffering a psychotic episode and frying your battery and ECU.

▼ The increasingly fat steel arches grafted on to this old body have evolved to cover fat alloys and 2004 tyres in exactly the same way as new model 911s have evolved.

Look for rust in the areas where drains have become blocked, and then if you buy the car make sure the drains stay clear from now on. Old screen seals let in water front and back, and early bonnets have a foam insert which is perfect for retaining damp, so look for rust bubbles wherever there's a foam insert.

Targas leak and that causes a lot of rust, particularly at the bottom of the roll hoop. The extremely high cost of new Targa roof seals means many will leak for years before new seals are fitted. Encouragingly, they have a stronger sill structure to start with, so if you're rebuilding big time it may be an idea to rebuild with Targa sill panels, maybe even modified and used on a coupé shell. A good practice is to budget for an extra 30 per cent in repair time, panels and costs during major rust repairs, to pay for the additional unpleasantness that lurks beneath the panels that will be taken off.

Something worth knowing is that if you're thinking about hands-on body restoration, galvanised steel is a bitch to work with. The remains of the zinc plating interfere with the arc and make smooth welds difficult. It takes time and patience to learn to deal with it. On balance, a fairly nasty pre-galvanised 911 could be both a better buy and easier to deal with than a later medium-rusty galvanised car.

As always with a second-hand car, check the VIN number (on the screen pillar after 1969) against the registration documents, and check that those and the other numbers match the type and spec of the car, and that those numbers don't relate to a stolen or written-off car. Check also that the ID plates on the car are original and not put there by some unscrupulous dealer.

Check for wrinkles on the bodywork inside the front compartment and the wings all round, which indicate accident damage. If you can't find any, it's either undamaged or repaired well enough that it doesn't matter.

If the wing returns on post-1969 cars have no textured finish under the paint, the wing may have been replaced. Check under floor mats for floorpan rust.

ENGINE

2.7-litre magnesium-cased engines do not have a good reputation. Apart from the studs falling out, they leak worse than a Royal Oilfield motorcycle. The later Dilawar studs were supposed to expand and contract at the same rate as the magnesium engine casings, but they still fall out. An engine can have several pulled studs and still run adequately with no audible blowing, at least

not yet, so what you need to do is take the rocker covers off and check the studs for the correct torque figures. Check the cylinder compressions at the same time.

You also need to check the engine numbers to find out just what engine you're looking at – it's easy to change the engines, which is both an advantage and a disadvantage. It may seem extreme to start taking a car to pieces before you buy it, but you can't take a chance on being landed with an unexpected 2.7-litre engine when you thought you were deliberately and expensively buying another 911 model in order to avoid a 2.7. Even if you've balanced the risks and decided to go for a 2.7, you want to avoid being stitched up with one just before a massive repair bill rather than after it. You also need to know what engine you're buying when it comes to replacing the clutch and other components, so you might as well get under there and find the number now as do it later.

Before parting with a wad of your hard-earned, you need to consult the more heavy-duty Porsche reference books to crack the codes for the second number as well as the main engine number, then you can find out what carbs, smog gear or whatever the engine was originally supposed to be fitted with, and knock more off the price if it isn't.

If the timing chain on a pre-1981 car is rattling, look worried about it, shake your head doubtfully and demand more money off, but be aware that you can retrofit 1981 or 1984 tensioners which work better. Don't rev an engine with a rattling chain until after the tensioner has been replaced.

Valve guides wear out, particularly in pre-'77 cars, resulting in lots of blue smoke on starting up and on the over-run when you back off the throttle, but they can wait until you feel like dealing with them or until the next overhaul.

The later the car, the more electronics are involved, and some Porsche electronics don't like high temperatures. It's a shame that they're all kept in the hot engine bay, then: however, the Bosch Motronic system seems to be stable and reliable even when regularly cooked.

It's rumoured that some 3-litre engines are approaching the 500,000-mile mark without overhaul, so that's worth bearing in mind for long-term ownership.

A compression test is a good guide to engine condition; so is reluctance on the part of the seller to submit the car to one.

GEARBOX

The 915 box goes from 1972 to 1986, and is a good strong gearbox. The Getrag G50 box fitted from 1986 on is apparently the dog's plums, but while that's excellent news if you're buying a later car, the box sadly can't be retrofitted to earlier cars without fairly significant complications.

The rubber-centred clutch fitted from 1978 is known as the 'exploding clutch' in the trade. It can be replaced with a better one, but it's another bill to pay.

911 gearboxes are generally pretty good, although the intermediate bearings can fail on earlier cars, particularly on 2.0 and 2.2-litre ones. You can hear a whine in all gears except top if the bearings are on the way out. If you're rebuilding a gearbox yourself, it may be useful and financially helpful to know that some worn gears can actually be reversed and put back in rather than expensively replaced – giving you another 100,000 miles before you have to cough up any money for new parts.

BRAKES

Brakes are simply not a problem with any year of 911. Each improvement in power was paralleled by an increase in braking capacity, and you will get no more problems with Porsche brakes than with any other older car. The only warning is on dodgy right-hand-drive conversions, on which there may be bodged mechanical pedal linkages.

MAINTENANCE AND REPAIRS

STRUCTURE

On a 911 that has had a tough life, or that you are planning to give a hard time on a regular basis, there are a few structural repairs that will come up sooner or later. One is across where the back suspension sits. You can get an expert Porsche body man to make a seamless repair here, or you can get a MIG welder and beef it up with a bit of scaffold pole, depending on your budget and squeamishness. Both will work, and neither will be externally visible.

Rather more readily apparent is the cracking of the seam towards the back of the outer sills, which will eventually appear on well-hammered 911s as rust. The body flexes here, and as a result the paint flakes off, rust gets a hold and the whole thing begins to look nasty. It's not a huge job, but it has to be done properly and expensively. For a car that's a sporting toy rather than a concours entrant, a bit of extra beefing-up here will also stiffen the shell. At the back of the top of the rear wing, by the window, you also get stress cracking for the same reason, also requiring a repair.

Aftermarket alarms/immobilisers can generate a few nightmares, as they are connected to various parts of the electrical system and their components are of variable quality. You can get all kinds of electrical foul-ups which may not be the car's fault at all. If there are various intermittent electrical problems, consider replacing the alarm system with a hidden tap on the fuel line or a micro-switch on an ignition wire, and use a circular lock covering the steering wheel, then get the alarm taken out altogether. It's better to employ an alarm fitter for this rather than to do it yourself, because if the alarm has been wired in well, lots of the connections will be carefully hidden.

ENGINE

The old joke at the Porsche factory says that to change the spark plugs you need an asbestos octopus. On the up side, there's no radiator to go wrong. On balance, it's still a genuinely practical idea for an amateur to service and look after his own 911 in his own garage.

If you're rebuilding or interfering with an old oil system at all, it's a good idea to fit a new stainless steel oil tank and oil lines, as condensation in the old steel tanks causes rust flakes to get into the oil and thus into the engine bearings, which we definitely don't want.

You can pre-emptively bin the dodgy 1975 airbox on UK cars, because in the UK you merely have to achieve set emission levels depending on the year of the engine – how you achieve those levels is up to you and your local Porsche club tech bunnies to work out, and you don't have to include dodgy Porsche airboxes and red-hot extra smog boxes under the cylinder heads.

If it's possible to find copies of the proper

▲ Lenses are available both new and second-hand at autojumbles and swapmeets. The prices reflect the value of the cars – a replacement 1975 American bumper isn't going to cost you much compared to a clean 356 steering wheel.

▲ A set of factory RS wheels for $4,500 sounds pretty pricy, but if they're the real thing... Start seriously buying at an autojumble just as they're packing up their stands: most people will take a silly offer rather than taking stuff back home again.

Porsche workshop manual for your model of 911, it's well worth doing. Some of the Porsche club areas do have a set for consultation, which can be useful even if you're not allowed to spread them out on the garage floor and get oily thumbprints all over them. Photocopying them for personal use would be illegal, but then so's double-parking and buying peerages.

For some reason alternator failure seems to be regular on 911s, particularly in the US, so you need to fit a voltmeter. Sometimes just stopping and starting is enough to get one charging again, but if you don't know it's not charging until your headlights go dim and your engine cuts out, that's no help. There's also the risk of a dodgy alternator boiling the battery and frying the electrics – an expensive nuisance on any 911, but possibly terminal on an earlier 996, as the repair bill would be catastrophic.

The clutch cable plate and tube on the body are a weak point. Stress fractures are inevitable in the end, even with a standard clutch, and they happen even faster if you have a beefy uprated clutch. A spot of agricultural steelwork sorts the fracture problem out inelegantly but permanently. A good trick is to retrofit a 3.3 Turbo clutch spring, which is adjustable and allows you to balance the pedal pressure to perfection. This also reduces the stress on the bulkhead.

The suspension spring plate caps can crack after a while, and then the post forces its way through the pressing. Extra metal and some webbing is the solution.

IMPROVEMENTS AND MODIFICATIONS

STRUCTURE

The same modifications listed as maintenance are also an improvement mod to the structure of the car – anything that stiffens up the shell can only be a good thing, as the suspension works so much more effectively if mounted on a stiff shell.

Backdating to prettier and lighter body components is discussed on the forums at www.ddk-online.com and www.forums. pelicanparts.com.

Possibly the most cost-effective way of stiffening the car is a commercially available rollcage, which can also be bought as a drill-and-bolt kit rather than welded in. This will also give you a much better chance of walking away from a crash.

Spot-welding as a method of shell construction is primarily just a cheaper way of doing it, but also allows a degree of shell flex which is okay for road cars, and makes life quieter and more civilised. If you want your 911 to be stiff and accurate, and if you're working on the shell yourself, take the time to continuously seam-weld as much of the shell as you can reach. This is a routine part of traditional rally car preparation, for good reason.

Strut braces to keep the MacPherson strut towers the same distance apart will also make a big contribution to shell stiffness. Lowering the whole car, particularly getting it back down from the giddy heights of Land Rover-style US bumper regs ride-height, will lower its centre of gravity and make it sit better. The front end is already adjustable, so it's a matter of measuring it and getting the ride-height on both sides even. Camber, toe-in and bump steer are all affected by lowering the suspension. A full alignment will sort the first two, but if the front's too low the steering will kick until you raise the rack height. The rear end calls for slightly more dismantling, and involves moving the rear torsion bars round by a few splines to match the front ride-height. Your alignment check should include the rear suspension as well. Turbo tie-rods are another useful upgrade for 911s: they sharpen up the steering. You can also get stiffer aftermarket torsion bars.

Anti-roll bars should be retrofitted to some of the early cars which are inexplicably missing them, and bigger bars can make a useful improvement to the roll characteristics of all 911s, without spoiling the ride much. Note how the standard anti-roll bars keep getting bigger as time goes on.

New halogen headlights are a good idea. If you can, change just the bulb to save money, but don't touch the new glass bulb with your fingers as the sweat marks cause overheating and early bulb failure. Replace the rubber seals around the lights as well to keep the headlight bowls dry.

MECHANICALS

If you buy a 1975 911, bin the heat exchangers and airbox straight away. The airbox on '75 cars is not only prone to blowing up if you squirt the throttle at the wrong time, it also lets the engine drift off tune. However, a good 1973 costs $20,000 while a good 1975–80 car costs $10,000 – and it doesn't cost $10,000 to sort this problem out, making a '75 much better value.

Some say that the 2.7-litre engine's problems are partly due to inadequate cooling – so replacing the original fan with an 11-bladed one has to be worth doing, even if this is just a rumour.

If you're making exhaust manifolds or getting them made, include additional bolted flanges with gaskets somewhere in the tubing design. This seems to prevent stress fractures due to vibration, and it certainly makes the manifolds easier to get off and on.

If the engine is out, change the bush on which the clutch actuating arm bears when you change the clutch. If the bush wears right out, the ball on the arm snaps off.

The biggest individual improvements to the car can be quite small, but can yield disproportionately big benefits. Big alloy S brake calipers with big vented discs and Teflon hoses are a major bonus to an earlier 911. The right steering wheel and a redesigned and more comfortable seat can make a big positive difference as well, and can completely change the driver's abilities and enjoyment of fast touring and track use. Sometimes, though, it's necessary just to brace yourself and cough up some big bucks for improvements. A set of Bilstein struts and shocks costs a substantial amount, but the improvement in the car will be both significant and permanent.

A useful little improvement can be achieved by fitting a short shift gear lever, which also gives you the benefits of new bushings at the same time and will sharpen up gear-changing nicely. This isn't as simple as it is on old Fords, as the assembly has to be stripped and rebuilt; but it is still an amateur job, although tricky.

An affordable route to a tasty set of wheels is to buy the occasional battered and scruffy Fuchs wheel whenever you get the chance until you have a set of five. They can even be 'kerbed' and can have slightly damaged or flat-spotted outer rims, although if they're buckled in terms of the relationship between the rim and the bolt-hole plane they're scrap. If they're salvageable you can take them to a wheel refurbisher to get them repaired and get the centres powder-coated in silver, black or any other colour, or have them painted the same colour as your car, and then get the outer rims diamond-cut for a rather fab polished alloy finish. They should then be clear-coated. This will instantly transform a scruffy old affordable Porker into something nicer without breaking the bank.

PRICES

Nowadays, 1970s Porsche prices seem to be rising, with some fairly silly sums being asked for horrible cars. 1972 averages out on eBay at $12,000, with prices from $4,000 to $20,000. The middle and late 1970s seem similar as a snapshot, but one that seemed a good buy was a 1979 Targa with two days to go and bidding up to $12,600. It would be heading for maybe $15,000 or about ten grand in pounds. This looked clean and solid, the only downside being a fairly gross whaletail whose removal would probably entail a boot lid repaint. The car overall looked worn in rather than worn out, and was quite encouraging as a sample of '70s US prices. $20,000 is still going to get you a nice affordable 911, but don't leave it too long.

BEST BUYS

An ugly but solid 2.7 has to be the best bet: look for flat paint in a vile colour, nasty US bumpers and cracked seats, all of which can be taken care of in the UK for a lot less than buying a shiny Carrera.

▼ A California autojumble offers several seemingly solid and presentable 911s for sensible prices. If you know what you want and how to check its faults, you can do a good deal here.

CHAPTER 4

911: 1981–90

white socks and cocaine

Affordability rating ★★★

The end of the 1970s and the beginning of the 1980s saw unemployment figures of four million, and a 30 per cent collapse in UK manufacturing. The Porsche-buying classes were affected as well, and the company faced some difficult times. However, that nice Mrs Thatcher's culture of individual greed made some people rich as the 1980s progressed, and two of the favourite badges of financial success became a red 911 and a cocaine addiction.

A lot of money was made in the City during this period, and a lot of red 911s were bought and flaunted by aggressive and flashy individuals. It's difficult to write about this without sounding like a snob, but everybody's a snob in their own way. The 911 became strongly associated with greedy City yobbos and wannabe City yobbos, rather like modern Bentleys and gangsta rappers today. By the mid-1980s it was very unlikely that the driver of a 911 would be let out of a side street if anybody had the option to cut them off.

However, more 911s were sold during this decade than during the 1970s, so the company ended the '80s in better shape than they had ended the '70s.

Nowadays, that generalised automatic dislike of 911 drivers has to a great extent faded away, although the inevitable statement made by driving a Porsche will still annoy some people and make others envious. If you do enjoy being envied, a 1980s 911 doesn't look markedly different from a 1990s 911, as the styling is evolutionary rather than revolutionary – so as far as most non-petrolhead people are concerned, any 911 will make you look rich and successful. The affordable Porsche budget is after all half the price of a new Honda, which would make you look either boring or bored or both. Even a 1981 Targa looks a lot more expensive than it actually is.

◄ **I'm told that an Audi is now the cool ride for the thrusting young merchant banker. In the '80s it had to be a 911.** [Porsche AG]

BASICS

Body	Galvanised steel monocoque coupé and convertible.
Engine	Rear-mounted air-cooled flat six, normally aspirated and turbocharged.
Gearbox and transmission	All-synchro five-speed.
Suspension	Front, independent MacPherson struts, lower wishbones, longitudinal torsion bars, anti-roll bars. Rear, independent, semi-trailing arms, torsion bars, telescopic shocks.
Steering	Power-assisted rack and pinion.
Brakes	Discs all round.

Fuller specifications and further detailed technical information can be found in Chapter 15.

All 1980s Porsches are at least 20 years old now, so the accumulation of ever more complex electrical and electronic widgets in later 911s means the addition of ever more potential widget failures, and the repair costs of these vary between Raymond Weil and Rolex levels, while we're on the subject of status objects.

Something worth reflecting on is that a Carrera weighs 1,380kg, compared to a 1967 911S at 1,100kg, so you could take the view that middle-aged spread has by now changed the nature of the beast. Is that now closer to what you want from a car, or further away from it?

HANDS ON

As time went on, the 911 got heavier, more powerful and more luxurious. It's a matter of personal preference where along this continuum your frock is blown up highest: you have to decide what you really want a 911 for. You need to test-drive several. My own preference would be for pre-1970, although I have to admit the 1972 Carrera is quite nice too. The earliest cars are light, raw and slightly naughty, and later ones are mature, civilised and safer. The 1980s cars are getting into middle-aged spread territory, with bigger engines to provide enough power to keep up.

We've covered all the main issues in the previous 911 chapters, and an '80s 911 is basically the same beast as a '70s one but heavier and more powerful, and with slightly safer handling.

Another part of the equation is that at some point the rising cost of buying and maintaining newer 911s will take them out of your personal affordability range.

EVOLUTION

1981	911SC Cabriolet revealed at Geneva show with 204bhp, 146mph (235kph), rear wipers. Cats fitted to US cars.
1982	SC available with Turbo front spoiler and rear wing. Bigger alternator, more wiring.
1983	Cabrio in production, new cam chain tensioner design. Flat nose, 330bhp are options. Carrera 3.2 gets 231bhp, better chain tensioners. Oil cooling in front wings, LSD option. 911 Turbo look gets optional Turbo brakes and suspension. Electric heated mirrors, two-stage heated rear windows for Cabrio and Targa. Carrera top speed is 152mph (245kph).
1984	911SC becomes Carrera. Capacity of 3-litre engine becomes 3,164cc, electronic injection appears, bigger brakes for Turbo, bigger anti-roll bars, leather seats all round.
1985	Total sales of 911 since 1963 reach 200,000. Side impact beams appear, and electric seats. Turbo now has air conditioning.
1986	Warranties extended to two years with unlimited mileage. Suspension improvements, 9J x 16 rims.
1987	G50 five-speed gearbox introduced, seats improved, slant nose with retractable headlights optional. Total number of 911s made reaches 250,000. Cabrio and Targa available with turbo. Electric roof appears.
1988	Carrera 2 launched, best road manners yet. Club Sport offers 220lb (100kg) weight saving, lighter valves, higher rev limit.
1989	Carrera 4 offers 4WD, capacity now 3.6 litres, eight spark plugs, ABS brakes, auto tail spoiler, Tiptronic autobox. 911SC gets another 8hp, Turbo gets twin exhaust, bigger turbo, 188bhp. Sportomatic deleted. Electric windows, optional alarm. Seven-year rust warranty.

The most useful advice is to go down the year-by-year list of changes opposite and decide at what point the complications and rising purchase and ownership costs are not worth it. Personally I prefer to avoid elderly computers, although having said that, there is no substantial second-hand market for 911 computers, which suggests they're not generally a problem.

Power levels also rise inexorably, so that's also part of the story, but a rather more positive part of it.

In recent months I've had quite a bit of weekly hands-on contact with a 1982 911SC, as I now usually go for lunch on Saturdays in West Vancouver with a little group of serious gearheads who collect and thrash pre-war cars, one of whom bought the 911 in California and imported it into Canada to sell for a profit which is currently evaporating. This is about a 60-mile round trip from Tsawwassen in Baja Canada where I live, and includes some highway and some city driving. If the weather's good we take either a pre-war Bentley or an Aston Martin DB2. If the weather looks dodgy we use either the Porsche or my Jeep Cherokee. The owner thinks the 911 is generally okay as a car, but he's getting bored with the poor gearchange and is about to try a light synthetic gear oil to improve it. He may also replace the heavy rear bumper with a plastic one to improve the weight balance. The car

PRODUCTION 1981–90	
Porsche 911 Carrera	
1983–89	
Coupé	35,517
Targa	18,468
Cabriolet	19,987
Porsche 911 Carrera 2 &	
Carrera 4 (964)	
1988–93	
Carrera 2 Coupé	18,219
Carrera 2 Targa	3,534
Carrera 2 Cabriolet	11,013
Carrera 2 Speedster	930
Carrera 4 Coupé	13,353
Carrera 4 Targa	1,329
Carrera 4 Cabriolet	4,802

is also smogged and really quite slow considering it's a fairly light car with a 3-litre engine.

The handling on long, smooth curves is good, but after covering some miles in it, I think the same handling could have been achieved without the fairly harsh ride. If it can be done with a bike-powered Lotus Seven, it can be done with a 911. The fast part of the regular Saturday trip is okay in the Porsche, but I'm just as happy to use the Cherokee. It has a smooth 4WD gearbox, it rides better, and at roughly

▼ **An early '80s 911SC coupé, in a dashing shade of orange, and the open road – a recipe for big smiles.** [Porsche AG]

▲ **Tombstone seats are worth having, if only to reduce whiplash on being rear-ended.** [Porsche AG]

▼ **Some Porsche interior trim can be visually quite upsetting, and also very much dates the car. It's replaceable though.** [Porsche AG]

1,400kg/4,000cc/200bhp/240lb/ft compared to the 911's roughly 1,200kg/3,000cc/200bhp/200lb/ft, the Jeep's nearly as fast. Although I would have to concede that the Jeep is much more likely to fall over during an elk test.

With increasing experience of a 911, I'd probably tend to choose a 944 Turbo or a 928 instead, as they both offer better handling and performance for less money.

HISTORY

Between 1978 and 1982 the Turbo went up to 300bhp, which is fairly muscular. In 1980 the 911 gained 8bhp, and the Turbo got a twin-outlet exhaust. All engines got new ribbed valve covers with better gaskets. Electric windows appeared, as did an alarm system. The Sportomatic gearbox was binned.

1981 saw the factory rust perforation warranty extended to seven years, which can only be a good sign. Indicator repeaters appeared on front wings, the non-turbo European 911 got 204bhp, and the dashboard knobs were illuminated. The 911SC achieved a 146mph (235kph) top speed and a 0–62mph (0–100kph) sprint of 6.8 seconds. The improved non-exploding clutch disc was available from 1981.

1982 saw an old design fault finally sorted – the cam chain tensioner was now operated by engine oil pressure. Nothing worrying appeared during 1982: an improved roof-rack system made it easier for yuppies to carry their skis to Courchevel. Side-window demisting was a useful addition, as was a bigger alternator to deal with increasing electrical demands. Some visual tarting-up appealed to the fashion-conscious non-mechanically-minded buyer – lookalike Fuchs-styled wheels with black centres and shiny outer rims, and Turbo lookalike wings and spoilers.

The Cabrio launched in 1983 was based on the Targa shell, with additional stiffness added to the floorpan. There was a new flatnose option using pop-up 944 headlights, but a current asking price is £35,000. If the flatnose styling appeals to you, a better option is a 1983 911 with a flatnose replica kit from Showcase-Bodyparts.com at $1,000. Electric heated mirrors, rear seat belts and a 'pre-silencer' top the list of not-interesting options, but leather seats and a new stereo for the Cabrio would be nice. Well worth having is 1984's upgrade to the K-Jetronic fuel injection system. In 1984 the 911SC model became the Carrera with a 3.2-litre engine producing 207bhp, and got a matching brake upgrade.

The Swiss were now becoming obsessive about

exhaust noise, resulting in even more silencing and a special Swiss-market second gear to reduce revs for their government's drive-by quietness measurement.

The top Turbo option was now 330bhp, with 5.2 seconds to 62mph, and it topped out at 168mph (270kph), or 171mph (275kph) in flatnose form. 1984 also saw many of George Orwell's depressing predictions coming true, and saw the 911SC replaced by the 911 Carrera 3.2 with digital Motronic fuel injection, a reinforced crankcase, an even bigger alternator, an extra oil cooler and the new oil-pressure-fed timing chain tensioners, reducing significantly the chance of breakage and piston-to-valve contact. The new engine format achieved 207bhp on low-grade fuel, and a limited slip differential was an option.

The 'Turbo-look' non-turbo 911 model now came with the option of some genuine improvements as well as cosmetics: Turbo-spec suspension, four-pot brakes, 16in rims and low profile tyres. There were many wheel options, and also some options to upgrade anti-roll bars and shock absorber rates.

Complications/luxury upgrades now included electric windows, heated mirrors, a headlamp power wash, a leather-rimmed steering wheel and automatic climate control on the coupé and Targa models. Cabriolets sported standard leather seats. Coupés reached 152mph (245kph) and got to 62mph in 6.1 seconds.

The Turbo look, somehow very '80s, was available on Targa and Cabrio as well as coupés in 1985. Good ideas included beefed-up suspension specs, a shorter and sharper gear lever movement, 2mm added to the anti-roll bars and side impact beams in the doors. Other ideas that may lose their initial gloss due to old and corroded electrical contacts include thinner electric seats, central locking, air-conditioning and heated screen-washer nozzles.

1986 saw another mix of good, bad and in-between. The good includes yet thicker anti-roll bars and a new ten-year rust warranty, indicating serious confidence in Porsche's rustproofing techniques. Neutral changes include the beginning of seriously fat low-profile wheels and tyres with 9J x 16 alloys sporting 245/45 tyres. Also neutral was the make-up mirror, rather beside the point in a 911, and bad was the non-Turbo versions' dropped transmission cooler and lower power.

From 1985–6 the 959 appeared, which was a slightly tamed racing hi-tech tour de force, and is something of a footnote because we can't even afford a service on one, never mind buying one. Also, the one guy at Porsche who could sort out the 959's 1980s electronics has now apparently retired…

During this period and post-2.7, the warranties on Porsches became much more extended as the cars' unusual reliability made it safe for the factory to do so. Good marketing and advertising ensured that people now thought Porsches were reliable as well as fast.

Turbo engines in 1987 became available for Cabriolets and Targas. Catalysed engines still made 217bhp, not too bad, and a big bonus was the new bigger and stronger Getrag G50 gearbox. The engines had been getting more and more powerful and the drivetrain needed a boost to match. The G50 came with an hydraulic clutch – usually an improvement over cable operation.

The Carrera was now giving 217bhp, with the Turbo at 282bhp. Electric seats were introduced (which can be plundered and fitted to earlier cars – most Porsche seat fittings are interchangeable).

The convertible roof on a Turbo was now electrically operated, and electric operation was optional on non-Turbo versions. This is bad news – an ageing manual convertible roof can be gently fiddled up and down, but an ageing electric one either works, or jams and breaks. New leather cladding on the electric-mirror control knob, on the other hand, isn't a worry.

1988 saw a milestone – the 250,000th 911. The passenger seat was now electrically operated, and the wheels were ever fatter Fuchs alloys – 7J x 15 fronts and 8J x 15 rears. The Carrera Club Sport took

▼ The 1982 oil-pressure-operated cam chain tensioner can be retro-fitted to earlier engines: well worth doing.
[Porsche AG]

the same tone as the 944 Club Sport, with a lighter shell, stiffer springs and lots of trim left out to the tune of 220lb (100kg): its engine made 321bhp and with lighter valves it revved to an enthusiastic 6,840rpm.

A major change came in November '88 with the 911 Carrera 4, which had a completely new bodyshell under an outer skin that still looked like a 911 although 85 per cent of the body panels were new. Drag coefficient was 0.32, a useful improvement, and a very cute feature was a spoiler that rose from the body at higher speeds and retracted at lower speeds. The running gear was also completely new: torsion bars were out and the new shell featured MacPherson struts front and rear, with coil springs. Transverse links were used at the front, and aluminium semi-trailing arms at the rear. Anti-roll bars could be found at either end. More dramatically, the Carrera 4 was four-wheel-drive. Brakes matched the performance with ABS and four-pot callipers on vented discs at all four corners. Wheels were 6J x 16 front with 205/55 tyres, and 8J rears with 225/50 tyres.

A new 3.6-litre engine featured a vibration damper, magnesium chainboxes, 11.3:1 compression, twin ignition distributors, ceramic port liners and an air mass sensor rather than an air flow sensor. However, that high compression ratio and variable-quality modern fuels meant that the knock-sensing on each cylinder was crucial rather than just a piece of interesting techy progress.

The AWD system delivered 69 per cent of power to the rear wheels and 31 per cent to the front, but was also electronically controlled. Better heating was welcome – air-cooled 911s need all the help they can get – but the introduction of power steering was getting further away from the original character of the 911. However, 5.7 seconds to 62mph (100kph) and a flat-out 162mph (260kph) were more to the point. The twin mass flywheel, intended to stop a low-speed gearbox rattle, turned out to be a bad idea and caused problems.

1989 was the last year for the Carrera and for the 5.2-seconds-to-62mph Turbo, which had only just achieved a five-speed gearbox. It also saw the introduction of the Speedster: sadly, prices for them are still silly.

The Carrera 4, having made its debut and initial splash, was in 1990 offered in assorted cheaper versions. Coupé, Targa and Cabrio could be bought with 2WD, smaller brakes with fewer pistons,

▶ A crash-damaged or stolen and recovered project is quite a good option: you can't afford a late 911 Cabrio on a £10K budget, but this one is worth a lot less than a complete example. Check the car's legal status before going anywhere near it.

▼ Somebody's had the car quite well painted after the repairs, and the shut lines around the doors look good on both sides. It's worth investigating a little more, then.

▼ The wings are straight and the inner wings look okay too, so the body damage was basically either quite light or has been well repaired. It will need some replacement bumpers and trim and a sort-out of the scruffy interior.

vacuum rather than high pressure brake hydraulics and Tiptronic, the first Porsche semi-automatic gearbox for a couple of decades.

At the end of the 1980s the next economic slump hit, so rather than developing an expensive new engine the 930 engine was unearthed again and beefed up to 3.3 litres and 320bhp.

WHAT TO LOOK FOR

Most of the issues described in the previous two chapters apply to 1980s cars as well, so study all three to get a realistic picture of the period and budget that will suit you.

STRUCTURE

Modern galvanising is good news, but it doesn't stop rusting, just delays it. After 19 years the ten-year factory rust warranties are now further out of date than Dannii Minogue. Even so, you're probably still looking at cosmetic rather than structural rust on '80s cars, unless they've been

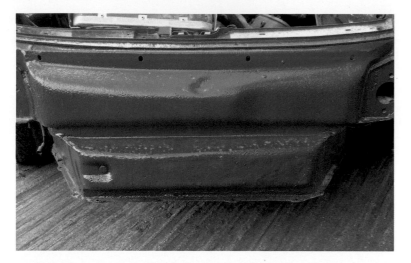

▲ **This substructure at the front has been visibly straightened out, but on close examination everything looks adequately straight. It's worth getting the car to an alignment shop for an inspection, and then making an offer.**

▲ **The engine is all there, and nobody has been interfering with it. That's good news.**

▶ **Bad news is that the airbag's gone off, which means the car has had a relatively significant thump.**

in an accident. Repaired accident damage can start creeping corrosion anywhere there has been paint damage and repair work, and there's also the possibility of compromised shell rigidity if panels have been straightened rather than replaced.

Electric windows do not always age well, and, obediently observing Sod's Law, always fail in the down position in the rain. The advent of alarm systems tends to be bad news, as their components are deliberately concealed throughout the car's wiring. Useful against thieves, less useful to stranded owners.

ENGINE

The new oil-pressure-driven cam chain tensioner was fitted in 1983, and was a significant improvement. It can be retrofitted to earlier engines, but any post-1983 car already has that advantage.

A *Road and Track* editor recommends the post-1984 injection system as a significant improvement.

Digitalised fuel injection is another word for computer. When working, computerised fuel injection is more efficient. However, capacitors do not last indefinitely, and nor do sensors and corrosion-prone connections, which provide even more roadside strandings and fat repair bills than the computers themselves.

Premature valve guide wear occurs with the 3.2 engine. Look for rich blue oil smoke in the mirror on the over-run after high-speed cruising.

TRANSMISSION

The 915 gearbox goes from 1972 to 1986, and is a good strong box, but the bigger boxer engines and hard driving put it under stress: if you think about it, the reason for the introduction of the G50 is that a stronger box was needed. The Getrag G50 gearbox fitted from 1986 on is apparently even better than the 915 box, but while that's excellent news if you're buying a later car, the G50 box sadly can't be retrofitted to earlier cars without fairly significant complications. G50/00 is the European spec version of the gearbox, and the USA G50/01 box has slightly closer ratio gears.

The exploding clutch that spits rubber bits everywhere, mentioned in the last chapter, was fitted until 1981.

Turbo models pre-G50 should have the beefed-up four-speed G30 gearbox, and post-G50 they should have the G50/50 with reinforced end casings.

MAINTENANCE AND REPAIRS

STRUCTURE

Electrically-operated convertible tops are complex and involve considerable forces and several electric motors, neither of which is good news when the structures reach a certain age. One Cabrio was recently on sale very cheaply because of a broken roof mechanism, which gives you an idea of the potential cost of a repair. Regular lubrication and keeping everything in adjustment will help.

ENGINE

The Carrera 3.2-litre engine can suffer from very premature valve guide wear, which means a top end rebuild. Keep an eye open for high oil consumption.

DRIVETRAIN

Post-1986 cars with the G50 gearbox also have an hydraulic clutch, which is simply a better way of doing it. You can usually get home if it leaks, it's smoother in operation and it doesn't pull through the mounting on the bodywork. Just keep an eye on the fluid reservoir level, although if it runs out you can often get home by topping up and then pumping the pedal to get a clutch and resting your foot on the pedal to retain pressure and keep going, before bleeding it through properly later.

IMPROVEMENTS AND MODIFICATIONS

STRUCTURE

Backdating 911s is all the rage now, and replacing big fat 1980s bumpers with small, light '70s bumpers is a smart move aesthetically as well as offering a useful weight reduction.

The introduction of MacPherson struts cuts costs, but it also means leaving a gap between the strut towers for the luggage space. All MacPherson strut cars suffer from movement as hard driving makes the monocoque bend and the strut towers lean towards each other. Aluminium strut braces bolted between the tops of the two struts complete the fourth side of the square and stiffen the structure up nicely.

There are panel kits to make a 911 look like a 959.

ENGINE

Retrofitting the oil-pressure-fed cam chain tensioner is worthwhile.

It may be worth thinking about a 'standalone' computer, which replaces the standard computer and is programmable by laptop – expensive, but in skilled hands very effective for getting the absolute most out of an engine. You also have the cheaper option of 'chipping' the original computer to take it much closer to the real potential of the engine. Many upgraded replacement computer chips provide better torque and power curves as well as more and smoother power than the original manufacturers' programming, which seems odd but is definitely true in many cases. Steve Wong's chips seem to have a good reputation. Many upgrade chips are rubbish, so do your research.

Earlier single-wire cylinder head temperature sensors are unreliable and best changed for a two-wire sensor.

DRIVETRAIN

Upgrading to a G50 gearbox would be nice, but this is a big and complex project. It would normally be better to stretch to a later car with a G50 already fitted.

PRICES

In the UK, prices on 1980s 911s seem random although high: the importance of condition seems to outweigh that of the year, although 1990 does seem to precipitate something of a leap in the prices. Many 911s on offer suspiciously cheaply seem too good to be true, and probably are. The number of UK cars with a dodgy history is remarkable, and Porsches are both fast and desirable, so they do attract the attention of the unwholesome. Checking each potential purchase for theft and write-off accidents would be prudent. You may still choose to buy a previously damaged car, but don't pay five grand over the odds for it. Down the American west coast, the average price of an '80s 911 is around $15,000, or £9,000 – still quite accessible.

BEST BUYS

As 911s get newer, a trip to the US west coast to get top value becomes a better idea. Look for a car with flat, shabby paint and a rough and cracked interior, as you have some control over the cost of a paint job, and second-hand interior trim in the UK is available as it doesn't get destroyed by too much sunlight.

There's a diminishing returns aspect to the later 911s – there are improvements as time goes on, but there is also a distinct rise in cost and complexity. Porsche repair costs can be massive. If you know what you're doing, or have access to skills at sensible prices, buying a damaged or faulty car could net you a bargain. On the other hand, buying a later car just before a major failure without the expertise or resources to repair it cheaply… could spoil your whole day.

Personally, I'd think about 1987 as a good year for the '80s – the tough G50 gearbox is worth having, but there aren't too many computers yet.

CHAPTER 5

911: 1991–6

coming of age

Affordability rating ★

The 911 of 1996 was an entirely different beast from the first 911 of 30 years previously, but it was still a rear-engined air-cooled flat six. The introduction of water-cooling really meant the end of the true 911. There will doubtless be much discussion of that in saloon bars the length of the land, but it's a significant enough watershed, as it were, to draw the line. As far as I'm concerned, there are no water-cooled Beetles, and there are no water-cooled 911s either. The discussion is academic for our purposes anyway, as later water-cooled Porsches will not be in affordable territory for a while yet.

The affordability of 1990s 911s, apart from their purchase cost, is also compromised by their increasing complexity and the inaccessibility of repairs to people without a Porsche-supplied diagnostic computer.

However, we'll take a brief look at the 1990s 911s: they will eventually become affordable, and club members will always find ways of getting things done without spending £125 an hour at a dealership.

◀ **Rather like mistresses, car designs become more plump and more expensive as time goes on.** [Porsche AG]

HISTORY

The Carrera 4 continued to develop with its four-wheel drive and a new coil-sprung chassis which could be fitted with either a two-wheel-drive or four-wheel-drive set-up, according to model and budget. The Carrera 4 had a 3.6 twin-spark 247bhp engine and the concurrent Turbo version put out 315bhp. The automatic spoiler also made its appearance – it buzzes up when a particular speed is reached, but doesn't retract until you get back down to 5mph or so, so that everybody can see that you've been going dead fast. Top marketing, that. In 1991 the Carrera RS

BASICS

Body	Galvanised steel monocoque coupé and glass-roofed coupé, plastic/alloy bumpers.
Engine	Rear-mounted air-cooled flat six, turbo option.
Gearbox and transmission	Five-speed and six-speed all-synchro depending on year and model. Tiptronic semi-auto five-speed option.
Suspension	Front, independent MacPherson struts with coil springs, lower wishbones, anti-roll bars. Rear, independent, semi-trailing arms, MacPherson struts with coil springs over, anti-roll bar.
Steering	Power-assisted rack and pinion.
Brakes	Discs all round.

Fuller specifications and further detailed technical information can be found in Chapter 15.

▼ **The trendy blobby fashion details of the 1990s can't disguise the classic shape of the 911.** [Porsche AG]

was introduced, with 260bhp, and this is another much-copied car. Our budget won't get near a genuine example of these sought-after iconic Porsches, but replicas abound, and you can always make your own if you like the look of a particular RS or whatever.

1993 saw the introduction in the US of the RS America, which was a good idea. A little cheaper, a little lighter, based on Carrera 2 mechanics and a Turbo-look body with good brakes and suspension, but not turbocharged. The European Turbo of that year was making 376bhp and was good for 180mph (290kph). In 1993 there were more comprehensive and lengthy warranties and a range of new finance options, and the stiffening of the Carrera chassis to match the continuously increasing power.

The following year the Carrera 2 became just the Carrera, and the Carrera 4 was lightened and fitted with a more sophisticated limited slip differential between the front and rear axles. Traction control was improved, and the semi-automatic Tiptronic box was fitted with control paddles on the steering wheel in imitation of Formula 1 – more good marketing. Customers buying Porsches purely for their engineering and performance got a six-speed manual box instead.

All flat six engines got better internal balancing, lost their harmonic balancers and the need for one, and were fitted with lighter con-rods. The

3.6-litre engine now produced 272bhp, and both Carrera and Carrera 4 claimed 179mph (288kph). The 928's rear suspension system, known as the Weissach axle, was introduced to the 911, again slightly steering the weighted wheel in a corner to discourage the car from spinning into the scenery. Mind you, with the car now able to corner at 1G on a sticky surface, the handling was pretty sharp despite the engine still being in the wrong place after 50 years.

Prices were down in an attempt to get some life into a dead market, and gradually the sales numbers turned the right way again. 1996 brought with it a remarkable new Targa design, with a huge glass sunroof that slides back into the bodywork. The new 400bhp Turbo was strongly influenced by the 959, although by now the electronics were rather more reliable. The late Turbo was more of a 959-influenced roadgoing supercar than a showpiece hi-tech racer fitted with registration plates. Whatever: the result was a 50 per cent increase in sales and a much healthier-looking future. This is where we bow out, though – it's going to be a while before these cars slide beneath £10,000. 1998 is also really the end of the line for the 911 concept, as the introduction of water cooling really makes it a different car in the same way that getting rid of the Boxer would do. RIP the 911. There will be plenty of argument about that, but not here.

PRODUCTION 1991–96

Porsche 911 Turbo (964) 3.3-litre/3.6-litre 1991–92/1992–93

3.3-litre Coupé	3,660
3.3-litre Cabriolet	6
3.6-litre Coupé	1,437

Porsche 911 Carrera/ Carrera 4 (993) 1993–97/1994–97

Carrera Coupé (272bhp)	14,541
Carrera Cabriolet (272bhp)	7,730
Carrera Coupé (285bhp)	8,586
Carrera Cabriolet (285bhp)	7,759
Carrera Targa (285bhp)	4,538
Carrera S Coupé	3,714
Carrera 4 Coupé (272bhp)	2,884
Carrera 4 Cabriolet (272bhp)	1,284
Carrera 4 Coupé (285bhp)	1,860
Carrera 4 Cabriolet (285bhp)	1,138
Carrera 4S Coupé	6,948

Porsche 911 Carrera/Carrera 4 (996) 1997–2001

Carrera Coupé	31,135
Carrera Cabriolet	23,598
Carrera 4 Coupé	12,643
Carrera 4 Cabriolet	9,411

Additionally, in 2001–02, limited run of 911 'Millennium' Carrera 4 Coupés, with special trim and 'ChromaFlair' paint

▼ The definition of a 911 is that it has an air-cooled flat six at the wrong end. Otherwise it's not a 911. [Porsche AG]

▲ Even the later 911s kept to the original dash styling.
[Porsche AG]

1991 The Carrera RS was lighter by 10 per cent at 2,712lb (1,231kg), with 260bhp, and 7.5J front and 9J rear wheels. The Turbo engine was now 3.3 litres, and had a bigger turbocharger, Bosch K-Jetronic injection, electronic ignition, a bigger oil cooler and 320bhp. The chassis had stiffer springs, cross-drilled rotors, bigger callipers, ABS, 17in 'Cup' wheels (with offsets that made them unsuitable for retrofitting to earlier cars), 7J x17 with 205/50 ZR17 front tyres, 9J rear with 225/40 ZR17, Weissach-style rear-end steering and handling improvements, a leather interior, an upgraded cassette player, airbags, acceleration of 5.0 seconds to 62mph (100kph) and a top speed of 168mph (270kph).

1992 The 911 RS was lighter and stiffer with a hand-welded shell. On the cosmetic side, the 'Turbo-look' could be applied to the Cabrio. The 'Exclusive' model turbo featured hotter cams, a revised intake and heads, 355bhp, 4.7 seconds to 62mph and a 174mph (280kph) top speed.

1993 The Speedster was back, with 250bhp and a cut-down screen. The 911 RS America had 17in 'Cup' wheels, a fixed rear wing, electric windows, central locking and an alarm. The 911 turbo got new pistons, 360bhp, a limited slip diff, bigger brakes, a 20mm lowering job, 8J x 18 front wheels with 225/40 tyres, 10J rears with 265/35 tyres, and a 198mph (318kph) speedo with a 174mph (280kph) top speed. There were assorted expensive limited editions.

The new smoother 993 body had wider wings, more luggage capacity, a bigger electric spoiler, ellipsoid lights, a new 3.6-litre engine with a stiffer crank, lighter rods/pistons and 272bhp, a six-speed box, multi-link rear suspension, an active brake differential and LSD, double action twin tube shocks, better brakes with Bosch 5 ABS, 7J x 16 wheels with

▶ The very tail-heavy proportions are revealed in this rather unkind shooting angle.
[Porsche AG]

Carrera 2

▶ ▶ For most of the 911's production life, it relied on big rear-end rubber to keep a grip.
[Porsche AG]

205/55 tyres and 9J x 245/45 rears and a redesigned interior. Performance was 5.6 seconds to 62mph, with a top speed of 168mph (270kph).

1994 The 993 Cabriolet had a self-deploying wind-blocker, and the 'Exclusive' version came with new cams, 285bhp and 3.8 litres. The 'Motorsport' version came with 299bhp and a top speed of 174mph (280kph). The Carrera 4 in coupé and Cabrio form got 272bhp from 3.6 litres, and was manual only.

1995 1995 saw the duplication of Tiptronic controls on the steering wheel. The twin-turbo RS and GT2 models offered less turbo lag and 408bhp. Cooling was improved with the fan turning at 1.8 times engine speed rather than 1.6. OBD (On Board Diagnostics) were improved. Options included 18in hollow spoke wheels, in 8J diameter with 225/40 front tyres and 10J with 285/30 at the back. Xenon headlights, air conditioning and a rear wiper added to sophistication, or to complication, depending on your viewpoint.

The final and fastest 911 was the GT2 with a Turbo body, big spoiler, aluminium doors and 430bhp. The power was controlled by an electronic LSD with asymmetric lockup under load. It was lower and stiffer and ran 9J x 18 front wheels with 235/40 tyres at the front and 11J with 285/35 profile rears, topping out at 183mph (295kph).

1996 The 1,000,000th Porsche rolled out on 15 July. The 3.6 got 285bhp, and the new two-wheel-drive Targa appeared, with a slick sliding glass roof in three parts – the wind deflector, the sliding section and the rear window. The Carrera 4S featured a wide body, an extending spoiler, a six-speed gearbox, all-wheel drive and lowered suspension. The alarm was now remotely operated and the phone in the car was hands-free. The Vario-Ram tuned-length intake appeared, and the 3.6 got bigger ports and a cam and piston change. The 'Exclusive' got 3.8 litres and 300bhp and the Turbo engine now made 430bhp.

The Carrera S was available as a coupé in narrow or wide fittings, with a stock or Turbo body, and with Tiptronic. It had two-wheel drive and used spacers to get its wheels out to meet the fat body, which actually cost 3mph in top speed. The RS was dropped.

1997 The swansong Turbo S had twin turbos, 424bhp and a bi-plane whale tail, and the 911 story closes with the change to water cooling.

Water cooling has brought some fairly breathtaking prices: if you wear out the discs and pads on your late model GT2, the replacement cost is £10,000, coincidentally our theoretical budget for an entire car. Porsche are now the world's most profitable motor car company, and the word Affordable is dissolving into the mist.

▲ The longer front overhang on the later 911s balanced the car better, reflecting improvements in its manners over the years. 'Cup' wheels will look dated quite quickly. [Porsche AG]

HANDS ON –
The owner's view

Jeff Jeeves has many good things to say about his 993 Carrera 4S. His '67 911 featured in Chapter 2, but although the '67 is his favourite he's been very impressed with the later 911 as well. This is the one with Turbo wheels, flares and brakes but no turbo. The performance is apparently awesome; the car is reliable, agile, docile, very quick and safe. For covering ground very quickly, it would be hard to beat. It is one of his 'sensible' Porsches, and its high-speed cross-country abilities, reasonable fuel consumption and reliability change the picture slightly when it comes to affordability. Unless you have a family to tote around the place, you could reasonably use a 993 911 as an only car, which means you could redirect

the money you would otherwise have had to spend on some boring saloon. Porsche engineering is still generally of higher quality than some other manufacturers, and that should help to keep the running costs reasonable, if you look after your car well. Jeff's car has cost nothing much to maintain during his ownership – a 24,000-mile service at a Porsche dealer cost £250 and nothing of any significance has so far broken or failed.

As far as flavour goes, the physical monocoque is still basically the same as a 911, and he feels that some of the essential character and DNA of the original 911 remains in the late-model air-cooled 911s. However, as far as he's concerned the 993 911 is really the last of the breed.

Jeff did try out a water-cooled 996 with the new shell, but he didn't really take to it. He didn't like the way it drove, or the styling, or the water-cooled sophistication: the noise was also wrong. It didn't really suit him any more. Which is not to say there's anything bad about it, just that it's strayed too far away from the original 911 concept for that particular Porsche enthusiast to accept it as the same car. As Jeff owns several 911 Porsches covering a wide range of models and years, his opinion is worth listening to.

WHAT TO LOOK FOR

Largely as for '80s 911s, but blue smoke means walk away.

STRUCTURE

You're not looking for rust so much as repaired accident damage. There should be no visible defects in undercoatings. More electrics and electronics mean more potential and potentially cross-related problems, so check that absolutely everything works.

ENGINE

With the cost of repairs and the decreasing opportunities to repair late Porsches yourself, a full professional check would be the smart move. Be sure to get compressions checked. Cylinder compressions should all be within ten per cent of each other. Blue smoke on the over-run indicates valve guide wear: repair cost can be between £500 for valves and £5,000 for guides. Some valve gear parts have been failing at 60,000 miles.

TRANSMISSION

The Tiptronic gearboxes and the all-wheel drive systems are complex and electrically and electronically controlled. Make sure there are no funny noises, and run through all available functions several times. Test-drive hard enough for the car to reveal any drivetrain faults it might have.

SUSPENSION

Something to ponder from the affordability viewpoint as these cars get older and eventually become accessible is that a boring old sensible full-profile tyre is 80 per cent of the tyre's width and maybe 6in (150mm) deep, and can deal with potholes. A 35 per cent profile tyre is only an inch or two (25–50mm) deep and will not survive a significant pothole. Nor will its rim. One pothole could mean buying two rims and four tyres…not affordable at all.

MAINTENANCE AND REPAIRS

ENGINE

The Carrera 4 twin mass flywheel is not 100 per cent reliable, but was improved for 1992–4.

IMPROVEMENTS AND MODIFICATIONS

STRUCTURE

Any shell with MacPherson struts will benefit from a brace between the strut tops.

ENGINE

Mocal sell an effective aftermarket thermostat-controlled oil cooling kit, which helps keep oil temperatures in a safe range.

TRANSMISSION

Gear linkages can get sloppy and baulky, and it can help to replace the bushes throughout the linkage.

PRICES

Out of affordable territory, mostly, unless you can find a mess and sort it out. A brief surf around Seattle, LA and San Francisco reveals a few possibles – a 1990 Cabrio with a broken roof for $16,000 and a stolen/recovered coupé for around the same. The average price of the shiny and fully functional ones is $37,000 plus shipping, taxes and all the rest. The 1990s are still essentially out of reach.

BEST BUYS

The only affordable 1990s 911 buys are damaged or stolen.

CHAPTER 6

924

the Audi GT

Affordability rating ★★★★★

The Porsche 924 is derided by many as an Audi GT fitted with a Volkswagen LT van engine. This is excellent news for the hunter of affordable Porsches, as it has rendered a rather good Porsche almost worthless. There is truth in the Audi/VW van scenario, but it's not as straightforward as some would have you believe. The 924 was indeed designed as a VW or Audi GT, but it was designed at Porsche by Porsche designer Harm Lagaay under Porsche styling chief Tony Lapine. And the car does indeed have a VW van-derived engine, but the 924-spec version of the engine was fitted with a forged steel crank and Bosch K-Jetronic fuel injection and gave a solid 125bhp.

The Porscheness of the 924 only comes sharply into focus when you realise what has been achieved with engineering creativity and relatively cheap VW parts. The gearbox itself is shared with post-1973 Audis, but it's in a Porsche alloy housing and is relocated to the back of the car and connected to the engine via a torque tube.

A front-engined GT with a rear gearbox and transaxle? This is radical, interesting engineering, never mind where the parts come from. One of the results of this thinking is a front-to-rear weight distribution of 53 to 47 per cent, which is approaching perfect. Add to that a high polar moment of inertia for safe stability at high cornering speeds, and fully independent suspension all round, and you have a car that handles so well it's spawned its own race series. Do affordable Porsche buyers care if the front struts, rack and rear trailing arms came from a Beetle and the wishbones came from a Scirocco? Only when it comes to paying VW prices rather than Porsche prices for replacements, I submit, M'lud. Not that VW prices are necessarily particularly cheap: those Scirocco wishbones can now be overhauled, but for a long

◄ The only thing cheaper than a 924 is the classic insurance required to drive it. [Porsche AG]

BASICS

Body	Steel monocoque hatchback with detachable front wings. Galvanised monocoque underbody.
Engine	Four-cylinder water-cooled 2-litre iron block, with alloy OHC head. Bosch K-Jetronic injection. 125bhp. 924S has Porsche 944 engine fitted. Turbo, 170bhp in Europe, 143 in USA/Canada/Japan.
Transmission	Via torque tube to rear-mounted four-speed (later five-speed) manual gearbox/clutch/differential assembly.
Suspension	Front, MacPherson struts with coil-over dual action shocks and lower control arms, optional anti-roll bar. Rear, independent with trailing arms, transverse torsion bars, dual action shocks, optional anti-roll bar.
Steering	Unassisted rack and pinion. 924S power-assisted.
Brakes	Disc front, drum rear, with servo.

Fuller specifications and further detailed technical information can be found in Chapter 15.

EVOLUTION

1975	First 924 made in November.
1977	Rear suspension improvements in August.
1978	New trim, optional dogleg-pattern five-speed gearbox.
1979	Conventional H-gate gear selection. Breakerless ignition. Automatic option. Horrible interior options. Turbo version appears.
1980	Suspension stiffer, anti-roll bar standard. Carrera GT launched, then GTS, GTS Rally, Carrera GTR: relatively rare, expensive.
1979	924 Turbo appears. Many detail upgrades and toughening of parts.
1983	Last Turbos made.
1986	924 replaced by 924S with 2,479cc all-alloy 150bhp Porsche-designed engine.

▼ **Cutaway shows the gearbox/ transaxle placed at the back of the car for excellent weight distribution.**
[Porsche AG]

time the wishbone assembly had to be bought as a complete unit, which cost an outrageous £500. Doubtless buying them in a Porsche box would have added a significant additional premium.

The 924 quickly became a very good seller after a five-speed box had been fitted and the interior noise had been quietened down. Many people were very happy to buy a 924, Audi van or not, which means there are still plenty around to choose from.

The 924 is actually quite a lot lighter than the 944, and when a 2.5-litre Porsche 944 engine is fitted to a 924, it goes faster than a 944. That couldn't be allowed when the 944 was launched, so the 924S has a lower compression and a detuned ECU.

One of the advantages of running a 924 is that you don't need to own another car as well unless you have older children. The rear seats are definitely occasional, but the luggage capacity under the glass hatch is enough for a two-week touring holiday. In fact it's a pretty big space, although rather shallow, and could be very useful indeed for day-to-day use: a cheap 924 will never be a pampered Sunday car anyway.

Its cruising and handling abilities would tempt you to consider long-distance touring, too. The

PRODUCTION

Porsche 924/924 Turbo/924 Carrera GT
1976–85/1978–82/1980–81
Coupé	121,510
Turbo	12,427
Carrera GT	406

(plus 59 GTS and 19 GTR competition 'Evolution' models)

Porsche 924S
1985–87	12,195
1988 model year	4,079

◀ **Difficult to believe that this is a dealer price for a solid, functional Porsche with many years of useful life left in it.**

▼ **924s do bring the risk of dodgy 1970s colour schemes, but you can always repaint.** [Porsche AG]

drive from the UK to the Nürburgring through France comes to mind – some autobahn blasting, some good *Routes Nationales* and some tight wiggly bits. For a press-on touring trip a 924 would be pretty rewarding for good drivers, as well as being safer than most cars for drivers who aren't quite as good as they think they are.

The 944 and 968 are developments of the 924, and many useful upgrades can be retrofitted to earlier cars – so even if your budget is strictly 924, it's worth reading this and the next chapter and being aware of what can be raided from later cars.

HISTORY

▼ The smooth front aspect with its neat spoiler achieved a remarkable 0.34Cd drag factor, which does no harm to fuel economy.

The design brief for the 924 was developed by the joint VW/Porsche organisation that had generated the 914, and this new project was intended to replace the 914, which was not selling very well. The new car was to have been branded either VW or Audi. Then the joint VW/Porsche organisation was disbanded, at which point VW owned the design. However, the oil crisis of the time brought into question for VW the whole concept of a high-end VW/Audi sports GT. Porsche plucked up their courage and bought the design outright, despite grim economic times. A regime and direction change at Volkswagen left the ex-NSU factory and workforce spare, so Porsche decided to work with the new blood at VW, to make and market the new GT car as a Porsche, and to build it at the NSU factory.

That the car had a van engine is also true to some extent, and was true for a while. The 924 engine is a 2-litre overhead-cam straight four with an iron block and an alloy head, developed by Audi at Ingolstadt from a VW design, and it was used in Volkswagen's LT van as well as being sold to the American AMC corporation. Its primary characteristics are good torque and toughness, ideal for a van. Is a strong, torquey van engine such a bad place from which to start developing a reliable and practical high-performance road car engine? Silly question, really.

Lots of people happily disagreed with the purists, and by 1979 the 924 represented 60 per cent of Porsche's sales: to some extent it sidestepped the social stigma of the 911's unfortunate association with City yobs and greedy bonuses.

◄ This is not an Audi. It's a Porsche design, constructed mostly by a different and lower-grade manufacturer. That puts it in the same company as a Pininfarina-built Ferrari, then.

▼ You even get a decent-sized boot and hatchback with a 924, although it's not as much of a genuine GT as a Reliant Scimitar.

▲ The interior is strongly Audi in flavour, which means crisp, simple, well-made and functional. A little detailing would have it looking like new in an afternoon.

▼ The seats are very much in the '80s German style – they feel rock-hard but are actually very comfortable indeed over long distances.

HANDS ON – The driver's view

The car I tried out as a sample of the 924 breed was actually a 924S, which represents the graduation of the 924 from an Audi GT to a much higher Porsche parts percentage including the engine. It still carries the van stigma but is becoming a pretty serious Porsche.

I would seriously have considered buying the 1989 example I test-drove at Lodgesports in Manchester, if I still lived in the UK. The car was in sound bodily condition with no real rust visible at all, and although the paint was mildly scruffy it would have come up nicely with a little T-Cut and an afternoon's work.

It only had 72,000 miles on the clock, which may

well have been true considering the general level of visible wear, and the engine was in fine condition. The gearbox bearings had just been replaced after the car had been traded in for a 944, and there was no drivetrain noise at all. The interior was rather grubby but in good condition, and a decent valeting would have brought it up very well indeed.

On the road, the car felt very stiff, solid and competent. Urban Manchester these days doesn't allow for much in the way of experimental tail-sliding to confirm the magazine reports, but contemporary reviews of the 924 universally praise the handling. A spot of roundabout action at increasing speed provoked no ill behaviour, merely protests from the tyres at a roughly equal volume back and front. No marked oversteer or understeer, and it felt as though it would just drift rather than doing anything embarrassing. The main impressions the 924S left me with were very good seats, plenty of low-down power, and a tangible rigidity of the shell.

The cockpit is austere but functional in '80s Audi style, although it becomes comfier and more flash as the model years go by. If a 924S doesn't present itself fairly quickly and you decide to compromise on bhp and buy a clean 924 instead, I don't think you would regret that either.

You don't need to go to California to find a good 924. The example I checked out at Lodgesports was very representative of what's currently available, and the price on the windscreen was a bargain £1,895. As far as the prices go, it doesn't matter too much whether a 924 has the Audi engine or the later Porsche engine – the car I looked at had the Porsche engine and was still way under two grand. I'm sure that waving a small wad of rumpled fifties would have got an even better price on it, and a private sale should be cheaper yet. Lodgesports are a small and helpful garage who specialise in Porsche service and race prep for the older models, and they often have good-value cars for sale. As well as the 924, there was also a 944 for sale at £1,995 with 184,000 recorded miles in good condition.

The Lodgesport chaps like 924s and 944s a lot, and choose to race them rather than to race 911s, although they have the option to do either. They recommend the 924 as a top car available for pocket money, with the reservations that the gearbox bearings wear out and the electrics are slightly dodgy.

WHAT TO LOOK FOR

STRUCTURE

Check for rust – on early cars the bodyshell is galvanised, but the doors, bonnet and front wings aren't – and in any case, as I've already said, galvanising merely delays rust rather than stopping it. So still check thoroughly before spending any money.

Check the electrics – minor malfunctions are not a big deal, but when buying every fault allows you to look doubtful, squeeze your chin and demand more money off the price. Very old and generically complex electrics and electronics are in the process of becoming more and more of a problem for cars now becoming classics.

Battery boxes are always worth checking for nasty rust beneath the battery, as blocked drains keep the area damp and batteries tend to leak acid.

Check that the upper door hinges aren't cracked, or the doors will fall off.

Dashboard cracks can appear – check for poor repairs.

As regards trim, the door handles, the column stalks, the ignition lock and even the handbrake are straight out of the Audi/VW parts bin. However, it's all good well-made stuff with no cheap corners cut, and it all works well. 1980s Audi engineering has a lot going for it. Given the popularity of the 924 for racing, pull the carpets up and check if there are holes drilled in the floor by the B-posts. If there are, that means it's probably a retired race car with the rollcage taken out.

Damp carpets can mean the sunroof seal is leaking.

Door gaps should be an even 7mm all round. If they're not, check very carefully for accident damage. Check underneath and inside panels where possible for damaged galvanising and localised rust.

The general buzz is that the 924 is not altogether

up to Porsche's 1980s engineering and quality standards, but then not many cars are. It's still a high-quality German car, and at the prices we can get one for these days it will do very nicely indeed.

ENGINE

The VW/Audi engine is a good one and is not a reason to reject a standard 924. It's generally wise to avoid the 924 Turbo, which doesn't have a good reputation. One problem with the 924 was poor hot starting, due to engine heat and fuel vaporisation, which can mean opening the bonnet and churning the engine over for five minutes before it will fire up: that can only get worse with a red-hot turbocharger in the engine bay as well. The 924's Turbo conversion was very involved and complicated and added 60lb (27kg) to the engine,

▲ **Seats fold down to provide really quite a useful load area.**

◀ **This is the VW van engine that all the negative fuss was about. It has a special Porsche-spec forged steel crank, a reliable fuel-injected 125bhp, lots of torque and is as tough as old boots. It even says Porsche on the cam cover. All sounds pretty dreadful, doesn't it?**

which resulted in suspension changes as well as other concomitant engineering changes, such as the relocation of the starter motor to the other side of the engine. There were never that many 924 Turbos made, so turbo-specific spares are a problem. The power is only up from 125bhp to 150bhp (plus 60lb added weight) so you're not really missing much.

The hot-starting problem is generic until after 1980. Open the bonnet, wait a while, try again. Improvements in fuel pump location etc can be retrofitted from scrapped later cars, or you can always cut some louvres in the bonnet.

If you decide to buy a 924 Turbo and the owner doesn't let the engine idle for a few moments after your demonstration drive, don't buy the car. If that's not done, the oil gets cooked, and the turbo probably is too. The reason for this is that the turbo is red hot and is cooled by engine oil, and if it's switched off directly after hard use the oil boils in the turbo and then deposits caked hydrocarbon crud in it. Idling the engine for a few minutes gets the worst of the heat distributed safely around the whole engine.

Blue smoke on the over-run usually means valve guide wear. Constant blue smoke is usually bore wear.

As regards matching engine/chassis numbers – as affordable Porsche buyers we don't care whether the engine number matches the chassis, as long as it's a good engine. However, lots of people do, so you can knock more money off the asking price if the engine is 'wrong' for the car.

TRANSMISSION

Gearbox noise indicates that a regular 924 gearbox bearing failure is on the way. Replacement is £500 at Lodgesports in Manchester, so even if you're nowhere near Manchester use that information to get a good repair price at your local independent garage.

SUSPENSION

Steering wander suggests misalignment: could be adjustment, could be bent pressed-steel front wishbones. Check tyres for odd tyre wear patterns as described in Chapter 14.

MAINTENANCE AND REPAIRS

STRUCTURE

A great deal of the detail on a 924 is sourced from VW, so parts replacement, although expensive compared to Ford, is not expensive compared to Porsche. If a door handle or something breaks, try a VW/Audi shop first. Familiarise yourself with what can be bought from VAG parts bins without the Porsche premium being added.

ENGINE

Expect some valve guide work at around 90,000 miles.

Electrics on 924s are getting elderly now, and did not have a good reputation to start with. Keep a spare cold start relay and a fuel pump relay on board.

TRANSMISSION

Gearbox bearings are a problem that comes up occasionally, and the job costs around £500 – so be prepared to have to pay that bill now and again with a really long-term car.

Hot-starting problems can be helped by adding a non-return valve after the fuel pump exit, and by using a big battery with enough grunt to keep the engine churning until it fires.

IMPROVEMENTS AND MODIFICATIONS

STRUCTURE

The shell is pretty good, and is already stiff. Adding a rollcage will improve any production car's torsional rigidity and safety. You can update the exterior styling with wider 944 wings and bumper mouldings.

Better seats from 944s, 911s and in fact most other Porsches can also be used, if you want to upgrade to leather or racing buckets.

ENGINE

A 924S is a 924 with a 944 engine in it, but detuned to stop its lighter weight making it faster than a 944. Most of that lost power can be reclaimed quickly and easily by changing to a 944 ECU, although replacing the pistons to raise the compression probably isn't worth doing on a car of this value.

A 944 Turbo engine assembly complete would liven up a 924 nicely.

BRAKES AND SUSPENSION

944 brakes would also be an economical upgrade, as they're shared with the 924 Turbo.

Second-hand 944S suspension is even better value, with thicker anti-roll bars and a little extra stiffness. A top buy for a DIY project would be a cheap 924 Turbo with a suspect engine, because the drivetrain, gearbox and suspension are much upgraded: bin the turbo engine and fit a late 944 motor.

Later wheels tend to be bigger with fatter tyres, and are interchangeable between 924 and 928, although 968 'Cup' wheels introduce offset and width complications.

PRICES

Usable 924s can be bought from £1,000 upwards with a current MOT.

BEST BUYS

Later rather than earlier cars, as trim and noise reduction improved as the years went by. At £2,000 for a good one, you really can't go wrong. The earlier dogleg-first-gear Getrag five-speed box is good for racing but a minor nuisance in town driving. A 924S gets you a Porsche rather than an Audi engine. Keep an eye open for a 924 Carrera GT – 400 of them were built for racing homologation, and they had stiffened and lightened shells (930kg), Bilstein suspension with titanium rear booster coil springs, 12in and 11in wide rims under fat poly arches, and took the Turbo engine figures from 210 to 320bhp and from 202 to 282lb/ft of torque. They won't be cheap, but on the other hand nowhere near as many people will be fighting over them

as they would for a similarly modified factory hot rod 911.

Absolute best buy has to be a 924S, partly in terms of Porsche authenticity and pure Porsche power, and partly because you can enjoy applying inverted snobbery to 911 owners whose engines originated in Volkswagen Beetles.

▲ **924 Turbo, bad idea. 944 Turbo, good idea.** [Porsche AG]

▼ **Telephone dial wheel styling is dated.** [Porsche AG]

944 and 968

the Porsche GT

Affordability rating ★★★★

The 944

If you're uncomfortable with the van engine concept and don't want to spend any time justifying it when somebody jealous starts going on about vans, buy a 944. You can tell your tormentor dismissively that your 944 has a purer Porsche engine than a 911 Carrera. That's quite true – the flat six 911 engine is still a development of the VW Beetle engine, but the slant four in the 924S and 944 is based on the design concepts of a pure Porsche engine, the V8 from the 928.

The 944 Turbo can apparently match a normally aspirated engine for reliability and long life, and water-cooling rather than oil-cooling the turbocharger seems to have made it last as long as the engine, which is excellent news.

The 944 is still essentially a 924 under the skin, although the skin does begin to look progressively sexier and more muscular. The aluminium Porsche engine with its balance shafts was smoother than the previous Audi item as well, and fluid-filled engine mounts smoothed things out yet more.

The dash is in the Porsche style, but much more modern, organic and oval. The drag coefficient is still a milestone 0.34, and there are continuous small improvements such as cast aluminium semi-trailing arms replacing the pressed steel ones.

The 944S2 runs a 3-litre development of the same 2.5-litre engine, and achieves 208bhp without a turbo. Lodgesports in Manchester have much experience of the 924 and 944, and raced a 944 in 2003, replacing an earlier 924 racer. Top handling, they say: perfect weight distribution. Note that as Porsche repair and race-prep specialists, they can acquire and race whatever reasonable-budget Porsche they choose – and they chose a 924 and then a 944.

◀ **Buying a 944 could cost several hundred pounds more than a 924.** [Porsche AG]

BASICS

Body	Steel monocoque hatchback with detachable front wings, fully galvanised.
Engine	Porsche-designed four-cylinder water-cooled 2,479cc alloy block, later 2,990cc. Twin balance shafts, liquid-filled engine mounts. Alloy OHC head. Bosch K-Jetronic injection. 163–208bhp naturally aspirated, 217–247bhp turbocharged.
Transmission	Via clutch and torque tube to rear-mounted five-speed manual gearbox/differential assembly.
Suspension	Front, MacPherson struts with coil-over dual action shocks and lower control arms, optional anti-roll bar. Rear, independent with (later cast alloy) trailing arms, transverse torsion bars, dual action shocks, optional anti-roll bar.
Steering	Rack and pinion, power-assisted on later models.
Brakes	Big discs all round, with servo.

Fuller specifications and further detailed technical information can be found in Chapter 15.

EVOLUTION

1981	Launch.
1983	Power steering option.
1985	New swoopy dash. Turbo S on sale, offering 220bhp.
1986	Twin-cam 16v 944S, 3 litres, 208bhp, one year only.
1987	ABS, upgraded suspension.
1988	Turbo SE 250bhp, upgraded drivetrain.
1989	944 is 2.7 litres. 944S2 is 3 litres, 211bhp. Cabriolet launched.
1991	944 models replaced by 968.
1992	Stripped-out Club Sport available.
1994	Optional torque-sensing LSD, optional serious suspension and brake upgrades.
1995	Model deleted.

HISTORY

The launch of the 944 meant that the VW/Audi van engine was finally consigned to history, and a new engine designed and built by Porsche was introduced. This 2,479cc OHC slant four shared a lot of its design and some of its manufacturing machinery with the 928 engine, although the two actually have no major parts in common. In spirit the 944 engine is effectively half of the V8 from a 928, and gives 163bhp.

The naturally aspirated 2.5-litre four got a new head with 16 valves and more power, although the Turbo version retained the eight-valve set-up. The wings began to bulge out as bigger wheels and tyres appeared. By 1989 the 944S2 offered 16 valves, 3 litres, 211bhp and 207lb/ft of torque, and 149mph (240kph). This cost somebody £31,000 in 1989, but a couple of decades later you'll still get 90 per cent of the car for around 10 per cent of that original price.

The Turbo version took the power figures from 163 to 217bhp with serious torque, giving a top speed of 155mph (250kph) and some very useful mid-range grunt. The Turbo S featured the 16-valve engine as well as the turbo, and power was 247bhp. The turbo is a much better installation than that on the 924, and proper water-based turbo cooling gave it a long life.

PRODUCTION

Porsche 944	
(944 Lux in UK)	
944 Series I (1982–84)	64,486
944 Series II (1985–87)	41,174
944 (1988)	5,480
944 2.7-litre (1989)	4,426
Porsche 944 S/S2	
1986–93	
944 S (1987–88)	7,324
S2 Coupé	9,352
S2 Cabriolet	6,980
Porsche 944 Turbo /Turbo SE	
1985–88	
Turbo Coupé	17,627
Turbo S Coupé	1,635
(1989–91) Turbo Coupé	3,738
(1989–91) Turbo Cabriolet	528

▶▶ **Continuous updates sat well with the harmonious body design of the 924/944/968.** [Porsche AG]

▼ **This car is superior in almost every way to a 911 for about 20 per cent of the cost, and still looks like an expensive Porsche to most people. Why wouldn't you?** [Porsche AG]

▲ Brian Schneider has taken an old 944 and added lots of parts from newer cars to build a very nice low budget car.

▶ Brian's car has a more modern swoopy dash than the old-school square German '80s number in the 944.

▶ Brian has bolted in a set of very nice leather 968 seats. Second-hand trim from crashed newer cars can be quite reasonably priced if you keep your eyes open and search eBay regularly.

▶ The boot is a decent size, with plenty of room for the luggage and shoes of even a high-maintenance weekend companion.

HANDS ON – The owner's view

A long-term hands-on view of the 944 comes from Brian Schneider, whose 1984 944 was bought in 1992 for $1,200. Brian has two 911s as well as the 944, and prefers the 944 to the 911s. The 944 out-handles both of them and is just as reliable, so he prefers to drive that most of the time. One of the 911s is a '97, which has such a tiny mileage on it that he's decided to keep it just as an ornament.

Brian's 944 is a hodgepodge of parts from different years, according to which particular bits he fancied. He's used some new parts and acquired many more from junkyards and on eBay. The nose and front wings are from a Turbo. Brian has put about $7,500 into the car, but much of that is in uprated suspension and wheels. If you just count the repairs and running costs he is really only into the car for $4,500, including the initial repairs. That's over 14 years, and works out at about $400 a year including the purchase price. He recommends buying one at about $1,500 and budgeting about twice that to get it into good condition if you 'shop smart'.

The rear-end mechanicals are unpopular with Brian, as it's all rather tight and tricky to get at. It's a nuisance having the gearbox at the back, but dynamically that's the best place for it.

Fortunately the rear-mounted gearbox on a well-serviced 944 is unlikely to have to come out. Many will last 200,000 miles and will still slickly synchromesh into first gear at 7mph (11kph).

WHAT TO LOOK FOR

STRUCTURE

When buying a 944 remember that the shell is still a 924, although galvanising helps. Look for and complain about rusty battery trays and rust on the corresponding panel on the other side of the engine bay.

One detail that's quite nice is the swoopy dashboard that came in with the 944 and updates the interior compared to the rather 1980s angular dash that remained with the 924.

Look for dark blue, green and brown paint colours, as these are unpopular and harder to sell, and therefore cheaper to buy.

ENGINE

The important test for the condition of the engine belts is to listen for a whine from the front end, which should be audible. If it's silent, that means the tension's wrong and there could soon be trouble with the roller bearings and an £800 bill with the engine having to come out. Check for service bills with regular belt changes.

A front crankshaft oil seal leak can be dealt with during a timing belt change, but a rear oil leak is an engine-out job.

The bores of the 944 engine are aluminium (alusil), and need regular oil changes. Check for colour and consistency of current oil: thin, low and black is bad. Check maintenance records if possible, and check the newness of the oil filter, which is inaccessible and may not have been changed much by lazy owners or mechanics.

Oil in the water and the resultant white emulsion in the radiator can mean a blown head gasket, a warped head or a damaged radiator, although failed oil-to-water heat exchanger seals are also quite common. Walk away. Turbo engines tend to blow head gaskets, which can result in coolant leaking into the cylinders, causing galling of the cylinder walls. Check the sheaf of bills for head gasket work, and look for blue exhaust smoke.

TRANSMISSION

A noisy clutch can indicate that its rubber disc is on the way out. The repair involves stripping the shaft out.

SUSPENSION

Check wheels for damage, as they're expensive to replace. Check both the inside and the outside edges, and while you're down there check the wishbones for damage.

Front wheel shimmy is common but is not usually down to a single reason. Can be expensive to eliminate. Steering racks are prone to failure.

MAINTENANCE AND REPAIRS

STRUCTURE

Grab some spare electric window motors when you get the chance – they're a weak point, although failure is an irritation rather than a major problem. Body parts are expensive if bought from Porsche, and cheaper pattern parts are less likely to fit well, so for 924 and 944, second-hand genuine parts are the way to go. Make sure the engine bay water drainage flaps stay clear.

ENGINE

Change the engine drivebelts and cam chain tensioner as soon as you buy a 944. Thereafter change them religiously every 30,000 miles. A failed belt on an interference engine means piston-to-valve contact and a bill that's even bigger than the resulting bang.

◄ The battery area is always prone to acid leaks and rust, so make sure it's kept clean and any acid damage is repaired quickly.

◄ These drain hole flaps must be kept clear, or horrible body rot in an inaccessible place is a possible result. Check when buying, and then keep the holes clear.

◄ The pure Porsche engine gets the car well away from its VW/Audi origins, but not as far as Porsche snobs would like. Excellent – that'll keep the prices down, then.

◄ The belts at the front of the engine should make a whining noise if all is well. If they're quiet, they're out of adjustment. Walk away.

Turbo models can suffer from cracked exhaust manifolds, but they can be repaired by welding. Engine designers often seem to forget how heavy turbochargers are, so adding some bracing to the manifold while welding it anyway may be worthwhile.

One key thing you need to know about the 16-valve engines is that there is a small but serious design fault in the cylinder head. The cam chain tensioner can let go after a while. The chain then jumps and strips the gear teeth off the cams, which results in an engine full of shiny metal mince followed by a terminal rebuild quote. Worse news is that because of that, there are now only a few spare second-hand 16V heads available. The cam chain tensioner only costs a fiver, so when you buy a car, change the tensioner as well as the cam belt. Even if you get a full history including a recent belt and tensioner change, just do it again. The existence of a garage receipt for new belts merely proves that a receipt was written, not that any work was done.

16-valve engines have weak (and expensive) cast camshaft gears, but all you can do is check them periodically for cracks.

Oil in the water is more likely to be a leaking heat exchanger seal or radiator fault than a head gasket. Good news is that the 944 remains a DIY possibility for general maintenance and repairs. A head gasket change takes three hours for somebody experienced, and should take a day for a cack-handed amateur with previously clean fingernails and a Halfords socket set. Porsche parts prices don't get cheaper just because the cars are old, but with the number of scrapped 924s around it's very possible to run one just from the second-hand spares market.

If the rear main engine oil seal fails, the good news is that it can be replaced without taking the engine out.

It's better to leave changing timing belts to

an expert. Timing belts and cam chain tensioners should be changed every 30,000 miles.

The liquid-filled engine mounts wear out and need changing regularly. The job is simple but time-consuming as you have to drop the crossmember and jack up the engine. Don't bother with Porsche Original Equipment parts for this repair, as the cheap alternatives last just as long. It's worth checking the OE prices, though – some Porsche parts prices are ludicrous, but some are still reasonable. Belts and critical engine parts should always be Porsche products, but are in any case unlikely to be available anywhere else.

IMPROVEMENTS AND MODIFICATIONS

STRUCTURE
New interior parts can be very expensive, but the Internet is an excellent source of good second-hand parts. 968 seats fit the 944, just like 911 seats. Even four-way powered seats can be bought for reasonable prices by hunting around, so keep your eyes open.

Replacing the nose of an ordinary 944 with a Turbo nose and wings is a stylish upgrade – the Turbo nose is longer and offers different proportions from the normal 944 styling.

ENGINE
As ever, improving incoming gas flow gets more power, and upgraded ECU chips add power by allowing components to run much closer to their real limits, at a calculated risk to their longevity. The best way to get really significant performance is to start with a Turbo – a bigger turbocharger, chipping, higher boost limits and an intercooler will add up to some serious horsepower, and you can mix and match cheaper Japanese turbo goodies with the Porsche parts.

WHEELS
Some 17in 'Cup' alloys from 993s are around for sale, but check the weight – they may look exactly right, but if the rims feel too heavy they're fakes. Bad fake wheels at 149mph (240kph) are not good news, and if you don't survive the resulting prang you won't be able to go and have a bit of a chat with the guy who sold them to you. There's also the matter of getting the right rim offsets. Find a good performance wheel shop from which to buy tyres and get them fitted, even if you buy your wheels privately elsewhere, and make sure the offsets are right. 'Cup' wheels on a 944 need spacers to get the rim edges in the right place relative to the wheel arches and the suspension.

▶ The fluid engine mounts make the cabin a civilised place to be until they wear out. Vibration is the clue, and replacement is simple but tiresome.

They make a big difference to the car, though – the fat low-profile tyres make the car much more sensitive and touchy, and the wheel is much more responsive. Standard wheels and tyres will feel less nervous, which may suit you better depending on how you use the car.

BRAKES

It's better to buy non-Porsche brakes, as long as the brake manufacturer has a good reputation. Each £100 spent on, for instance, Brembo or Willwood (Willwood offer particularly good value) is going to get you bigger discs and more calliper pots than the same £100 spent at a Porsche dealership. Porsche will be buying the brakes in from somebody else anyway, so you might as well cut out the mark-up and the middleman and buy direct – the idea being to achieve less bang per buck, as it were. Mind you, when the press tested the 924 brakes on the track at its launch, the standard disc/drum set-up outlasted the tyres, so there's nothing at all wrong with standard Porsche brakes in good condition.

SUSPENSION

Second-hand 944S and Turbo suspension is a useful budget upgrade, giving thicker anti-roll bars and a little extra stiffness. A good shock option that seems to work well is Koni adjustables set at their max stiffness.

PRICES

944 prices are kept low by the sheer age of the cars and by the high numbers made: really good ones start at just a few thousand, and projects show up on eBay for just a few hundred.

BEST BUYS

The 944 may be missing most of the charisma and the soundtrack of a 911, but it's also missing most of the price tag… and none of the performance. Any solid 944 in good mechanical condition has to be a top Porsche bargain.

Top value 944/968 has to be a Turbo if it can stay together, which it will tend to do because the turbo is water-cooled. Less good value but rather nice would be a Cabrio 944.

▲ The low prices of 944s combined with their excellent handling makes them a natural choice for low-budget racing.

▼ Turbo Cabrio is a top car, but van-engine snobbery damages its value. Just what we want to hear! [Porsche AG]

▼ The 968 is still a development of the 924, and there's nothing wrong with that. [Porsche AG]

The 968

The 924's doors and some of the engine design and chassis lived on in the 968 launched in 1991. At 240bhp (achieved with variable cam timing and manifold development) and with a six-speed gearbox, the 968 will be as much fun as a bag of monkeys when good ones depreciate to within affordable range. They're getting close, as the earliest ones go back to 1991.

There is a regular version, a Sport version and a Club Sport. There are also a very few Turbo S models, but that information is academic as the numbers are insignificant. The Sport is – well, sportier than the standard 968, and the Club Sport is a lighter stripped-down version supposedly for club racing, and is fairly hard-core. Club Sports initially cost 20 per cent less, which may or may not help with financial accessibility, but they are quite basic.

The engine is apparently rather noisy for a car of this period, and has a cammy feel – so you need to wind it up to get a real kick out of it. Weight distribution is finally the perfect 50/50 front to back, and the weight at around 3,000lb (1,360kg) is light enough to allow pretty serious performance.

However, the 968 is not very competitive with its period Japanese rivals, and the engine seems to be rather rough and a little flat below 3,000rpm, so prices may depreciate into real affordability sooner rather than later. They won't depreciate anywhere near as fast as the Jap rivals, though...

BASICS

Body	Steel monocoque hatchback and convertible with detachable front wings, fully galvanised.
Engine	Porsche-designed four-cylinder water-cooled 2,990cc alloy block. Twin balance shafts, liquid-filled engine mounts. Alloy OHC head with four valves per cylinder, variable valve timing.
Transmission	Via torque tube to rear-mounted six-speed manual gearbox/clutch/differential assembly. Optional Tiptronic semi-automatic gearbox.
Suspension	Front, MacPherson struts with coil-over dual action shocks and aluminium lower control arms, optional anti-roll bar. Rear, independent with (later cast alloy) aluminium trailing arms, transverse torsion bars, dual action shocks, optional anti-roll bar.
Steering	Power-assisted rack and pinion.
Brakes	Big Brembo vented discs all round, with servo and ABS.

Fuller specifications and further detailed technical information can be found in Chapter 15.

HISTORY

Launched in 1991, the look of the 968 finally got away from the Audi-tainted 924 shell, as the 968 bears more of a family resemblance to a 928. Something important to traditional Porsche customers is that the 968 was built in Zuffenhausen rather than by Audi.

The understated styling to some extent belied the serious performance.

Suspension remained 924-based but much further developed, with the settings very similar to the 944 Turbo for a more sporting than touring feel. The bigger brakes necessary for a 150mph car were also fitted, inside 'Cup' wheels of 16in and 17in diameter and low-profile tyres with a maximum width of 255.

The 968 was discontinued in 1995.

WHAT TO LOOK FOR

STRUCTURE

Check Club Sports for bolt-holes suggesting previous rollcage fitting, as you don't want to buy a shagged-out ex-race car. As dealers tried to shift the last few years' production, the options were loaded on, so later cars have more toys. Check for broken headlight housings, which are rather fragile.

ENGINE

As 944 but with variable valve geometry, so there are more components to go wrong. The engine is also very powerful for a naturally aspirated straight four, so you want to see fresh oil and hear no rattles.

GEARBOX

Tiptronic gearboxes may well reduce values, as they are semi-automatic.

MAINTENANCE AND REPAIRS

ENGINE

The main engine belt should be changed when you buy a car unless you know for sure that it's been done recently. A garage receipt is not sufficient proof. If you plan to keep the car, consider replacing the water pump and belt guide rollers at the same time, which many owners do.

GEARBOX

There is a control relay for the Tiptronic box that may fail – check the electrics before assuming that problems are more serious.

TYRES

Avoid using tyres with less than a 40 per cent

profile, as the ride becomes harsh and the tyres tend to tramline.

IMPROVEMENTS AND MODIFICATIONS

BRAKES

It's possible to upgrade the brakes to larger 928 S4 items.

PRICES

At the time of writing, several 1992–4 968s with around 120–150,000 miles were on auction at eBay for between £7,000 and £10,000 with classified dealer ads starting around £10,000 and rising to £15,000. A personal appearance at a dealer with a wad of fifties would probably massage those prices down, if you didn't have the confidence to take a punt with bidding at the £5,000 level.

▲ The 944 evolved into the 968. Changes were subtle, but quite extensive. [Porsche AG]

▼ The 968 still looks like the old 924 despite a new shell. Cheaping out on designing new doors may not have been the smart move: just changing the door handles from the Audi ones wasn't enough. [Porsche AG]

CHAPTER 8

912

two pots short?

Affordability rating ★★★

Depending on your perspective, the four-cylinder 912 can be regarded as a poor man's 911, or an interesting car in its own right, or as the spiritual successor to the 356. From members of 912 clubs and registries you're going to get variations on the latter two answers.

With a reasonable top speed of 115mph (185kph), it's not a slow car for a classic, and high-speed driving is relatively quiet and comfortable. However, compared with the unburstable 911 engine with lots more main bearings, the 356SC and 912 engines do reveal their limitations. A well-serviced 911 engine, given a reasonable amount of luck, and regular enthusiastic but not over-enthusiastic exercise, will achieve very high mileages indeed. However, the 912 engine will usually be capable of 80,000+ under normal driving conditions, and much less if the car is driven like a 911. There is a temptation to try to keep up with the abilities of the shared 911/912 shell and suspension, but the four-cylinder engine has definite limits. Treat it as a sports tourer rather than a performance car and you could get over 100,000 miles out of it between rebuilds. That's respectable for a car made in 1965, but rebuild costs are something to think about when choosing between a 91l and a 912.

In the UK the 912 was not a big success, as most people buying a Porsche wanted the whole six cylinders. This seems odd when you compare even the 912's reasonable athleticism with the rather sad performance and handling available from what the British were building as 'sports cars' in the early 1960s. Even the feeblest Porsche represents pretty good performance and excellent handling compared to the Morris Minor-based Frogeye/MG Midget/Sprite and the Austin A60 Cambridge-based MGB. Neither of those is what you might

◄ **The 4-cylinder budget 911 has a significant following in its own right.** [Porsche AG]

BASICS

Body	Non-galvanised steel monocoque coupé and Targa.
Engine	Rear-mid-mounted air-cooled 1,582cc flat four from 356C, detuned to 90bhp. Later, VW 1,971cc injected flat four.
Gearbox and transmission	Four-speed all-synchro with optional five-speed.
Suspension	Front, independent MacPherson struts, lower wishbones, longitudinal torsion bars. Rear, independent, semi-trailing arms, torsion bars, telescopic shocks.
Steering	Unassisted rack and pinion.
Brakes	Unassisted discs all round.

Fuller specifications and further detailed technical information can be found in Chapter 15.

EVOLUTION

1965	Launched April, Targa launched September.
1966	Wider track.
1967	Five-dial 911 dash, safety door locks, new engine mounts.
1969	Longer wheelbase.
1969	912 deleted.
1975	912E introduced: a 911 with 1,971cc *Einspritzung* (injected) VW 411 engine.
1976	Galvanised shell.
1976	912E deleted.

▼ **The Targa with the soft-top rear is a slightly weird-looking animal with a reputation for leaks, but with the rear section down and the Targa roof off, you've got almost a full convertible.**

call a sophisticated thoroughbred, and a 912 would stack up pretty well against them in most respects even without a 130bhp six.

Unfortunately, a good 912 is quite rare in the UK compared to a 911, although the occasional example can be found.

There's no point in duplicating here the information in the 911 chapters about the year-on-year structural and non-engine-related mechanical features of the 912, as it really is a 911 with a different engine. To find out what to look for, check out the warnings in the 911 chapters, as the information is identical.

912 enthusiasts will tell you that their cars handle better than the 911 because they're better balanced. That's certainly true to some extent, as there are two fewer cylinders hanging off the back of the car behind the axle. The 912 is about 250lb (115kg) lighter than the 911, and the weight is undoubtedly better distributed – the 912 is 56 per cent biased to the rear compared with the 911's 59 per cent. On the other hand, most of us might feel that 40 more horsepower and flat-six exhaust pipe music makes up for the 911's relatively minor handling shortfalls compared to the 912.

The earlier 912s had the last of the 356SC engines, with different air filters and a new exhaust knocking 5bhp off the 356 spec to give you 90bhp. Not a slow car, but not a very fast one either. The engine may be cheaper to overhaul than the flat six if you use some short cuts, but it's still pure Porsche, so the bill is not going to be a small one by any standards, and can now rival a 911 rebuild invoice.

Production was originally quite healthy, but the proportion of 911/912 shells fitted with four-cylinder engines declined as the 911 and its flat six became iconic. It also logically follows that the 912 was genuinely the economy model 911, so perhaps upgrading it with a flat six isn't such a heretical thing to do after all.

If you're on a really tight budget and still want a Porsche that looks like a 911, you'll be pleased to find out that although the 912 went out of production in 1969 when the 914 was launched, it came back briefly for a second generation with a Volkswagen engine. You can be very relaxed about the cost of running the 2-litre VW engine if you decide to retain it, and ethically you can be much more relaxed about replacing a VW engine with a Porsche engine even in the form of a flat six. The '70s 912s carry huge bumpers in the US and an extra 400lb (180kg) had been gained over the years, so the later 912 needs all the help it can get in the urge department. Again, revising a 912 by fitting lighter early bumpers helps with weight and appearance.

Overall it may be the look, feel and engineering quality of the Porsche that you like, and you may decide that higher performance is not worth paying for – in which case an earlier 912 with its 356 heritage going straight back to 1948 is a very worthwhile classic car for anybody with the sense to see that, and it could suit you and your chequebook very well indeed.

HISTORY

In many ways the 912 mirrored the process of continuous development that hallmarked the 356. The electrical system was now 12-volt, and there was an optional five-speed gearbox (universal in the USA), making fast cruising that much more civilised and offering better ratios to make use of the available power when pressing on through the curvy bits.

It seems that the 912 was more popular in the States than in the UK and Europe, because not all Americans wanted the maximum performance, and many found the price of the 911 version indigestible. The 911 was to become the mainstream Porsche from the early '60s on, but it cost some 30 per cent more than the 356SC it replaced – quite a big price increase for even a pretty loyal customer to swallow.

Continuing to offer the existing 356SC engine in the new 911 shell as an economy model would not only retain the customers who wouldn't pay another 30 per cent for their next car, but would also bump up the numbers of 912/911 shells being made, resulting in significant savings due to economies of scale, and keeping the cost of making the 911 down. This was good commercial thinking, and over 30,000 912s were sold. At first the 912 sold twice as well as the 911. However, Porsche felt that the engine had come to the end of its development life in its final 912 form, and you can see where they were coming from. There was no further development of the 912 engine.

Other than the engine, the improvements made to the 911 through its life were mirrored in the 912, so later models have a wider track, a 2.25in (57mm) increase in wheelbase and so on.

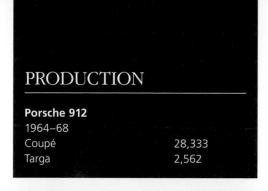

◀ The 912 engine may look like a Beetle four, but is pure Porsche: not as reliable, sexy or powerful as a six, and not as cheap to run or as tunable as a Beetle motor. A good excuse to look for a bargain 912 with a dud engine and play with it, then.

Having been pensioned off in its original form, the 912 came back to life several years later, after the 914 was abandoned. This was a relatively easy task, as it basically meant just fitting some 911s with smaller engines. This time Porsche committed heresy themselves and fitted the second-generation 912 with a Volkswagen engine. The economy-model mid-rear-engined 914 had also used the VW 411-based engine that was fitted to the 912E in 1975. E stood for *Einspritzung* or injection rather than Economy. The 912E carried on with this VW engine until 1976.

▼ As far as most people are concerned, this looks like a top sexy classic Porsche sports car. Irrespective of the engine size or format, it's also a nice car in its own right, and very affordable compared to a 911.

▶ Jim Giordano (www.giocars.com) sells Porsches in Washington State at auction prices, many of them abandoned projects. He's familiar with shipping them to Europe. This 1969 912 Targa is well restored for $12,500.

▶ The soft Targa rear screen is often replaced with the more waterproof and quieter glass alternative. Jim says try both, as the semi-convertible feels really nice.

▶ The interior of this car is not perfect, but it's very nice. British weather is much kinder to interiors than the US, so the UK may be a better source of good second-hand interior parts.

HANDS ON –
The owner's view

The 912 club scene in southern California is healthy, and there are 1,200 owners on the registry, with 400 active club members. Many owners such as Bill Bennett are involved in the 912 club as well as the 912 section of the Orange County area of the main American Porsche club. The UK club scene is also thriving, so there is plenty of help and support available for those rebuilding a car, and lots of social action to get involved with once it's on the road.

Bill owns a nice example of the rare early Targa variant with the soft back window, and feels no need for any additional cylinders. There were only 600 Targas built with soft windows, which is rather a shame because they're effectively full convertibles with a substantial rollover bar, and replacing a glass Targa rear window costs a bomb compared to a plastic one. The cheapest of these soft-roof Targas costs around $9,000, which is still well within our affordable budget. The coupés cost from $5,000 to $10,000, with $15,000 being the maximum price for a seriously good one. Bill's car has been no trouble at all, and it was a smart move on his part to buy the best he could and just look after it. He subscribes to the 'spiritual successor to the 356' group of 912 enthusiasts, and regards the 912 as offering the same basic character and engine as the 356, but with more effective streamlining and better suspension. It's also much more affordable than a 356.

Dave Hillman is another 912 enthusiast who had rather a different experience from Bill Bennett's trouble-free Targa – Dave paid $8,000 for what looked like quite a good 912, but the car has since hoovered up $25,000 in repair and restoration costs. Despite the amount of money thrown at it, the car still has some remaining 'issues', as Dave delicately puts it. That sort of money is way above the possible value of a 912, and underlines his advice to buy the best you can possibly stretch to in the first place to save money later. However, Dave is cheerful enough about his car, and certainly part of the fun for him is in fiddling with it at the weekend and then complaining about how much hassle it is and how much it costs. This is after all his hobby, and if playing about with it

◀ This red Targa from the same source is much rougher, but is only $6,000, leaving a lot more for improvements. It's still quite solid, though, and would not need a massive restoration to be usable.

costs some money, so be it – you don't expect to make a profit from going skiing either. Dave's horror stories are catalogued on his website if you want to commiserate with him and to find out where his 912 trouble spots were. He also runs a 912 talk site. The Internet is a good source of lots of information about the 912, apparently – but you have to bear in mind the perennial computer/Internet problem of rubbish in, rubbish out. There's certainly lots of useful information on the net, but on the other hand any idiot can post whatever drivel they want on it as well. Dave Hillman has made it his mission to collect all the useful non-drivel information on the 912 in one place, so check out his site (www.912bbs.org) and see what he has to say.

912 register president Jeff Trask was quite happy to show off the rusty bits of his otherwise very nice 912, and to recommend checking the floorpans, under the engine, the sills, and the bottom of the front wings as trouble areas. He also peeled back the rubber cover over the sill panel to reveal the only serious rust on his car. If a prospective seller doesn't want you to pull the rubber on the sill panel back and have a look underneath, listen to the alarm bells going off in your head and walk away.

WHAT TO LOOK FOR

STRUCTURE

The 912 is a 911 with a smaller motor, so it suffers from exactly the same structural problems. These change year by year in exactly the same way as a 911, so the same information applies. Study the 911 chapters as well as this one.

With a 912 you are less likely to suffer from dangerous bodged repairs, because to be blunt they're a lot less worth repairing than a badly damaged 911. A cut and shut job, in which the front and back ends of two write-offs are welded together to make more or less one car, is less likely. However, general structural and rust repairs are also less likely to have been carried out for the same reason, so on balance you're more likely to get original rust than bodged repairs.

The major problem with British-bought cars is rust. With Californian and other dry state cars, you can budget for a set of new window rubbers and

◄ The area around the front sidelights is a favourite for rusting, and the lights and lenses themselves are vulnerable. However, Porsche autojumbles offer many cardboard boxes full of replacements.

◄ The bottom of the back edge of the front wings has a tendency to crumble. If the rest of the wing is in good shape, cutting the rust right out and fitting a big patch panel can get a good result without spoiling the fit and front door gap of the original front wing.

◄ If you peel the cover off the sill and see something nasty, there is a stonking bill wafting towards you, as this is a major structural member of the shell. If a seller won't let you remove the screws and take the sill cover off for a proper look, walk away.

▶ The front of the luggage compartment floor is a favourite place for rust and for evidence of crash damage. Check it carefully when you're looking at a 912 or a 911.

▲ **Oil leaks are part and parcel of most old and affordable cars. Look on the bright side, though – at least it stops the central tunnel from rusting.**

MAINTENANCE AND REPAIRS

STRUCTURE

As 911 – same car. Note that Targa seals are grotesquely overpriced – you can spend £500 stopping the rain getting in.

ENGINE

Check valve clearances regularly.

You would probably only have to rebuild a 911 once in your life if it was a weekend car, but I'd budget for two rebuild invoices for a 912. If it does come to a rebuild, it may be cheaper to use a 356SC crankshaft rather than a 912 crankshaft – the rev limit is slightly lower with the 356 crank, but the price of buying it could be quite significantly lower.

Shasta Design offer what seem to be realistic prices on non-original replacement crankshafts and piston/cylinder sets, so repairs may be more of a realistic option if you don't insist on all the bits coming in Porsche boxes.

Parts for the smog devices on the 1968 cars in particular are unobtainable. Fortunately for UK buyers, smog gear can simply be dumped if it can't be repaired. 'Visible smoke' from the tailpipes during an MOT test is all you have to worry about for pre-1973 Porsche-engined 912s. The later VW-engined 912 merely has to be in reasonably good mechanical condition to pass the later emissions tests with no problems, and of course the VW engine costs pocket money to replace or repair compared with any Porsche engine.

GEARBOX

If the car jumps out of gear when going over major bumps, replace the engine mountings with stiffer 911 ones.

IMPROVEMENTS AND MODIFICATIONS

STRUCTURE

Structural and performance improvements are the same as for the 911, but with the limited power available from the 912 the removal of the massive and massively heavy '70s American bumpers will yield even more of a performance improvement, as well as equalling the aesthetic improvement achieved by removing them from a 911.

The 912 is around ten per cent lighter than a 911, and better balanced, so continuing to remove weight to add performance is the way to go. Lowering the suspension and fitting a strut brace to stiffen up the front suspension by keeping the

damage to the paint and trim from the sun instead. The window rubbers have to be regarded as a service item with a limited life in the US, as once they're cracked, what little rain falls is let straight into some very vulnerable areas. California, the West Coast and the dry states are the best hunting ground to find a good one.

MECHANICALS

A 1968 912 is a good car to import into the UK, as the unobtainable 1968 smog equipment, if defective or missing, can render that particular car unusable in California. A '68 912 taken for a failed smog test as part of the purchase will immediately fall in value faster than a Daewoo. However, as long as it doesn't emit visible smoke it will be fine for UK use.

Otherwise, you're looking for evidence that the car has been thrashed to keep up with its 911 looks, as well as indications of high mileage. Look for smoke and rattles from the engine, and blue smoke on backing off the throttle indicating valve guide wear. If receipts suggest that the engine hasn't been replaced or rebuilt in the last 80,000 miles, research the price of a rebuild before completing any negotiations or writing any cheques.

The later VW-engined cars were only made for a short period, and are a good buy. Porsche snobs are snotty about them because they have a VW engine, but affordable Porsche enthusiasts will enjoy paying peanuts engine bills for exactly the same reason. If nobody but you has the sense to buy them, so much the better for getting a good deal.

◄ The engine is functional but has not been rebuilt in recent years. You'd want to check it very carefully, or even think about a transplant.

front wings the same distance apart will also help the handling.

ENGINE

There's a limit to what a 912 or 356 crankshaft will take, but the later VW engine as fitted to the second generation 912 (and which can also, of course, be retrofitted to the first generation) has been the subject of considerable aftermarket development. The Californian desert buggy and the VW drag racing worlds have evolved some monster 2,550cc VW air-cooled fours containing serious kit such as chrome-moly I-beam conrods, and fuelled by electronic fuel injection systems with superchargers, turbochargers and nitrous oxide. A fairly strong 2.5-litre performance version of one of these engines fitted to a 912 would blow quite a lot of 911s out of the water without even breathing hard, and a good turbo set-up on a big Beetle engine in a 912 would humiliate most 911s. You could even leave the 912 badges on to add insult to injury.

Fuller specifications and further detailed technical information can be found in Chapter 15.

HYBRIDS

Even at the risk of being lynched by 1,200 registered owners and 400 club members, it has to be pointed out again to those in search of an affordable Porsche that the four-cylinder 912 engine can be replaced with a six-cylinder 911 engine. As far as Porsche were concerned, the 912 was an economy version of the 911 anyway, and is essentially the same car. There were initially fewer instruments and always fewer cylinders, and the price reflected this. The deleted instruments can be sourced at reasonable prices at Porsche swapmeets and autojumbles, and in any case the full set became standard equipment in the 912 from 1967. Fitting 911 badges would definitely be uncool, but perhaps a hybrid 912/6 badge would be the way to go? Either that or no badges at all.

There's also the matter of rescuing otherwise doomed cars – nobody would bin a good 911 just because the engine had blown up, but the 912 is generally worth a lot less. That situation inevitably means that many are still being scrapped that could be saved by a 911 transplant. Again, just like a kit Speedster-converted scrap 356, any kind of bastardisation has to be a better option than the crusher.

PRICES

A random eBay cruise revealed one 912 in the UK, a nice-looking ex-California coupé with a 914 engine and the bidding at £6,000. On the other hand, a similar surf on the American information superhighway nets us eight cars with the bidding at an average price of $4,000. Which more or less mirrors the above.

BEST BUYS

Best buy has to be a solid, drivable California car with faded paint and cracked seats. It's worth noting that the US export 912 came with the five-speed box as standard, and that the 901/902 gearbox was used in the 911 as well – the only difference is the gear set ratios.

CHAPTER 9

928

from supercar to sold as seen

Affordability rating ★★★★

My own experience of a new Porsche 928 in the 1980s still seems current 20 years on, according to what I'm being told now. A fashion photographer friend of mine with a useful private income went to Germany and bought a 928 new from the factory. I was also in fashion photography at the time, mostly doing test shots for model agencies. Tough job, but somebody had to do it. Quite a bit of time was spent driving around Chelsea in that 928, and there's very little room in the back seats, particularly with a model on your lap.

The 928 is a bargain luxury express for those in the front seats, and has nice little touches throughout such as the rear-seat sun visors. Rear-seat passengers may get a slipped disc trying to get in or out of the car, but at least they won't be dazzled by the sun on the way to the chiropractor.

The owner in question complained to Porsche frequently and vociferously about the car's electrics, which were not very good. In the end he got rid of it before the warranty ran out, and bought an Audi Quattro, in which everything electrical hooted, flashed and buzzed to perfection. However, although the 928's electrics may not ever have all worked at the same time, it did always get where it was going, and it was top fun charging down London's Westway at 4:00am before there were any speed cameras, and before the police had anything fast enough to catch it.

Your experience of a 928 a couple of decades further on is likely to be similar, apart from the Westway and the models on your lap. Of course your luck could always change as far as the models go. The annoying electrical hassles on a 928 won't change, but then you're not paying the price of a one-bedroom flat for a brand new supercar, so the electrical gremlins won't be anywhere near as annoying. Your 928, should you

◀ **928s for me, mean happy memories of mildly misspent youth, although the car in question was traded for an Audi Quattro because of its dodgy electrics. [Porsche AG]**

BASICS

Body	Fully galvanised steel monocoque hatchback with aluminium and plastic exterior body panels.
Engine	All-alloy OHC V8, with 16 and later 32 valves.
Transmission	Via torque tube to rear-mounted five-speed manual or three- and later four-speed automatic gearbox/differential assembly.
Suspension	Front, independent with upper wishbones, lower trailing arms, coil springs over shocks, anti-roll bar. Rear, independent with transverse links, coil springs over shocks, trailing arms and anti-roll bar, Weissach anti-skid rear steering geometry.
Steering	Power-assisted rack and pinion.
Brakes	Vented discs all rounds, with servo.

Fuller specifications and further detailed technical information can be found in Chapter 15.

EVOLUTION

1977	First 928 made. 4.5 litres, 240bhp.
1980	928S has 4.7 litres, 300bhp.
1983	S2, and autobox gains fourth gear.
1987	S4, 5 litres and 32 valves, 170mph (275kph).
1988	GT with manual gearbox and 330bhp.
1992	GTS, 5.4 litres, ABS, 350bhp.

▼ **The 928 is conceptually similar to a 924, but with four extra cylinders.** [Porsche AG]

choose to buy one, will now cost about the same as a decent sofa.

Much maintenance work is carried out by Porsche specialists on the electrics and electronics of 928s. Even if the mechanics are genuinely doing their best and spending ages tearing their hair out trying to get your 928 sorted, they still have to charge by the hour. It will be worth your while investing in a Haynes manual and a circuit tester, and some of that clever electronic-widget spray from Radio Shack that makes things work.

The 928 has an imposing physical presence and looks huge, but that's mostly illusion – it's not big at all, just 10in (250mm) longer than a 911, although it is pretty wide at 74.4in (1.9m). The smooth and curvy shape of the 928 is actually dating very well: as far as most people are concerned it could still look like a brand new car rather than a design from the mid-'70s, as soon as you've updated the wheels and tyres.

HISTORY

Part of the thinking behind the 928's design brief was that the 911 was getting old, and couldn't be relied upon to continue selling forever. In the event, the 911 did indeed continue to sell more or less forever, but that probably seemed unlikely at the time.

The 928 shared more of its design with the 924 than the 911. The new V8 flagship cruiser was designed to face increasingly random and unpredictable American emissions and safety regulations. Water-cooling would ensure quietness in case American noise regulations turned nasty, and the sheer size of the engine would provide enough power to survive carrying lots of extra new smog gear and still give a respectable performance. The idea was also to have a crack at the Mercedes/Jaguar high-performance GT market in America rather than concentrating on pure sports cars.

The 928 arrived with a 4,4/4cc all-alloy overhead-cam 240bhp V8 with electronic fuel injection, driving a rear-mounted gearbox and transaxle with a driveshaft running in a torque tube. The shaft went straight through to the differential in top gear, to cut down on the noise of the usual indirect Porsche top gear. The gearbox was initially an automatic three-speed supplied by Mercedes. Five-speed Porsche manual gearboxes

PRODUCTION

Porsche 928	
1977–82	17,669
Porsche 928S/928 S2	
1979–1983/1983–86	
928S	8,315
928 S2 and S3	14,347
Porsche 928S4/GT	
1986–91/1989–91	
17,894 (including Clubsport models)	
Porsche 928 GTS	
1992–95	2,831

▲ Keep it simple. The understated, subtle curves of this mid-1970s design simply don't date. Pop-up headlights are a little passé, but the general shape is still modern.

◄ The 928 S2 is a good one to pick – there are some updates and improvements, but the electrics are generally still electric rather than electronic.

◀ **The alloy V8 will last for hundreds of thousands of miles if well serviced, but secure the sump plug to keep all the oil in or its life is measured in minutes.**

▶ **The interior is pretty sumptuous. Early epileptic/ migraine chequered cloth seats can easily be replaced by later 928 seats: you can't go wrong with black leather.**

▶ **When you move the adjustable steering wheel up and down, the whole instrument binnacle moves up and down as well. Very slick, and a mechanical system so it shouldn't go wrong.**

were also an option, and the automatic box later became a four-speed and also became the standard fitting.

Suspension was independent all round, featuring wishbones at the front and an interesting semi-trailing arm design at the back, with geometry that made the outer wheel toe-in slightly on hard cornering to cut the risk of an oversteer skid or spin – the Weissach axle.

Porsche inevitably started improving the performance of the 928, and the S model went up to 4,664cc and 300bhp. In 1990 the S4 version came with twin-cam heads and a boost in capacity to 4,957cc and 316bhp. The 928 was always a genuine supercar, and that point was well made with a 171mph (275kph) flying mile at the Bonneville Salt Flats, in a standard car with the catalytic converter still fitted.

The swansong was the 928GTS of 1992, with 5,397cc, 350bhp and 369lb/ft of torque. The end of the line came in 1995, which means the newest 928 is nearly 14 years old.

HANDS ON – The owner's view

Yorkshireman John Oakes runs a very nice 928 that's worth £5,000 tops, even though it's not really that far off its new condition. The car was bought for £34,000 by its first owner and had £5,000-worth of extras fitted when it was delivered, which John is now enjoying, having paid less than ten per cent of the original price. The car was painted a Mercedes metallic blue, with special matching blue leather and contrasting piping. It has a little sunroof that can't be any bigger because the roof is too small, and it used to have a top-of-the line stereo radio cassette player. Cassette players are almost as out-of-date as eight-tracks, but the ten very high quality speakers are just as tasty now as they were then, and a new CD head unit brings the sound system into this century.

John sees his 928 as a useful tourer with either emergency rear seats, or enough storage space to take his wife on a two-week holiday with as many clothes as she needs. He also quietly enjoys looking seriously rich in a just a few grands' worth of old Porsche when people spending £30,000 on a new BMW just get to look like sales reps. The number of people who know that John's car is only worth

£5,000 is very small indeed, and it still looks like a supercar, for the cost of a second-hand Hyundai.

The car was his daily driver, but its 16mpg city fuel consumption and car park vulnerability led him to buy a disposable Ford for day-to-day use.

The Porsche's fuel consumption at speed on the autobahn is also frighteningly poor, but then the people who could afford to pay £34,000 for this 928 when it was new, and then £70,000 for its replacement, don't have to bother about fuel economy at 150mph. The small fuel tank is a nuisance for high-speed autobahn cruising, as there's no point in driving at 150mph and then losing more time than you've saved by having to stop and fill the tank up every hour. Used at UK speeds the big V8 achieves about 20mpg on average, which isn't bad at all. This car has 180,000 miles on it, but with care and frequent fresh oil it should go on for a long time yet – there's one 928 on record with 700,000 miles on one engine, according to John.

There has been no trouble with the car that he would really blame it for: the transmission let go when the internal pump shaft broke, but at least it wasn't a Porsche-built transmission with loads of Porsche OE repair parts required, or it might have been the end of the line. Repairing the Mercedes transmission was expensive but manageable. One or two oil cooler hoses also burst, just through old age.

This car isn't raced as such, but it does spend some time on the track. With only three speeds, the likelihood of being able to get exactly the right revs for exiting a corner is infeasible, and the car is also pretty hefty at 3,500lb (1,590kg). The handling is excellent, but it is hard work punting a big automatic round the smaller British club circuits, which is where most track day action takes place. John keeps a set of bald track tyres on the original Porsche alloys that came with the car. The original wheels have been replaced with a cool new set for the road that really modernise the whole car, which was not a hard job considering how dreadfully dated the telephone-dial wheels were. Even calling them telephone-dial wheels is itself pretty old hat – when was the last time you used a phone with a dial?

WHAT TO LOOK FOR

STRUCTURE

Structurally, the news is good. The 928's shell is well galvanised and rust is still rare even now. The outer panels are aluminium, and the front and back bumpers are made of deformable ABS plastic.

Bad news/good news is the mad twisty-chequered op-art seat fabric on early cars, which you will either

◄ Electric seats were the last word in sophistication when the car was new, but old electric seats after 20 years of damp could give you a few hours of contact-cleaning entertainment.

◄ The back seats are something of a joke, but the car will technically seat four in an emergency. Non-petrolhead wives can be reassured that this makes a 928 a sensible, practical, cheap spare car.

◄ The hatch reveals quite a reasonable boot, which becomes a good luggage space when the vestigial rear seats are folded down. The car is then a genuine grand tourer, with room for plenty of luggage for a French touring holiday, for example.

◄ A set of new wheels in a suitable style will immediately update the whole car. Owner John Oakes keeps some bald tyres on the old rims as low-budget slicks for track days.

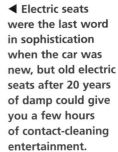

► Most of the car is galvanised, but the fuel tank support straps aren't. Aftermarket stainless steel replacements are now available.

▼ The radiator is a complex unit with several functions, and will thus be horribly expensive to replace with a new one. Flush it every couple of years and keep it full of good antifreeze at the right concentration, which will protect the aluminium cylinder block as well. Buy a good second-hand spare when you get the chance.

love or hate. I think it's fab, but then I don't suffer from migraines: although I probably would if I drove a chequered 928 for too long. Later and leather-clad seats bolt straight in, so the epileptic seats aren't a big problem anyway. Seat adjustment is electric, so the seat wiring all needs to be functional.

The only regular rust problem is the steel strap that holds the plastic fuel tank, just inboard of the plastic rear bumper. A full fuel tank weighs a lot, so a strong retaining strap is important. However, there's now a stainless steel aftermarket fuel tank strap available at 50 per cent of the Porsche price that sorts the problem out permanently. Check for accident damage inboard of the deformable plastic front and rear bumpers, as the bumpers simply return to shape if bashed.

Galvanising lasts for about 25 years on steel car bodies, so do the maths – and check very carefully for rust underneath and wherever you can get at. Drive both expensive and cheap 928s before

making up your mind what your budget level and model type should be.

Shock absorbers are worth checking, as the car's 3,500lb weight is hard on them.

Check that everything electrical and electronic is working correctly, and knock big bucks off the price if it isn't. The climate control/air conditioning is very complex, although some problems can be solved by recharging and by replacing hoses. The systems become increasingly complex as time goes on and more features are added. While basic air conditioning is simple enough, Electronic Climate Control is markedly less so. A two-stage electronically-controlled rear window defogging system containing electronic parts that have been parked outside in the cold and damp for 20 years may still work fine. Or it may not. If it compromises half a dozen other circuits as well when it resigns, you will probably wish they'd provided a cloth for the rear window instead. It's nice to have a climate-controlled glove box – say goodbye to melted summertime Mars Bars. It's not worth putting up with much electronic grief for, though.

ENGINE

Elderly electronic fuel injection is always a worry, mostly because of bad connections through corrosion. I was told by a car electronics company that well over half the 'faulty' exchange ECUs they get in are working just fine: it's a dodgy earth, or current backing up into the wrong place that causes problems, as often as not. Keep all engine wiring connections clean and sealed and there should be no major worries.

Headlamp beam height adjusters can break – check they're functional.

Check for white goo in the radiator cap. Some emulsion is inevitable in cars that are not used much, but too much goo suggests that one of the head gaskets has gone. That needs fixing quickly, as the emulsion will clog up the radiator and then you'll face an even bigger problem. While checking for white goo, check for red or pink goo as well, in case there's any leakage into the coolant from the transmission.

Check the radiator condition carefully – it's a complicated item that cools oil, water and transmission fluid, and a new one costs £500. If buying in California, even buying for UK import, get a DMV smog test. If the car fails it's labelled as a 'gross polluter', which has something of a negative effect on its cash value. A major pre-purchase inspection should reveal some problems, even if there aren't any worth bothering about. Another chance to chew your lip, shake your head and have another go at lowering the price.

GEARBOX

The manual transmission on the 928 had a tendency to wear out synchro rings and bearings, the bearing largely because the car weighs nearly two tons, and the big torque from the V8 puts some significant stress on them. A noisy manual gearbox is not something you want to hear. The two-bearing torque tube in the automatic cars lasts less well than the three-bearing manual version: torque tubes take eight hours to change.

MAINTENANCE AND REPAIRS

STRUCTURE

Keep the salt washed off the body and wheel arches, and touch up the occasional stone chip. If the tank straps are steel and still sound, clean and paint them to stop them rusting. While you're at it, paint the road springs as well: springs sag through rusting away, not through fatigue. Shocks need replacing when they wear out, but springs can continue indefinitely.

A useful move is to get your hands on a used set of the nine-volume Porsche 928 repair manual.

Wheel alignment is important with a 928, as a kerbing can knock the whole geometry out of line, affecting both handling and tyre life. A straightened-out car will feel much better and won't wear out its tyres. When the car is jacked up and then lowered, the wheels need ten miles of driving before they have settled into their correct position and can be aligned. Don't use a shop that doesn't know this, or they will probably set the camber with too much of a negative angle, which will trash the inside edges of your front tyres.

Power windows fail in the down position sometimes, in which case cleaning the contacts on the back of the centre console switch can help.

Some people have had several radiators let go, so keeping an eye open for a spare one on eBay would be sensible. Speed bumps also sometimes take out radiators.

ENGINE

Although the mass of machinery under the 928's bonnet looks daunting, it all breaks down into comprehensible subsystems and can be mostly be dealt with on a DIY basis.

A new alternator from Porsche is £450 so get the old one rebuilt if it rattles or fails – the problem is usually just one or two diodes and possibly a bearing and it should cost well under £100 at a local auto electrical repair shop, if you can find one. Buy a spare alternator in advance.

The oil should be changed every 3,000 miles

◄ When buying and during ownership, check the inside of the oil filler cap for whitish oil/water emulsion goo. This probably means a head gasket's gone, and also means your expensive radiator is getting clagged up with the same stuff.

◄ The high pressure hoses for the various fluid systems in the car are quite highly stressed, and should be checked for condition and changed if they look corroded or bulgy. Expensive, but not as expensive as not replacing them. Ask Mocal in Isleworth to quote for replacements, rather than Porsche.

◄ Most 928 gearboxes are automatic. This is good, because the big V8 does give a manual gearbox a hard time, and the autobox is a cheaper Mercedes one rather than Porsche-made.

in a car that's used hard but not used very often, and the sump takes 8.5 litres of oil each change. However, the good news is that you don't need to use awesomely expensive synthetic engine oil. The Porsche V8 is still basically a 1970s design, and modern synthetics and semi-synthetics are too thin and runny for the larger internal clearances of older engines. If you use a low-viscosity modern synthetic, the drop in oil pressure will be frightening. What the engine needs is a good quality 20/50 with a thicker old-fashioned viscosity, which is helpfully still available at a reasonable price. Keep up with the bad news on modern oils, which are offering less protection all the time as additives are removed for environmental reasons. Currently, racing or motorbike engine oils still offer good protection.

Service kits for the 928 are £55 plus oil, which is reasonable, and the service kit for the Mercedes transmission costs £18. The 928 oil filter is very big, and works very well: some people even use them on other cars if they have room. When servicing, use OEM plugs and wires to avoid potential misfires and EFI problems.

Check ageing oil and coolant hoses regularly, and replace them before they let go. The timing belt needs changing every 50,000 miles, and so

does the chain tensioner on the 32-valve engines. This is a design fault shared with the 944 engines, which are closely related to the V8. However, none of it is a very big deal to sort out: start with taking the radiator out and you can then see what you're doing and where everything goes. If you don't know for sure how old the belt and tensioner are when you buy the car, change them straight away. It's also worth changing the water-pump, upper and lower hoses and thermostat at the same time. (Check the new thermostat before fitting by dropping it in boiling water – just because it's new doesn't mean it works.) The differential oil cooler is separate, and the condenser for the air conditioning is in front of the radiator.

The torque tube on the automatic cars only has two internal bearings compared to the three on the manual cars – but it can rattle harmlessly for a long time. If it starts squealing it's time to sort it out, about an eight-hour job.

There has been a useful development recently for 928 parts in that some of the OE suppliers to Porsche have started selling parts for older cars direct to the public – look for the number 928 on castings, which means they're definitely the same parts that were supplied to Porsche.

One small but potentially terminal problem arises with the sump drain plug on the 928 – it has a tendency to come loose and eventually to fall out. If that happens and you don't realise it immediately, the engine will seize. The seizure wrenches and spins the main bearings round in their housings, and the engine block is then scrap. If you want to keep a 928 for a while, drill a hole through the visible part of the drain plug, then wire the plug to the engine side of an engine mounting so that it can't unwind itself.

A rebuild (on a rebuildable engine rather than a scrap one with a spun main bearing) generally costs about £4,000. That probably isn't a good investment, given that an older and rougher 928 with a second-hand engine good for another 250,000 miles could be bought for £500 with some hunting about, even if you had to buy a whole car just to get the engine out of it.

It may not be very scientific advice, but it seems that little-used 928s have a tendency to 'sulk', and not to run well if left for a while, so regular use is a good idea.

GEARBOX
Gearboxes may eventually become difficult to change from first to second as synchro rings wear, but even so they can still carry on for years. Learning to double-declutch vintage style to match component spin speeds is an alternative to replacement.

IMPROVEMENTS AND MODIFICATIONS

STRUCTURE
Mad/funky chequered acid-trip seats can be easily swapped for plain leather from later cars. Almost any modern wheels will update the entire look of an older 928. In general, the mechanical improvements and mods that you would have wanted to make have all been done by Porsche as part of normal development – so apart from taking advantage of 2009 tyre technology, sensible mods involve upgrading to later second-hand 928 parts.

ENGINE
This idea may bring death threats, but Chevrolet 350 Corvette engines can be used in place of a seized Porsche V8 engine if no scrap engine donors present themselves. Corvette V8s are also aluminium engines, with serious horsepower and quite cheaply available, and are best used with an overdrive GM 700R4 autobox. Just don't open your bonnet at Porsche club shows, as not all Porsche enthusiasts have a sense of humour.

BRAKES
When buying new major brake parts, the same rule applies as for 924s and 944s – you will get better braking for your money by buying bigger and better Brembo or AP brakes than by applying the same budget to new replacement Porsche brakes. Good second-hand brakes from a later 928 may offer better value and more pots.

PRICES

One of the useful things about rich people is that they don't want second-hand supercars, so depreciation on the 928 is almost as rapid as its 0–150mph time. Excellent news for affordability.

928s start in the UK at just a couple of thousand pounds for an early example that's a little rough but usable. In some ways it could make good sense just to run a succession of cars at this level, keeping them going with help from others breaking 928s, and scrapping your own one in turn when something major lets go.

Going up a grade to £5,000 will get you a really nice early 928, well worth looking after and preserving, or possibly a fairly well-used S4. Taking it up to the top of our affordable budget at £10,000 you're looking at a seriously nice S4 or even a GTS – if you really feel the need for 171mph.

eBay UK yields bids on 928s from £700 to £5,000, with five for sale on a random day in February 2010. A dealer was asking £9,000 for a 61,000-mile concours S4, but it attracted no bids. Bids, in fact, are noticeable by their rarity. *Classic & Sportscar*'s classifieds had one LHD 928 with 95,000km at a price of £7,950 – but eight grand for a left-hooker in the UK looks as optimistic as a lemming with a pension plan.

Really superb examples may in the next few years gain some value as classics, but for the moment a few thousand pounds will get you a nice 928, no bother.

BEST BUYS

When buying a 928, the S2, rather than the later cars, is the one to look for. It has several useful improvements over the early cars, but retains the simplicity of being predominantly electrically operated rather than electronically operated – a crucial difference when it comes to DIY maintenance. However, general condition and price are much more important than the model number. Don't bother going to California to buy one – they're more expensive over there, and rust hasn't been a big problem in the UK.

CHAPTER 10

914

a proper Porsche?

Affordability rating ★★★★

The first Porsches were based on VW engines, and the 1970s saw the flat four coming back again in quite a big way with the 914. The power of the 1,700cc 914 at 80bhp is somewhere between inadequate and adequate, and the 1,700cc car's quarter-mile time is slightly slower than an MGB, which is not impressive and not in normal Porsche territory. However, the 914's mid-engined configuration means that the handling and cross-country performance are superb, and the later 2-litre engines improved the performance. The 914 is not just one of the cheapest of the older Porsches, it's also one of the best-handling Porsches ever, and will not turn round and bite you – an expert driver can choose which end of the car to drift round a corner first, and an inexpert driver will simply enjoy the fast, flat and neutral handling and remarkable grip. The long wheelbase and short overhangs make the handling stable as well as adhesive.

Remember that the Beetle four-cylinder air-cooled engine is inextricably central to Porsche's origins and heritage, so the 914 still has some Porsche cred. It also has 911 front suspension and the basic rear-end geometry of a 911. However, the engines were shared with the post-Beetle notchback 411E Volkswagen. You decide whether it's a real Porsche or not.

The rare 914/6 with its 911 flat six is an entirely different proposition, but the only way you can get one for £10,000 is to make one. Which is actually not such a bad idea.

Something to bear in mind is that having the low-budget Porsches built by VW and Karmann may be a cheap option compared to Porsche manufacture, but it still means they were built to a good German standard. It's not as if they were being built by Moskvich. Until quite recently there were genuine

◀ The 914 is a very good sports car at VW prices and with VW running costs: well worth a look. [Porsche AG]

BASICS

Body	Non-galvanised steel monocoque.
Engine	Rear-mid-mounted air-cooled fuel injected VW flat four, 1,700cc, 1,800cc and later 2,000cc.
Transmission	ZF five-speed manual gearbox in transaxle, some automatics.
Suspension	Front, independent MacPherson struts, lower wishbones, longitudinal torsion bars. Rear, independent, semi-trailing arms, coil springs over shocks.
Steering	Unassisted rack and pinion.
Brakes	Unassisted discs all round.

Fuller specifications and further detailed technical information can be found in Chapter 15.

▼ **This is where the engine should have been put in the 356/911. Handling on the 914/6 is significantly superior.** [Porsche AG]

EVOLUTION

1969	First 914 built.
1971	Changes to emissions gear.
1972	Trim upgrades, better seat adjustment, retracting seat belts, switchgear improvements, fatter wheels.
1973	Gear linkage improvements, 100bhp 2-litre engine option, softer springs. Fuchs wheel option.
1974	1,700cc engine enlarged to 1,800cc, power to 85bhp.
1975	2-litre becomes standard. Large, grotesque US bumpers fitted. Vapour lock problems cured – fuel pump moved away from engine. Air pump for US emissions.
1976	914 is deleted.

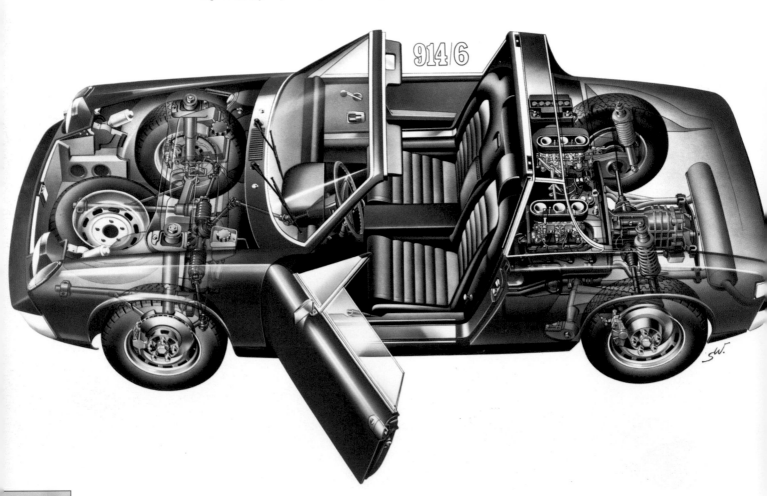

differences in material and engineering quality between the major manufacturers. For example Chrysler/Rootes, and for that matter British Leyland, made some pretty nasty, shabby cars in the 1970s, put together very badly. Volkswagen simply didn't do that. Incidentally, it will be interesting to see if the same sentence is written about the VW/Porsche Cayenne a few decades from now – we'll have to wait and see.

In some ways the 914 transcended the cost-saving compromise that spoiled the handling of the very first production Porsches, in that its chassis was mid-rear engined. That involved creative and tricky engineering, but not only was the mid-rear configuration finally achieved by Porsche in a road-going model, it was also offered to a much wider public as the bottom model of the range.

The 914 was never sold in vast numbers, and although raging rust has made it quite a rarity in the UK, there are still plenty about at bargain prices in the dry states of America. Even rarer is the 914/6 with a 911 flat six and wider track, wheels and tyres. This cost nearly as much as a 911 and obviously handled a lot better – estimates of the time said it

was about eight per cent better overall than a 911 – but not many people were going to pay 911 money for anything with VW connotations, even if it was a considerably faster and more competent car. In the case of the six-cylinder 911-engined 914/6 the bare bodies were shipped to Porsche for assembly, which partly explains their price and thus their rarity. However, you're unlikely to find one at all, never mind finding one within reach of our sort of budget.

More good budget news is that the fuel

▼ **Even if you can't find a good car in the UK, there are still some worth buying in the drier parts of Europe. This French one is obviously used for classic rallying or competition of some sort.**

▲ **The interior of the 914 is spartan, functional and cheap, much more VW than Porsche. However, this was the entry-level Porsche when new, so don't expect a climate-controlled glovebox. Garfield floor mats are not Porsche factory options, except in the Cayenne.**

An iron small-block V8 with some real power would change the nature and handling of a 914 completely, but some of the desert buggy people are getting very serious torque and power out of heavily modified 2,500+cc VW engines. A $4,000 914 with a $10,000 VW engine would probably cream most other affordable Porsches – in fact it would probably lift its leg over most Porsches ever built – and it would still be more or less original.

Something to consider is that many people, including Porsche themselves, have made hot-rod versions of this car, and the chassis and handling seem to be well able to cope with even very serious power. It's a shame that the original car was spoiled by poor engine performance and never achieved what it could have been capable of... but on the other hand it's excellent news that a car with this much untapped potential is unpopular enough to be bought for peanuts by intelligent buyers.

HISTORY

The Porsche/VW 914 was actually manufactured by Karmann to a Gugelot design. It was originally conceived as a front-engined GRP-bodied car, and the design was adapted by VW and Porsche for a mid-rear-engined car made in steel.

When launched, this new budget Porker delighted people who suddenly found that they could afford to buy their first new Porsche. It wasn't cheap, but it was cheap for a Porsche. It also kept the company in a position to carry on making more expensive cars for the very same people who were snooty about the 914. Not many people could afford to buy a new 911 or can now afford to buy its modern equivalent, but by returning to their roots with a budget Beetle-derived engine, Porsche brought the price of their economy cars within range of a much larger cross-section of the car-buying public. The new car was actually badged as a Volkswagen-Porsche in Europe when launched, and the price, although steep at over £2,000, was not as far out of reach as a 'proper' Porsche. The company were also able to keep their cashflow flowing and were still able to concentrate on their core purpose, which was to develop, make, race, refine and sell more rarefied cars for cognoscenti with fat wallets.

The car wasn't much developed during its life: the engine went from an inadequate 1,700cc and 85bhp to a slightly less embarrassing 2 litres. The engine size rose along with the family VWs from which the 914 took its engines. It seems to have been largely used as a cash cow, and was dropped when it was no longer needed and no longer selling well.

economy reported by a survey of owners, again when the cars were relatively new, found that they were getting 35mpg on the highway, 27mpg in city driving and 31 mpg overall – which is certainly on the affordable side compared to some Porsche fuel economy figures.

The only real problems posed by the 914 are rust and its sad performance. There's nothing stopping the low-budget Porsche enthusiast achieving a seriously nice car based on one, though. As far as rust goes, simply don't buy a rusty one. There's no need: good ones are still available in the dry US states, so spend a bit more time and find a really clean shell. Two options exist for doing something about the performance, the more difficult but more interesting one being to turn the car into a replica 914/6. That means a flat six 911 engine. The smart move has to be to actively look for the engine that everybody else is avoiding – the 2.7-litre one with the magnesium crankcase. Get the crankcase inserts fitted to stop the studs pulling out, then when the engine is back together try using a sealant on the outside of the crankcase wherever it's leaking oil. That whole project has to cost less than a good ready-to-wear 911, and you'll get the handling of a 914 combined with the punch of a 2.7-litre 911 in an even lighter car. You'll even get the music of the flat six.

If you want an easier life, build or buy a modified Beetle-based engine, which will bolt straight in. A trawl through a few Internet sites will give you a grip on the sort of power that is available from the Beetle-based engine-building fraternity. One specialist, for example, will sell you a 2,700cc, 200bhp naturally aspirated new VW engine for $6,500. Pop one of those in the back of a 914 and it's going to be somewhat livelier than the original 80bhp item.

HANDS ON –
The owner's view

Tom Ewing's car is a good example of a budget 914 bought in the south-western USA, which is realistically the best place to go to buy one. Apart from some conversions, all 914s are left-hand-drive anyway, and the few that turn up for sale in the UK are usually rusty. Tom's car is a little tatty, but it works well enough and it's structurally solid. He bought it through eBay, and paid a very reasonable $2,500 for it. Fortunately he lives in Chino, east of Los Angeles, and the car was for sale in San Diego, so he could just go and get it. Buying a car in the US through eBay can frequently require either a very long trip with a car trailer, or buying sight unseen and then shipping the car by road and rail, which would have to be a nail-biting business. I personally wouldn't do it. 'Immaculate Condition' is in the eye of the beholder, and buying an old Porsche without seeing it first is absolutely asking for the worst sort of trouble.

Tom traded a 1962 356 convertible for a Beetle in 1971. Looking back, that was perhaps not the best decision he ever made. However, as he's now retired and spends his time coaching soccer rather than earning money, he would have to make some serious sacrifices to fund buying another 356. Spending a couple of grand on a 914, an amusing sports car with a Porsche badge on it, wasn't much of a risk to take. Tom doesn't regret buying his 914 for a minute. He thinks the 914 is a hoot, he says that it's unarguably another convertible Porsche, and he likes the way the roof seals the weather out effectively and quietly, but can be removed in seconds and stowed in the back behind the engine without even taking up much of the boot space. There's also plenty of luggage space in the front, and all that without compromising foot room, of which there is still plenty. That's clever design work, as a mid-rear engine usually crams everything too far forward and pushes your feet to the centre of the car between the wheels – but the 914 works well in this respect.

Tom reports that his 914 also handles very well indeed, although the LA basin doesn't offer many challenges in this respect as there aren't any bends. However, he is planning a trip up Highway 1, which clings to the cliffs all the way up the California coast, and he's seriously looking forward to throwing the 914 round a couple of thousand sweeping curves and hairpins.

Another small but important point is that a 914 can be used by a couple, of which the feminine half may be more interested in luggage capacity than in handling, horsepower or historical air-cooled 356 legacies. In the 914, the luggage space is really good considering that the car is a mid-rear-engined two-seater: there's plenty of room for a good many female clothing changes, and still a corner for a spare T-shirt for the driver. (Do feel free to change the genders to suit your domestic situation.) It's all very well for Ferruccio Lamborghini to dismiss criticism of the luggage capacity of the Miura by suggesting that one send one's servants ahead with the luggage, but the word 'affordable' probably wasn't in Signor Lamborghini's vocabulary.

Tom's car may be superficially a little rough, but it's actually in pretty sound condition, and he's quietly working away at improving it. Problems so far are really limited to oil leaks and a tappet-securing screw, so he's been improving it rather than repairing it. He's currently hunting around for replacement side marker lights. Some US-only detail parts like that are hard to find, although in general the spares situation for the 914 isn't bad.

▲ Luggage space isn't bad at all for a small mid-engined sports car. Just about enough for a weekend away for two, with room for a good enough number of shoe options to ensure marital harmony. The Targa top stores in the boot without losing too much luggage capacity, which is clever.

◀ The seats weren't top quality in the first place, but their cheap and cheerful design makes them easy to repair, or you can opt for a posher retrim in leather. A good trick is to glue some freshly tanned leather under the seat every year or so to retain the expensive leather smell.

Many American owners have 'improved' the 914 big time with a V8, and one Californian bought his 914 new, drove it for two weeks, decided the power was pathetic and replaced the VW engine with a small-block Chevrolet V8. That car is still on the road, although after 20 years of drastic alteration it doesn't look or behave much like a 914 any more. It's useful to know that the engine bay is big enough to take a V8, though, as it gives you many options.

Joey Kulinna is a speed freak who realised what potential there is in a Porsche 914, and specifically bought his black one – one of 300 black ones from 1973 – to turn it into a monster. The mid-mounted V8 produces 620bhp at the crank and 552bhp at the wheels, and it runs through a Porsche 930 gearbox and suspension. The transmission contains $6,500-worth of modifications by Bobby Hart of California Motorsport, and should be good for 800bhp. The clutch is Kevlar with a 2,750lb pressure plate, and the weight distribution is absolutely perfect – Joey claims 2.3 seconds to 60mph, an average quarter-mile in 10.2 seconds, and a calculated top speed of 186mph (300kph). The brakes are also Porsche 930, four-pot callipers with 13.5in discs, but they're additionally specially vented and cross-drilled – Joey likes to have two units of braking horsepower for every unit of engine horsepower.

The suspension is all connected to the rollcage that discreetly runs through the whole car, but it is still essentially a much-modified Porsche 914 rather than a spaceframe made to look like a Porsche.

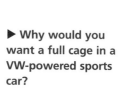

▲ **This 914 looks innocent enough at first glance, which is the way the owner likes it.**

▶ **Why would you want a full cage in a VW-powered sports car?**

▼ **That lot doesn't look as though it was ever shared with a notchback VW...**

▶ **Here's why – an alloy full-race Chevrolet V8 adds a little performance to the 914. This one was built for the Gumball Rally, and its top speed is still unexplored.**

WHAT TO LOOK FOR

STRUCTURE

Rust, rust, and more rust. Look for terminal structural rust in just a few crucial places. The battery tray in the engine compartment is vulnerable to battery acid attack as well as general rust, and once the battery tray has rusted out, the oxidisation continues beneath the tray, where the main suspension mountings live. It's scrap time if you're looking at one that's rusty here, as a proper repair will almost certainly cost more than the car is worth. The quick way of checking this before diving into the engine bay and underneath the car is to take a look at the right-hand rear tyre. If the tread on that tyre is worn out on one side and the opposite tyre is worn evenly, that means the trailing arm is already coming away from the chassis. Run away rather than walking away, but not before warning the owner not to drive the car any more and explaining why.

There is often nasty and well-concealed rust behind both the front and the rear lights, as they don't seal very well and form something of a damp trap. The advice is to strip all the lights right out, repair, treat and paint the whole area with a nice thick layer of sealer and paint, and then reassemble the lights and seal them with a discreet application of silicone to stop any more water getting in.

Also check the boot seams and the jacking points, and open the sill cover to look at the state of the sills. A good test for general structural strength is to sit a fat bloke in the passenger seat, then wind up the window and see if the door still opens. Be careful, though, as the 914's windows have a tendency to shatter.

Another minor gripe is that the trim was always coming unglued when the cars were fairly new, although tatty trim is actually good news when you're buying a car. It gives you something to suck your teeth and look doubtful about, but it only affects the price and not the performance or functionality of the car: all you then have to do, at your leisure, is to find better glue and stick the trim back on again properly.

MECHANICALS

Fuel injection misbehaves, despite later updating. The instruments and speedo are unreliable: check that they all work properly. Try the gear linkage out – on early cars, and if worn, it may be too horrible to consider.

There are a few semi-automatic Sportomatic gearboxes fitted to 914s, and if you find one its value will be considerably lowered as a result. Oddly enough, the same Porsche enthusiasts who

▲ This is where the trouble starts. Under this boot lid hinge is where the most serious crumbling begins.

◄ The battery inevitably leaks acid, and beneath it is the right-hand rear suspension mounting. Once that's gone the car is scrap. If you find a clean one, get a sealed battery and a plastic tray in place to keep it that way.

▼ Both the front and the rear light clusters leak, leading to some nasty creeping rot behind them. Remove, repair, replace with a rich lathering of silicone to stop them rusting again.

used to regard the Sportomatic with contempt are now lining up to buy Tiptronic gearboxes on newer Porsches, which are essentially a more sophisticated version of the same thing.

MAINTENANCE AND REPAIRS

STRUCTURE

914s, like old Fiats, can almost be heard rusting in the damp, salty and acid UK air. If you've got a clean one, keep the paint and underseal in good condition, and wash salt and dirt out of the wheel arches regularly.

The instruments in general seem to have a reputation for unreliability, so it's a good idea to collect some spares at swapmeets and autojumbles.

Fortunately they're still cheap. Another electrical foible is that the fuses relating to the fuel injection control box corrode, and then the engine suddenly stops. If you know where to apply a nail file, no worries: if not, you're going home in a breakdown truck.

MECHANICALS

Engine access is poor from the top, although everything is fairly easily accessible from underneath. That's fine if you have a pit, a ramp or a mechanic, but is a nuisance otherwise. The injection system is now elderly and proving to be rather a liability. It doesn't seem to have been the best system in the world to start with. The good news is that if the injection system is too much of a nuisance to bother with, you can simply change back to a set

▼ A 914 modified with a flat six will show you what the early 911 could have been capable of. [Porsche AG]

of second-hand VW 411 carbs, which will work just fine.

There's a little pulley wheel over which the clutch cable runs, and this wheel gets dirty and seizes. After that's happened the clutch cable doesn't last very long, so the wheel needs to be cleaned and lubricated regularly.

As the car is of Karmann/VW rather than Porsche construction, there's more of a tendency for bits to fall off. Check fuel lines regularly for fractures, as they spray the engine bay with fuel if they fail.

Adjust and lubricate gear linkages. Regularly clean fuses at fuel injection junction box, or replace with a bridge and modern fuses.

The engine bay heat does tend to get quite sweaty in high ambient temperatures, which can mean that the starter jams after a long run. This same engine bay heat can cause nightmarish vapour lock problems, and some owners have relocated the fuel pump to the front of the car where it's all much cooler. Porsche themselves relocated it there halfway through the production run. You can also add louvres or vents to the engine cover.

Mechanically the VW engine is simple, and is as reliable as any air-cooled VW, ie, not very. To confirm this, check all the ads for air-cooled VW camper vans, most of which are advertised as having just had a new engine fitted. Why do you suppose that is?

An Internet Google session with 'Porsche 914' as the subject will yield a lot of useful background and backyard information.

IMPROVEMENTS AND MODIFICATIONS

STRUCTURE

Although accessibility is limited, there's plenty of room in the actual engine bay – it was easy enough for Porsche to pop in a flat six with some minor rearrangement of the bulkhead, and lots of people have successfully fitted assorted V8s. One smart move is to get rid of the huge and very heavy impact-absorbing bumpers from the mid-1970s, and to replace them with the much more delicate and prettier early-'70s items.

MECHANICALS

The gearshift on cars up to 1973 is vague, rubbery and difficult to use smoothly, but those built after 1973 have a completely different and very good shift. It goes to the side of the gearbox rather than the back, and works a lot better. Bear this in mind when considering engine bay changes.

Move the fuel pump on earlier cars to the front, which Porsche did later in the car's life anyway. It gets too hot and vapour pockets prevent starting until the whole engine bay has cooled down. Better engine bay venting would be a good idea too. Driving in town in summer with the engine cover wedged slightly open would also be worth a try: it works on Cobras.

Power in standard form is rather feeble, but you can take the opportunity to fit whatever's currently available in cams, cylinders and pistons, carburation or injection from the racing desert buggy world if you want more bolt-on power. Many people seem to think it's a hoot to cram a V8 in, and I wouldn't disagree: with the rear-mid configuration, even the weight of an iron small-block doesn't seem to spoil the car.

A 2.2-litre 911T flat six engine, if you can find one, can be used to change a 914 to a close replica of a 914/6, provided you add wider wheels to match. The real ones are getting pretty desirable: try one first to see if you like it before getting seriously involved.

PRICES

There are too few 914s on sale in the UK to get a picture of prices, but they're not expensive – if you can find one it will cost just a few thousand pounds. Finding a good one would be more of a problem than paying for it. Much 914 production went to California: so should you.

American prices are also just a few thousand dollars, with something usable at around $4,000. Rust-free projects are available for peanuts, but make sure they at least roll, as importing drivable or rolling cars is much cheaper than shipping a crate of bits. The American 914 Club and TheSamba are good sources of 914s.

BEST BUYS

The later the better, not least because the 2-litre VW engine is the least feeble option and can easily be significantly beefed up at Beetle hobby prices. There's no LHD discount as virtually all 914s are left-hand-drive. They're very rare in the UK, although that just means they're rare, and not that they're valuable.

An Internet trawl reveals one for sale in the UK for around £3,000, with an apparent 15,000 miles on it since new. If there's nothing dodgy about it, and assuming its entire parked life has been spent in dry storage, that could be a good deal once the hydraulic and fuel systems had been cleaned out. UK cars will offer little choice, though – California beckons.

CHAPTER 11

356

from bathtub to jacuzzi

Affordability rating ★

The more you dig into the world of the 356, the more you realise that it's something special. When you compare it with its 1950s contemporaries it is in many ways decades ahead. 356 Porsches were and are expensive, but if you want good engineering you have to pay for it. Those who wished to work in the Porsche factory had to be time-served engineers with four-year apprenticeships behind them, and they didn't come cheap even in post-war Germany.

The car magazine and press reviews of the time were mixed, probably depending on the individual experience of the reviewer, and whether the car turned round and bit him or not. Rear engines and swing axles are basically mistakes, and the early 356s are unruly. The steering is also demanding: very light and direct, it makes cornering on the limit a delight, but will also twitch the car off the road in a skid unless handled delicately. Later 356 steering systems became heavier and more forgiving. For a seriously good driver, the milliseconds between the tail end coming slightly unstuck and the 356 spinning out are the area in which the seconds are shaved off laps and the real fun is to be had, and it's interesting that rally drivers now deliberately chuck the back end of their car out before every corner on the rough, to get it lined up for the next straight. This has become more or less standard 4WD and rear 2WD rally technique. In the 356's heyday, the Targa Florio and the Mille Miglia were both held on pretty rough roads, and most corners were taken in a controlled drift. That said, pushing your amateur luck in an early 356 is probably a bad idea. They handle very well compared to an Austin Atlantic, but just as in First World War radial-engined aircraft such as the Sopwith Camel, The Spin is just lurking there waiting for you. Maurice Gatsonides, who was a rally driver before inflicting

◄ A decent 356 will probably burst our affordable budget, but will pay us back in charismatic fun and long-term investment value. [Porsche AG]

BASICS

Body	Monocoque coupé, speedster and roadster bodywork in pressed steel.
Engine	Air-cooled flat four, rear mounted, 1,131–1,582cc.
Gearbox	Four-speed, later with synchromesh.
Transmission	Swinging axle from central diff incorporated in gearbox casing.
Suspension	Transverse torsion bars, trailing arms. Tubular shocks front, initially lever arms rear, later tubular all round.
Steering	Worm-and-nut, later worm-and-peg with damper.
Brakes	Initially cable, later hydraulic. Discs on 356C.

Fuller specifications and further detailed technical information can be found in Chapter 15.

EVOLUTION

1950–5	356 – bent flat or two-piece windscreen, 1,100cc, 1,300cc and 1,500cc engines. Some usefully cheap VW parts still used.
1956–9	356A – retains pudding-bowl shape, but 1,600cc engine offers useful additional power.
1960–3	356B – much higher front wing line, better headlamps; visibly closer to 911 styling. The Super 90 versions can achieve speeds of over 100mph (160kph).
1964–5	356C – more power and disc brakes; the 1600SC offers 95bhp.

▼ **Casually parked 356 Porsches are a rare sight in the UK, but there are still plenty about in California, in good shape and for a price on the high side of reasonable.**

the Gatso speed camera on us, lost control of a 356 that then spun through 720°, and found himself a helpless passenger until the car decided to stop.

From day one, the big, adjustable seats seem to have been superb. Again, racing success on the rough requires a well-secured driver who is using the steering wheel purely for steering the car, rather than hanging on to it in order to stay in his seat. The same comfort and support is just as welcome for any of us today. The seats in the 356 get a few per cent better with every year of development, like the rest of the car.

Many early 356s have a crash gearbox with no synchromesh, which requires learning the vintage driving technique of double-declutching to match the speeds of the gears so that they slip in smoothly and don't make horrible crashing noises.

This is not a big deal to learn, and it's satisfying to get the hang of it. It's also reasonably easy in a 356: with a 1920s Bentley, you'll still be crunching gears after owning one for 50 years. It may be that some of the bitching by the Press about the rear-end handling of the 356 was ironically the indirect result of the quietness and stability of the ride.

If you're doing 50mph round a 40mph bend on a rough road in an Austin Healey you're well aware of the heavy steering, the hefty but not particularly rigid chassis and body, the tyres shrieking and the axle banging away. However, the Porsches' increasingly subtle independent suspension and stiff monocoque could find you going a lot faster than you thought you were going, and you might well be too busy with the steering wheel to notice just what the speedo was actually reading.

Before buying a 356, it makes excellent general and financial sense to join one or more 356 clubs. It will cost several hundred dollars to buy a replacement steering wheel at a posh Porsche show, but something a little scruffier from a friend in the same club shouldn't break the bank – they won't be trying to make a living out of you like the show stall people. The social scene in a good club is also great fun, and some people will be actively restoring or repairing cars, so there's a lot of help and advice available for the asking. Others will have completed restorations way back, or have simply found and bought good original cars. Those are the people who spend their free time thinking of amusing places to drive their cars to with their club friends.

You simply can't buy a really good original 356 in the UK for £10,000, but you do have the chance to buy something usable for between $10,000 and $20,000 in North America, if you take fastidious originality out of the equation. The trick is to find out what the exact original parts should have been on a 356 and then complain about what's missing or altered. A reasonably priced 356 that retains its original engine and brakes is a rare beast, but later incorrect engines and brakes are better anyway. You're looking for an affordable 356, so forget about matching chassis and engine numbers except when you're knocking prices down. $15,000 can still get you a reasonable but not particularly original 356 coupé even now. The less original the better for affordability – low cash value and improved performance is just what we're looking for.

Speedster prices have gone crazy in the last few years. In 1998 a usable Speedster cost maybe $12,000. Nowadays a basket-case is $35,000. Prices go up and down, of course, and a wobbly stock market always causes a rush from company shares into other investments, including classic cars.

PRODUCTION

Porsche 356
(Stuttgart-built Pre-A)
1950–54

Coupé	6,252
Cabriolet	1,593
Speedster	1,234

Additionally one 356/1 mid-engined prototype and 52 rear-engined 356/2 production cars were handbuilt at Gmünd, Austria, in 1948–50 before the company returned to Stuttgart and proper production began

Porsche 356A
1956–59

356A Coupé	13,016
356A Cabriolet	3,285
(all 1300 and 1600 engines)	
356A Speedster	2,910
(all versions)	
356A Convertible D	1,330
(all versions)	
356A 1500 GS	447
356A Speedster GS/GT	167
GS Carrera GT Coupé	35

Additionally 204 356A Carrera 1600s with plain-bearing engines built in 1959

Porsche 356B
1959–63

Coupé T5 body	8,559
Coupé T6 body	12,038
Cabriolet T5	3,094
Cabriolet T6	3,100
Hardtop-Coupé T5	1,048
Hardtop-Coupé T6	699
1600 Roadster T5	2,653
1600 Roadster T6	249
(all engine versions)	

Porsche 356C 1600/1600SC
1964–65

356C/SC Coupé	13,510
356C/SC Cabriolet	3,175

One owner was offered and turned down $100,000 for his pristine 356 convertible in the early 1990s, and fortunately doesn't care that it's 'only' worth $75,000 at the moment. He bought the convertible for $23,500 as a nice clean example, but the door got dented and, as he puts it, that's when the madness started. The door skin was replaced, and the car then needed a paint job, so the old paint came off back to the bare metal, and then it all had to be put 100 per cent right before it could be painted again. The car in the end hoovered up $70,000 in restoration

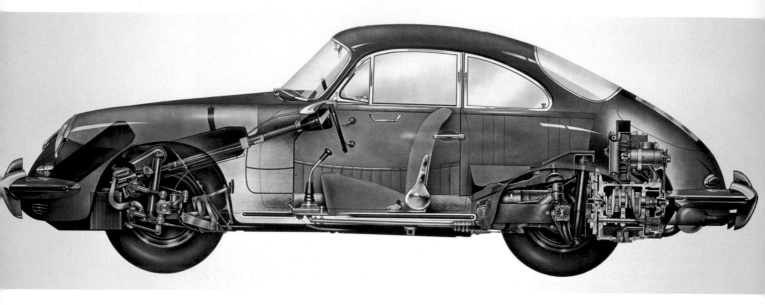

▲ The engine is entirely in the wrong place, but at least it's light. Take care on sharp corners. [Porsche AG]

▼ If you have a bashed or rotten wing on a 356, it could make good sense just to replace the damaged bit, as fitting entire 356 wings is coachbuilding rather than plop-on-and-spot-weld technology.

costs. However, it's one of his favourite cars, it's absolutely as new apart from where he's polished through the original chrome plating, and it's no more for sale than his absolute favourite, a '56 coupé, so the cash value really doesn't matter.

You can see the attraction of investing in classic cars: you certainly can't take a stock option out for a drive in the sun. Many classic-car speculators come a cropper in the end, but their loss is our gain. People who buy a $35,000 basket-case Speedster and put another $70,000 into a restoration that has its own inflation built in on top may get $120,000 back for it... but they're just as likely to miss the bus and have to dump it for $60,000 if the market goes sour in the meantime.

No Porsche was ever intended to be a Pebble Beach concours trailer queen, however. According to Porsche club legend, Dr Porsche attended the 1981 San Diego Parade, and on seeing rows of pristine concours-winning Porsches, said 'This is not what I intended for my cars.' Most of us would go along with that, I think.

For our purposes, old Porsches hold their value better than most classics, so you can perhaps think about a bigger budget on the basis that you're likely to realise a significant profit if and when you sell. Selling is not the subject of this book at all, but if you're going over budget to buy a relatively safe investment bet it does make sense, and we're pushing the limit for affordability by thinking about a 356 anyway.

In many ways it's better to either up your budget and go for something really good, or to go the other way and deliberately buy something quite nasty. The cars in between can look quite nice, but once you've removed the paint, the bodged rust repairs and the filler you'll often finish up with a near basket-case anyway. Many people have brought nice-looking cars back from California, popped them into the local garage for a quick MOT and then faced a £15,000 body restoration bill to get the car into a safe condition to drive. Buy a car that's an obvious mess and you can at least see what you're taking on, and you can make a good decision based on visible gaping rust holes rather than fillered-over and painted gaping rust holes.

Another good point to bear in mind, at least in the UK with fuel prices heading upwards past a fiver a gallon, is the excellent fuel economy available from the small flat-four engine. If kept in tune, which you will be doing anyway to preserve its condition, you can be looking at well over 30mpg driving reasonably.

You really need to get deep into the literature to get the full picture, and you need to look at quite a few cars to get a feel for what's good and what's bad, but essentially a 356 is cool, funky and fun, and a late one is competent and civilised enough to get quite a lot of amusing use.

HISTORY

The origins of Porsche cars go back to before the Second World War, with the Type 60K10. This was an aluminium-bodied racer intended to win a new Berlin–Rome road race, which was a political stunt to promote the relationship between the Nazis and the similarly unsavoury Mussolini regime in Italy. Unfortunately Hitler took his eye off the ball and invaded Poland instead.

After the war both Ferdinand Porsches, father and son, were imprisoned for their involvement in German military vehicle development. When they were released, options and finances were limited, and the original plan for Project No 356, a very light open rear-*mid*-engined sports racer, was canned in favour of the easily available Beetle floorpan. The British government were at that point pushing the People's Car as a way of getting Volkswagen back on its feet, although the Rootes Group, demonstrating the British motoring industry's usual flair for perceptive forward planning, apparently decided that the Beetle was a silly idea that wouldn't catch on.

356-001 was still basically a Beetle pan with an aluminium pudding-bowl body fitted: it looked aerodynamic, but actually wasn't that good in terms of drag coefficients. The engine was a 1,131cc Volkswagen air-cooled flat four with two Solex carbs and the compression ratio raised from 5.8:1 to 7:1, adding 15bhp to the Beetle's feeble 25bhp to give 40bhp. The car made a very respectable 80mph (128kph). Its first race was the Swiss GP in June 1948, and its first win was at Innsbruck in July of the same year.

Continuous racing meant continuous development, and the direction of development was towards excellent road-going performance. Much racing of the period was on bad roads, and the fully independent suspension of the 356 soaked up the bumps and kept the stresses on the driver and chassis low. The quality of their engineering meant that the increasingly Porsche-manufactured versions of the Beetle engine held together well, and although the cars were rarely powerful they stayed in one piece and remained consistently fast, resulting in a class win at Le Mans in 1951.

The fast touring ability of a good 356 as a usable post-war classic is much better than you would think. Road tests report that even with some of the smaller engine options, the earliest cars would cruise at 80mph and allow normal conversation, and the bigger engines would allow genuine hour-after-hour 100mph (160kph) cruising. This is when the Ford Anglia 105E was new and sexy, remember: the M1 was the only motorway, politicians still resigned when caught lying, there was no such thing as tights, and many British motorists were still choosing between an optional-extra car heater or wearing a thicker coat. Cabin heating as a by-product of an air-cooled engine is never the best option, but with the heater levers turned on and the rear windows cranked open, the windows on a 356 all stay clear of condensation and the cabin noise is still very acceptable.

You also get serious cornering agility with a 356, and later cars benefit from radial tyres: the Michelin X worked very well and tended to last a long time provided that the rather delicate sidewalls weren't abused. There is also generous cabin storage in the folding (and rather theoretical) rear seats for proper suitcases, not just a single squashy bag. Fitted leather luggage was available, and although a genuine set of 356 fitted luggage in usable condition would cost very silly money indeed, it would be a nice idea to root around antique/junk shops to get a set of period suitcases that would fit and look appropriate.

Continuous development through racing tamed the 356 to some extent, and an additional leaf spring across the back axle brought the handling much more within the amateur's reach. By 1958 a previously Porsche-hating journalist publicly declared himself converted to the cause by the later cars' much improved handling. The non-synchro crash gearbox was replaced in the early days with a patented and very good synchro system, resulting in a universally praised and very fast box which was later further improved by a shorter and more direct gearchange.

Firm rear suspension with softer front springing went down very well with the Press who had to drive the cars far and fast, and the high weight bias to the rear was countered by downforce from the pudding-bowl bonnet as the car went faster. This gave a very stable ride at high speed, at least in the absence of side winds, which tend to unsettle early Porsches.

A Porsche 356 Super 90 in 1963 cost £2,277. In descending price order, the competition included the hand-built AC Ace Bristol at £1,873, the beautiful Alfa Romeo Giulia Sprint at £1,597, the agile Lotus Elan at £1,317, the barrel-chested Healey 3000 at £1,045, and for ordinary mortals the TR4 at £929 and the MGB at £834. People were prepared to pay nearly three times as much for a dated 1950s Porsche design as they would for the pretty and superficially modern-looking 1960s MGB design, so there must have been something special about it.

▲ Owner Jack Brown chased this car for nine years, and now refuses to restore it because he likes it just as it is. Good man, Jack.

HANDS ON –
The owner's view

Porsche enthusiast Jack Brown is supposed to have retired, but he and his wife Margaret are busier than ever. They have to ration their time between the three 356 clubs they belong to, because there's just too much fun going on for them to keep up with it all. They're members of the 356 register, the So-Cal 356 club and the Alta Region 356 club.

Jack and Margaret are enthusiastic owners of

▶ This bent and superficially rusted bumper would be best repaired and refitted, because some of the repro 356 bumpers are only approximately the right shape.

▶ Jack's car was fitted with the wrong rear lights, probably in about 1959. They've been there so long they will be treated as original and retained. They're brighter and safer than the originals anyway.

several early cars, including immaculate examples of both an early coupé and a convertible. Jack's personal favourite, however, is the nasty but almost completely original '56 coupé pictured here. He's the fourth owner, and he started trying to buy the car from its third owner in 1992, when he discovered that it was lying unused in a Los Angeles garden. The car had been bought in 1986 by a Formula 1 engine builder, and the engine was started up and run briefly every year or so. However, the 356 didn't actually move for years, and just sat there doing nothing as the weeds grew up around it.

Jack called the owner every six months to hassle him to sell the car, and nine years later the owner finally came to terms with the fact that he was never going to do anything with the 356, and let Jack have it. The Los Angeles climate had been very kind to the coupé, and the rust was and is still limited to a few bubbles at the edge of the bonnet. The wheels still revolved okay, but the engine showed no sign of firing up at all. It turned out that the carbs had some sort of unidentifiable fluid and crud in them, and the carb casings had split: they were scrap.

In a remarkable new-old-stock coup, Jack found a Porsche mechanic who had removed a pair of Zenith 32PBIC carbs from a brand new 356 in 1956 to replace them with some bigger ones, and the unused carbs had then sat in his workshop for 36 years until Jack came along and bought them. Brand new 1956 carbs with 20 miles on them are a pretty reasonable originality compromise in a car that is otherwise just about as original as you will find. The seats had been painted a fashionable black at some point in the last 40 years or so, but with a few days' graft Jack was able to get the paint off and reveal the original dark red finish beneath. The seats are actually okay, and the interior isn't too bad generally, although the steering wheel looks rather sorry for itself.

There are some filled-over holes which were gouged in the wings during some very amateurish attempts to fit a radio aerial, and the bumpers and front panelwork are a little frayed. The rear lights are non-original but almost as ancient as the rest of the car, and in any case they're a little bigger than stock and slightly easier to see in the dark, so they'll stay.

Jack is now cheerfully fending off many offers to buy the car, which he gets just about every time he takes it out. Everybody wants to buy it, strip it and restore it to perfection, but Jack thinks that's just boring – nearly every other early 356 has already been restored, so this one will stay just the way it is, with as little as possible being done

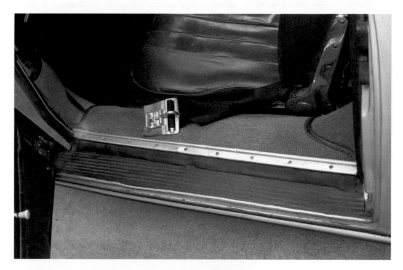

to it apart from repairs, servicing and new tyres. New screen seals are to be fitted soon, but that's effectively replacing a worn part rather than a restoration item, as the California sun hardens and cracks old rubber after a few decades, and this car does go out in the rain. It doesn't get pampered in any way, actually – it's regularly used for fast early-morning runs up Highway 1 to San Luis Obispo and Ragged Point, and Jack still enjoys throwing it round the sharp and demanding curves of the cliffside road. The directness of contact with the road has only recently been compromised to any real extent in Porsches, and the earlier the Porsche the more road feel you get through the wheel. Jack is realistic enough to admit that the car's handling has its limitations, but he points out that compared to almost any other sports car of the same period, the 356 is pretty good.

You won't be able to buy this car or anything quite like it, because this sort of absolute originality is almost unobtainable. People want this car enough to pay really silly money for it, but Jack says he doesn't need any more money. He has a Hudson to prepare for the Carrera PanAmericana race, he has a beautiful special-bodied Alfa Romeo, he has a perfect convertible 356, he has a nice old Ford truck still wearing its period turquoise paint after 300,000 miles, and he has a Boxster. He doesn't want anything else in life, so he really has no particular reason to want any more money. If you see him at a Porsche show, don't waste any time trying to buy his car.

His basic advice to affordable Porsche seekers would be definitely to think about a 356, but either pay the price and get a good one, or get a very rough one and learn to weld. He says the model doesn't matter: it's the condition of the individual car that's important.

WHAT TO LOOK FOR

STRUCTURE

What we're looking for is primarily rust. Early Porsche monocoques were hand-built, with the panels individually fitted to the bodies, which means good restoration is seriously expensive. Shut lines are fine, critical and very visible.

There are also some horrible rust points on the 356 which you might not think to look for. The front and back wings are single skin, so you would expect the usual A- and B-post rust. The big sill panels incorporating the heating channels inevitably sometimes transfer damp salty air as well as clean dry air and can rust, but the trickiest area is around the windscreen, where the scuttle and the screen pillars themselves rust out. This is

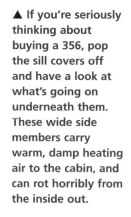

▲ If you're seriously thinking about buying a 356, pop the sill covers off and have a look at what's going on underneath them. These wide side members carry warm, damp heating air to the cabin, and can rot horribly from the inside out.

◄ The roof pillars and scuttle are in fine condition in this car, but if you detect any rust in this area, just walk away – it could well be terminal.

◄ The rear screen rubber has cracked in the sun. Screen rubbers don't last forever anyway, particularly in California. They need to be in good condition to keep water out of vulnerable bodywork areas, so they'll be changed soon on this car.

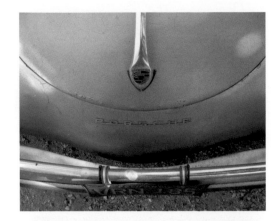

► The edge of the bonnet is bubbling slightly, which if you're going to restore it and keep it in the UK means there are several inches of significant rust that need to be dealt with.

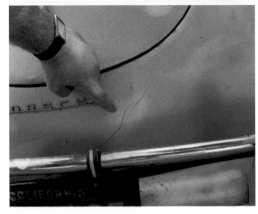

► There's no sign of rust inside the front panel, so this cracked filler is covering a dent. Not a big deal, but another reason to knock down the price when you're buying.

► The door hinges and door hinge mounting areas are in excellent shape, and the doors shut with a quiet click. No problem here, then.

a potential nightmare to repair. The base of the rear screen also rots out if the seals leak at all, and the bumpers rust out as well. Replacement bumpers are available, but are not always very accurate replicas.

There are some potential nasties under the bonnet, too – check the shapes of the inner wings for earlier crash damage, and carefully check the spare wheel well for rust. The fuel tank and its support metalwork also rust.

Additional points worth mentioning are that the rear of the front inner wheel arch and the A-post and related floor areas are complicated and expensive to repair, and that the front-to back longitudinal members are very important structurally. When checking over any 356, jack it up on its jacking points. Firstly, this reminds you to check that the jacking points are strong (and that they exist at all, for that matter), and secondly the door gaps should remain at the original 3.5mm. Even if they're not 3.5mm, the gaps should at least remain the same when the car is jacked up. If the car sags, either find out why and knock off 20 grand for a major substructure restoration, or save yourself time and trouble and just walk away. A car that is structurally weak enough to sag when jacked up is in dangerously bad shape, with the word 'scrap' hovering above it, and even if it looks like a peach now it will look like a piece of Belgian lace when the shell has been stripped and media blasted.

A dropped or sagging door that won't close properly is also a bad sign – it could be because of bad adjustment, worn hinges or a poorly repaired door skin, but it could also be because of a rotten or distorted A-post. An original Porsche door should have even and tight shut lines all round, and should click shut with minimal hand pressure. If you have to slam it something's wrong. Another scrapping point is major rust around the mountings for the torsion bars. If that's not pretty strong, you're in for some seriously expensive welding. The bulbous line down the whole side of the bodywork should be very smooth when you kneel down and look along the sides – investigate any ripples or odd shapes in the metal. Also, check that the external panels are still made of metal – bodging with filler can be very expert indeed. A magnet (held in a spectacle-polishing cloth to avoid scratching the paint) run along the body sides will soon establish whether the panels are steel or plod.

There is a really difficult-to-restore area in front of the windscreen where the wings join the scuttle. This was originally leaded, and the join should be made of metal and should be undetectable. With the bonnet open, also check the rim of the bonnet aperture. It should have quite a sharp angle all the way round, and any change in shape, particularly at the front, can suggest repaired damage. The frontal panelwork is vulnerable, and the spare wheel well and inner wings should be symmetrical and are again worth checking for filler. A thin layer of cosmetic filler on the outside of the shell is one thing, but filler on the inner wings is probably covering something up.

When it comes to the interior, bear in mind that re-trimming seats and re-carpeting is relatively affordable and can be done at home, but hard interior trim such as steering wheels can command silly money, not least because the cheap alloy metal horn rings broke after a few years 50 years ago, so people have been looking for good second-hand replacements ever since. Instruments wear well and are not madly expensive.

MECHANICALS

It's worth doing a compression check on the engine, because No 3 cylinder runs hot. It's near where hot oil collects, and there's a chance that the piston has picked up on the barrel wall or even seized in the past.

Establishing which engine is in the car can save you some money: if it's the wrong one, which it frequently will be at the sort of prices we're looking at, the financial value of the car drops. Privately you may well think a 912 engine is a better idea from a driving point of view, but anybody who is selling you a 356 with the wrong engine fitted doesn't need to know that. It doesn't help that Porsche's policy of usually offering three engine options and continuously improving and enlarging them results in a huge range of possible engines. The options new would usually include a Normal, a Super and something like a Super 90 for road cars, and sometimes four-cam Carrera engines for road and race use. We needn't worry about 356 Carrera variants, though, as they cost more than a divorce.

Six-volt electrical systems were dropped in the 1960s because they don't work as well as 12-volt systems. Essentially you get to choose between six-volt originality and 12-volt easy cold starting and visible headlight beams. Conversion is simple but quite expensive as it requires a new generator and voltage control unit as well as other onboard electric motors, and of course changing all the bulbs. A previously 12-volt-converted car is a definite bonus, but of course you should still moan about the resultant lack of originality and knock some more money off.

Gearboxes with synchromesh appear on later cars, which makes them easier to drive – but

◄ The rim of the bonnet opening is a good guide to previous accident damage, as it's difficult to get the smooth curve back. Feel with your fingers for irregularities, inside as well as outside.

◄ The bottom of the spare wheel well is another favourite area for rust and accident damage. Check above and below for anything that doesn't look right. The single-skin construction helps.

◄ The horn rim was made of cheap alloy, which broke about 40 years ago. Jack could spend hundreds of dollars hunting down a rare unbroken original replacement, but what the hell, the horn still works.

double-declutching is rather fun anyway, and easy when you get the hang of it, so it doesn't matter.

Porsche brakes are always good, and there are no particular brake problems on early cars.

MAINTENANCE AND REPAIRS

STRUCTURE

Once you've got a good shell in good condition, make sure it's permanently protected against further rust by applying a flexible coating and by touching it up wherever stone chips have revealed metal. The single-skin construction of early cars is a big benefit for long-term ownership, because you can see exactly what's going on and deal with it.

For the later cars closer to 1960 than 1950, you can go on the Internet and order a great many replacement panels with a credit card, which will be sent off to you the same day. For really early cars you're going to have to hunt down repair panels. That's fine if you enjoy the hunt, and many people do, but a late rather than an early 356 rust bucket is going to be (relatively) cheaper and more practical to repair.

MECHANICALS

Restoring an engine and box will require a mixture of rare and expensive Porsche parts and cheap and cheerful Beetle parts on an early engine, with more Porsche-made parts on a later engine.

There's no choke on most 356s – you just squirt some fuel into the cylinders by squeezing the throttle a couple of times, then fire it up and it settles down to an 800rpm idle quite quickly. There's a hand throttle on some models to set the idle as the engine warms up. The lack of a choke is probably one reason for the longevity of the engine – most people use too much choke for too long, which washes all the oil off the bores and promotes cylinder bore wear. Use as little throttle of either sort as possible until the engine has warmed up.

Regular oil changes are crucial, as ever, and much more so with air-cooled engines in which the oil provides cooling as well as lubrication.

An expert should be able to remove a 356 engine in 15 minutes, and if you're a competent DIY mechanic you should be able to look after one and work on it without major problems.

IMPROVEMENTS AND MODIFICATIONS

STRUCTURE

One improvement well worth doing is to get the fuel tank slosh-coated inside and out in plastic. This stops rust flakes getting into the carbs and the engine, and keeps the tank permanently protected.

With the gear lever so remote from the gearbox, it will improve most cars if linkage bushings are replaced and kept greased.

MECHANICALS

If you buy a car with no engine or a wrecked engine, you can instead use a 912 engine, which was the ultimate development of the flat four before the six-cylinder came in for the 911. You can also use a VW engine, of course, in which case you have all sorts of options in terms of power and reliability upgrades, not least of which is a 2,500cc base engine for low-tech but effective grunt – but you do risk being beaten up by men in blazers if you open the engine lid anywhere near a Porsche concours show.

There's a slight VW-related advantage in buying one of the earliest 356 Porsches, because from 1950 to 1953 they were still to some extent converted Beetles rather than Porsches, and carried a good many VW-badged – and therefore VW-priced – mechanical parts. The extra cost of every other part for an early car will probably more than cancel that out, though.

THE PLASTIC ALTERNATIVE

Given the high cost of either a clean, solid 356 or a wreck plus a restoration bill, let's look sideways for a moment at a slightly different way of achieving a 356 on a budget. How about considering a plastic-bodied Speedster conversion built from a scrap 356 coupé? You can't afford a real Speedster without selling your house, but once you've thought it through, a well-made semi-replica has a lot going for it.

A compromise between a Porsche and a replica can be constructed from the remains of a scrap 356 for quite a reasonable amount of money. Even with classic cars as relatively rare as the 356, there comes a point where the car is genuinely scrap and has to be abandoned in its original form. Let's face it, many 'restored' concours winners are virtually replicas anyway, but have been remade from new steel panels, which is apparently perfectly respectable, rather than GRP, which is seen as horrible kit car stuff. Serious crash damage to a mostly single-skin monocoque is simply not repairable, certainly not economically, and the same applies to serious rust. If the screen pillar area and the roof are gone, as well as the inner and outer wings, the A and B posts, the doors, lids and the floor, it's not worth repairing a coupé. An original Speedster or roadster in this state might be worth rescuing, but it would in any case finish up as a very expensive replica, if we're to be honest

▶ An abandoned project could be well worth looking at, as long as you can account for most of the bits, or enjoy hunting down the bits that are missing. Much of the work on this car is done, including major body restoration, so somebody will get a good Porsche for a good price.

about it. A scrap coupé that has reached its end as a workable car but is still complete could be worth rescuing and rebuilding as a glassfibre Speedster, though – if you retain the floorpan tunnel and the mechanicals, you retain the identity even if the rotten floorpan sheet metal has largely been replaced. The central tunnel usually remains strong, and you could replace the side floor pans and whatever else was rotten with a mixture of sheet steel and new modified Beetle metalwork, which is also usefully cheap. As much of the original car as possible could be repaired and retained to try to preserve some of its character.

The result would in reality be a bastardised half-kit car and the very idea will upset many people, but let's get real – a seriously wrecked or rotten 356 coupé isn't going to be repaired. Its steering wheel will sell for silly money at a show, and the glass, the engine and box and a few other bits will be sold on, but most of it will go to the crusher. If on the other hand the scrap coupé is recycled into a neo-Speedster by a sympathetic builder, any usable sections of the remaining steel bodywork and the glass set can be passed on to another owner to help keep another 356 on the road.

Being rebuilt as a fake Speedster and living on for far longer than a new steel car has to be a more desirable fate than the crusher, doesn't it?

The cost of such a project will also be pretty reasonable compared to a real Speedster. A replica body is going to cost a few thousand pounds, and the Speedster screens and roof aren't cheap, but part of the point of such a rescue project would be to recycle all you could of the original car – seats, clocks, door-handles, badges, trim, registration. You wouldn't be able to fool anybody who knew anything about cars that it was the real thing, so you don't get into the dodgy area of serious fakery – it's interesting to observe that there are now many more Le Mans Bentleys and Type 35s around than were ever built by Bentley or Bugatti.

INVESTMENT

Something to consider with a 356 is the investment potential. Investment is largely irrelevant to an affordable Porsche buyer, but if you add more

money to the buying pot for a 356 and buy well, you have the option to cash it in for a significant gain later. You may never want to, but this does mean you can go well over budget and still make a very sensible buy. The silver car spotted in Washington State is an example – a clean shell well restored, with its original matching-numbers engine, but partly dismantled. $25,000 US takes it away – well over the £10,000 budget by the time it's drivable in the UK, but its value is only going to go up.

PRICES

Speedsters: don't even think about it. Mid-1950s coupés in restored or original condition, $40–60,000. For later 1960s coupés, high $20,000s coming down to mid-$15,000s as they get rougher. Under $10,000 gets you a project coupé, but if it's an abandoned dry-state restoration with the rust already cut out and well repaired, that's not such a bad idea.

BEST BUYS

There isn't a particular year or model that offers an obvious best buy – with each individual car, condition and originality, or the lack thereof, are much more important. In general later cars are cheaper. Earlier cars are rare and cool, but later cars work better and are more practical. The only useful best-buy advice is Go West, Young Man: California is the best hunting ground for solid older Porsches.

THE AFFORDABLE PORSCHE

CHAPTER 12

Replicas

tributes or porky pies?

Affordability rating ★★★

This chapter will enrage some and intrigue others. I don't really look at any motor manufacturer through rose-tinted spectacles, although I am coming to respect Porsches to some extent as I write this book. The cars I enjoy most are hand-built ultra-high-performance sports/racing cars, also known as kit cars. Before you flip the page, let me tell you why I like kit cars best even after writing books about Ferraris and Maseratis. Some of the very best of Ferraris, Aston Martins and ACs were made on the Superleggera principle – a strong steel main chassis frame with lighter steel tubular structures carrying a lightweight body. Apart from Beetle-based buggies and their ilk, virtually every modern kit car is made in this way, but stronger. What weight there is tends to be carried very low down, and the GRP bodies are very strong in their own right. Torsional rigidity is immense, and kit car chassis stiffness and power-to-weight ratios can only be dreamed of by people making pressed steel monocoques with full glasshouses and power windows.

The purest of sports cars is the Lotus Seven, and the very same Lotus Seven is also the purest of kit cars. Even the reasons for manufacturing kits are different – production cars are built mostly for profit, but kit cars are built to realise the dreams of both makers and owners. We're talking hand-pressed Turkish-grind doppio espresso here, rather than commercial non-dairy fat-free decaf frappuccino. The kit car scene is where the maverick speed-freak engineers and designers live, and is the real edge of the automotive world. The fastest kit car of 2003, a roadgoing Tiger with two Kawasaki bike engines, achieved 3.15 seconds to 60 at Santa Pod: unofficially, on dry concrete it does the job in 2.9. The same guy made 2.83 seconds to 60 in 2005. While passengering in a 1,300cc, Hayabusa-powered carbon-bodied Fisher Fury during a track

◀ **The various Speedster replicas offer a very close replica of the Speedster, but as a practical new sports car rather than as a treasured classic. They're usually stronger, faster, handle better and will last indefinitely in casual daily use as long as you replace the floorpans every 15 years when they rust out.**

BASICS

Body	GRP replica bodies with internal tubular steel bracing for door hinges/dashboard/rear bulkhead. Also floor-stiffening structures, usually involving VW Beetle floorpan or spaceframe equivalent. Beetle pans can make registration/emissions tests and paperwork easier.
Engines	Beetle-based air-cooled flat fours: anything from donor engines at 1,300/1,500/1,600cc to monsters heading for three litres.
Transmission	Tough four-speed Beetle transaxle will take a lot of abuse. Five-speed Porsche transmission is an option, but tends to be noisy in a replica.
Suspension	Usually Beetle-based with adjustable torsion bars, coils over shocks, upgrades cheap and easily available. Late Super Beetle not usually suitable. Rear, usually Beetle-based torsion bars and arms, with upgrades again cheap and easily available.
Brakes	The more authentic replicas use Beetle drums, which are made more effective by lighter weight: disc conversions are cheap.

day shared with a Porsche club, we got chucked off the circuit for taking the mickey, because we were going past their production sports cars on the Bruntingthorpe back straight at about 150mph and then braking to 80mph to go around them on the outside of the corners: it was if the 911s were standing still. That's kit car life.

Many early Porsches are to some extent turnkey kit cars anyway, having been put together from a kit of parts largely composed of bits of other cars – fortunately using much of the same care and attention that most kit car builders apply to assembling their personal dreams.

So before you instinctively and conventionally deride a replica kit Speedster or Spyder as a horrible plastic bathtub, check out *Kit-Car* magazine, in which I write monthly, and also have a look at the last book I wrote for Haynes, *The Kit Car Manual*. Both of these will give you some facts to go on before you dismiss hand-built cars made with GRP, which come to think of it Porsche have used for bodywork themselves. The only danger of too much reading about kit cars is that you might decide to skip Porsches altogether and go for something faster and more edgy.

SPEEDSTERS

The fact of the matter is that you can't afford a genuine Speedster unless you're seriously loaded. Even if you are loaded, you still can't afford a 550 Spyder. However, for around 20 per cent of the cost of a genuine Speedster you can achieve maybe 80 per cent of the feel of the real thing – and you're getting a virtually new car that will last longer than you will. It's not a Porsche, but for those of us on normal incomes it's a Speedster all right. With a bit of hunting you can afford a ready-built second-hand Speedster replica for around the budget levels we're looking at. It doesn't really matter how old a GRP Speedster replica is, because apart from the floorpans it will never rust. Beetle floorpan sheet metal should be regarded as a consumable, and the better Speedster kits have their own Superleggera-inspired tubular frames anyway.

£10,000 will get you a kit Speedster that's used but in good condition. There are a few nasty Speedster replicas that have been bought and built

▶ This 356 is too badly crashed ever to be worth repairing, but if you wanted to achieve as authentic a Speedster as possible it would make a good donor car.

by incompetents, but in general the standards are high. The basis is a VW Beetle pan, which normally needs new floorpans either side, although the central tunnel usually remains rust-free. The Beetle floorpan needs to be shortened to fit the Speedster body, which is normally a professional job unless you're handy with a MIG welder. The body is normally quite a hefty GRP moulding with steel frame inserts that bolt to the floor and mount the doors.

If you're on a budget, you could consider building a Speedster kit from scratch. The cheapest currently available is from Pilgrim and the cost of their basic kit is £2,700 which is a good start. I don't have personal experience of the Pilgrim, but it certainly looks promising. The major player in the UK has been Chesil Speedsters, whose kit starts at around five grand. I have driven a Chesil halfway across Europe and it was a pleasure to drive, as well as being tangibly a high quality product. My favourite Speedster replica is the Intermeccanica from Vancouver, though. This has its bodywork left in the mould for two solid (and expensive) weeks to ensure that as the glass fibre body fully cures and hardens, its shape remains absolutely perfect. The Intermeccanica looks exactly like a Speedster, but has some modern technology secreted around it, including heated seats, which makes winter open-top motoring an entirely different experience. It's also a chance to own a car with an Intermeccanica badge, which puts you in pretty rarefied territory. In the 1960s Intermeccanica were up there with De Tomaso and Facel Vega, and way upmarket of mass-produced sports cars such as Ferrari and Maserati.

The use of a previously registered VW floorpan for a Speedster kit can sometimes be useful in avoiding tiresome and expensive government testing, and definitely helps with emission controls, as the vehicles' identities are based on an engine

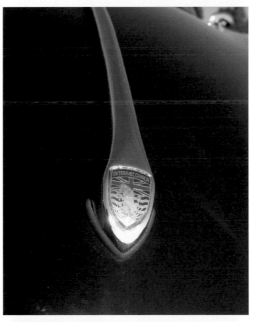

▼▲ The car looks pretty convincing until you notice the fat modern tyres, electric windows, high tech sound system and 170bhp.

◄ The Intermeccanica badge is fitted with pride: it's not a Porsche, but it's definitely a Speedster.

◄ Among other advantages offered by Speedster replicas, other than being able to afford one in the first place, are 12-volt electrics and halogen headlights, so you can see where you're going – 12-volt horns are a bonus, too.

► The interior is a pretty close replica, but features an Intermeccanica dash badge and a Nardi steering wheel. Replica original-style wheels are also available, although usable real ones fetch very silly money.

◄ The engine choice is up to you. The donor Beetle usually comes with an engine that resembles the power output of an original Speedster engine, but you can also fit a nearly 3-litre, injected and turbocharged monster. This Intermeccanica has a 2,332cc Beetle engine with Webers and 170bhp.

▼ The back end conceals a high-level brake light, mandatory on new cars but invisible unless the brakes are on.

that is too old to require injection, catalytic converters and so on. If you want an evil 2,500cc quad-Webered monster at the back of your Speedster rep, no worries as far as UK emissions go if your car is still legally an old Beetle.

If you haven't already thrown this book away and stalked off for a restorative drinkie and a sit down, have a look at the Speedster club website and have a chat with them.

SPYDERS

The legendary 550 Spyder was a rare and expensive sports racer from the heyday of Porsche's racing glory. Its excellent suspension and reliability gave Porsche a real edge in road races like the Targa Florio, the Mille Miglia and even Le Mans. Continuous sideways action over *pavé* and nasty roads battered other cars into submission, but the Porsche ironed out the bumps and kept going. The 550 Spyder was the true spirit of the 356 that Porsche wanted to build, with the engine in the rear-mid position. Compromises for luggage space and cabin room may have spoiled the 356 in some people's eyes, but the 550 had the lot – excellent power to weight, sublime handling (up to a point) and the beauty that often comes to machines built with an absolute purity of purpose.

However, like a Ferrari P4, you can't have one unless you're the dictator of a reasonable-sized country, or possibly a gangsta rapper with a good agent. You can't even get to sit in a 550 unless you're a pretty heavyweight motoring journo. The cost of buying one of the 65 cars made is about $400,000 to $450,000 if you can find one.

You can, however, get something brand new

and very similar in purpose to a Spyder, with a light spaceframe chassis, a highly tuned air-cooled flat four and a lightweight replica body the correct shape. The weight and weight distribution is going to be about the same. The real thing in lighter 550A form weighed 1,170lb (530kg), and the Beck 550 replica weighs 1210lb (550kg). In 1953, getting 140bhp out of a Beetle-based engine was a tricky business, but today it's easy, and the engine still weighs the same. The replica gets you 5.2 seconds to 60 and tops out at 130mph (210kph), and if you dare you can still run it on the same tyres as the real thing. That will get you, according to contemporary 550 reports, sublime cornering up to .82G, and 'evil handling' if you push it beyond that.

James Dean's 'Little Bastard' 550 killed him in the end, or at least driving it into a Hudson did. If there's insufficient life in your life and you need some real risk, a 550 replica on vintage replica tyres is going to be right up there. It's also going to be pretty close to the feel of the real thing, the only differences being a stronger body and engine and $400,000. It's up to you how close to the edge you want to push it.

In the UK, a respected name for higher-tech Spyder replicas was Technic/Martin and Walker, but they seem to be off the Information Superhighway for the moment. However, the GP Spyder, based on the VW floorpan, has been around since 1983 and is still available in a corner of Cornwall. I have reviewed the GP for a magazine, and it seemed quicker than a Speedster replica and more open to the fresh air. The amount of power you decide to indulge in is a private matter between you and your chequebook. I'd suggest that *Ultra VW* magazine is a good place to start researching bang-for-buck figures from VW Beetle-based engines. The Beetle floorpan will to some extent be overwhelmed by serious power, but that's either a problem or an opportunity depending on what kind of driving fun you're looking for. I used to make replica XK120 Jaguars under the Ayrspeed name, and my brother used his Ayrspeed in preference to his new Subaru Impreza for going to work, because with its 16in crossply tyres he could hang the tail out in the wet without even breaking the 30mph speed limit. A mid-rear-engined car will obviously handle much better than an overpowered XK-engined tourer with agricultural tyres, but that's the kind of fun you'll have with a Beetle-based Spyder as long as you stick with proper skinny tyres, crossplies if your nerves will stand them.

If you go the Beetle floorpan route you'll save money over a more serious spaceframed replica, and the use of a Beetle pan and registration can simplify the process and cut costs with getting the car on the road.

California offers a more serious car, in the form of the Vintage Spyder. Their car does use a spaceframe and either safer or faster rear suspension depending on how you drive. The rear end is now a coil-over-shock system rather than Beetle torsion bars, so location will be improved and suspension settings will be adjustable. The front end remains basically Beetle. A turnkey car starts at $25,000 less engine. At the moment, that translates as £16,000 or so, which is well over our £10,000 budget and still needs money spent on importing it if you're in the UK – but it is a brand new car. A more economical option is their kit at $14,000 less engine, which starts you off at maybe £9,000. You're looking at a year's worth of weekends to build such a kit, for a newcomer to the sport. A good sign is that the company is prepared to shift the firewall for very tall drivers, which suggests that they're flexible and still small enough for individual customers to matter. Before you buy anything at all, whether Speedster or Spyder, you need to find out as much as you can about the whole scene, and an excellent place to start is www.speedsters.com, the website of the Speedsters Club. This is a good and enthusiastic club that offers all a good car club can – help, tech advice, parts and cars at good prices, and a healthy social side for those who have finished building their cars or have bought them already built. There is also a Spyder section of the club, and the members will be very well aware of and up to date with what's good and what's not in terms of the kits available. In the USA the Spyder Club has a couple of hundred members, and although they're scattered all over a huge geographical area there's bound to be a cluster in SoCal.

911

There used to be fake 911s available in the UK, known as Covins. Their owners swear by them, but the cars tend to have water-cooled Ford engines, which aren't convincing. They can be chipped and turbocharged up to quite good power, but the kits were never fully developed. Some people have remade them with 911 engines and have re-engineered the suspension completely, but by the time you've done that you could have put the same effort and money into a rough 911 or a fake 914/6 and built something much better. From the rust point of view, they do have the very big advantage over a genuine 911 of not crumbling away under you, but apart from the rust bonus the Covin 911 replica isn't better, faster, cheaper or more available than the real thing, so you might as well just go for the real thing.

986/987 Boxster

back to the future

Affordability rating ★

The earliest Boxsters are now within reach, as early high-mileage examples are availabe for well under the ten grand level in 2010. Their relative newness means they offer poor value for money compared to the rest of the cheaper affordable Porsches mentioned in this book.

However, the basic idea of a small, relatively light (2,822lb/1,280kg) sports car with reasonable power, good handling and the engine in the right place can't be faulted, and if you really fancy one then it's worth the money.

The value problem is a triple whammy – firstly, Boxsters are still depreciating. Secondly, they are a truly modern car, which means that they're very complex and rely on interconnected electronics and computer technology to function. Many of their problems are out of the reach of amateurs and local mechanics, and increasingly all main dealers and larger garages are forced by car manufacturers to pay through the nose to keep up with factory diagnostic computers. Who do you suppose pays the final bill for that? This applies to all modern cars, not just Porsches.

Thirdly, the Boxster was a completely new design, which means the first couple of years of production are to some extent production prototypes – the first owners in 1996 were the test drivers, and it's their discarded cars we can just about afford now. These early cars will still be suffering from initial design and production faults that will have been sorted out during the following few years.

The Boxster is still a Porsche, though, so its general engineering standards will be higher than most. At least it's a proper purpose-designed sports car with a decent engine, not some cynical restyling of a euroshopper with the roof cut off and a good ad campaign.

◀ **Quite nice lines, and the later styling update hasn't been radical enough to make the older Boxsters look dated.**

BASICS

Body	Steel monocoque convertible.
Engine	Mid-mounted all-alloy DOHC water-cooled electronically injected flat six.
Transmission	Five- or six-speed manual gearbox, or five-speed Tiptronic semi-automatic.
Suspension	MacPherson struts with coils over shocks, anti roll bars front and rear.
Steering	Powered rack, later proportionate.
Brakes	Powered discs all round, ABS.

Fuller specifications and further detailed technical information can be found in Chapter 15 and in the Haynes Porsche Data Book.

EVOLUTION

1996	Launched as 1997 model. 201bhp from 2.5 litres.
1998	18in wheel option, side airbags, stiffer rear chassis, satellite navigation option.
1999	Xenon Litronic headlights, 18in wheel option.
2000	225bhp from stroked 2.7-litre engine, 250bhp from 3.2-litre S engine using 996/911 crank. Gearing change on fourth and fifth gears, bigger valves, four cats, rear suspension improvements. S gets bigger 911 brakes.
2001	Electronic Stability Programme option: comes with Motor Schleppmoment-Regelung which avoids engine-braking skids.
2002	Bose sound system, glass rear window, S gets bigger valves. Two extra bolts secure front subframe to bodyshell.
2003	Minor facelift, S gets bigger valves, stiffer anti-roll bars. Front and rear skirts change, longer side air intakes, eight extra bhp, 17in and 18in wheel options, better hood, rear window upgraded to glass rather than plastic. Variocam option.
2004	987 series launched, major facelift. Carrera GT style headlights, bigger side air intakes, bigger arches and wheel options, new interior, upgraded exhaust. Active Damping Control option, 911 style dash, side panels welded to floor as well as bolted.
2005	Base model gets 240bhp, S gets 280bhp. Stiffer chassis, wider wheels, variable-effort power steering.
2007	S gets 295bhp 3.4-litre engine shared with Cayman.

◄ The front end of the earlier Boxster is shared with the new 911, which might be annoying for buyers of new 911s – but they won't be reading this anyway so it doesn't matter.

The front end of the car up to 2001, and the basic engine design, is shared with the 911, meaning big savings for Porsche and some savings for you.

The list of faults below sounds fairly daunting, but these are mostly relatively minor, other than water leaking into the door jamb and taking out some or all of the wiring. Keeping your Boxster in a garage or under a tarpaulin would be a wise precaution. Premature wear of clutches, ball joints and wheel bearings is compounded by enthusiastic driving but is really down to inadequate design and component quality: on Boxsters they will be regular service items.

To some extent, a picture of a car's reliability is provided by customer reviews on the Internet. The reviews are partisan, and many 'reviewers' of performance cars are fantasists and have never driven one, but in general the proportion of yellow smiley faces to blue sad faces does parallel what I hear from mechanics and petrolheads. When I looked for a North American replacement for the Range Rover I used to drive in the UK, the reviews of Jeep Cherokees were mostly yellow with some blue, Chevy Blazers exactly 50/50 – half their owners say they're crap and half

say they're excellent – and the Nissan Pathfinder had no blue faces at all. That all corresponds exactly with mechanics' advice, which is also worth seeking out.

Boxster Internet reviews are nearly all yellow with just a few blues, so that's a good sign – they come out well in those reviews. Any ageing newer-generation car is going to have some reliability issues. Many of the parts and functions are more reliable than they used to be, but there are just so many more parts in them than there used to be.

▼ Humpback is quite dramatic and the detailing such as the exhaust tailpipe is funky. A nice-looking car.

HISTORY

The success of the 993 left Porsche plenty of time to develop the new 986 or Boxster, and they took their inspiration from the 550 Spyder. The Boxster was launched in 1996 as a 1997 model, to offer a cheaper and more accessible option for people who wanted a Porsche but couldn't afford a Carrera, and also to people who just wanted a small mid-engined open car. The design was by Harm Lagaay, and the car is visually the junior member of the Porsche family. The concept of an 'entry level' car becomes somewhat stretched when the new price at the end of 2006 was between £34,000 and £42,000 – but entry level Porsche it is nonetheless.

The concept of using bought-in sub-assemblies or modules made the car very profitable too – outsourcing the suspension/steering units, transmission, dash and wiring and other parts packages makes big savings. So does using more or less the same suspension for both ends of the car, with the extra pair of steering arms used as rear toe-in control rods – a clever move used in several rear-mid-engined kit cars 20 years previously. More clever yet was using most of the front half of the 911, as well as the engine design. This does not impress 911 buyers, but it's good news if you're a Boxster customer.

The Boxster was a commercial success from the beginning, and has followed the Porsche tradition of continuous improvement and development. Arrangements to provide extra production capacity in Finland turned out to be a smart move, and the Uusikaupunki factory has been kept busy. It's worth noting that the Finnish cars are certainly no worse that Stuttgart ones in terms of quality control, and possibly slightly better.

The base model was joined by a premium S version with more power and handling improvements, and there was a fairly major facelift in 2003/4. The car still looks basically the same, but there were structural as well as visual improvements, with a stiffer chassis. Power levels, as always, have risen with the passing years, from 201bhp from 2.5 litres at launch to 295bhp with the shared 3.4-litre Cayman engine.

HANDS ON – The driver's view

The Boxster I tried out was a 2003 base model. The interior had the same sparse functionality as German cars of the 1980s, and reverted to the flavour of earlier, more focused sporting Porsches. The car actually belongs to my next door neighbour Jim Norris, which although it provided a genuinely random example, did not permit me to test it to its limits: there are many ditches in the countryside south of Vancouver and I prefer to remain on good terms with Jim. Within reasonable limits the car shows no sign of any handling faults at all. The chassis is pretty stiff for a monocoque convertible, the engine is in the perfect place, the suspension is firm but not brutal, and when you get the hang of the Tiptronic gearbox it works well. If there were a clutch pedal option with the Tiptronic as well, it would be perfect. As it is, the box is smooth and crisp, and positive changing soon gets a rhythm going. In the UK this semi-auto would be a much better option than a manual gearbox, as gears are a waste of effort in crawling traffic.

There was quite a gap between my first taste of this Porsche and the photo session, and after 80,000km I could hear a wheel bearing going, the engine sounded a little rough, there was more mechanical noise, and the whole car felt significantly more baggy.

HANDS ON – The owner's view

The owner of this Boxster had been driving a BMW for a while and was bored with it, and his leasing dealer made him a tempting offer on the Porsche. He's not a particular Porsche enthusiast, but quite liked the idea of driving one and fancied a convertible, although he felt it looked rather like a midlife-crisis car. I encouraged him to take the car and skip the midlife crisis. A year later he was

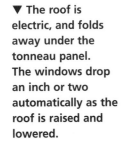

▼ The roof is electric, and folds away under the tonneau panel. The windows drop an inch or two automatically as the roof is raised and lowered.

◄ The cockpit is cosy and the driving position good. Black leather seats are worth looking for, as they always seem to look better the more worn they get: they also feel more comfy with age.

▼ The instrument binnacle tells you most of what you want to know, but the electronics are complex and really beyond amateur fiddling. Okay as long as it all works, but corrosion, vibration and leaks will inevitably take their toll.

◄ The Tiptronic gearbox is quite a good compromise for congested roads – you might as well have an automatic in the city, but a sequential clutchless manual is good fun for country driving.

▶ The front boot and dinky emergency spare offer genuine weekend luggage space, but if the luggage space is occupied, what are you going to do with a punctured 265/35 x 18in tyre and its 9in-wide rim?

▼ Rear boot also offers quite a big space for a small rear-engined car. But probably not enough space for your punctured 9J x 18 wheel and tyre.

still relatively happy with it – he's had minor hassle from jealous cops and the ball joints have worn out, and a minor engine fault occasionally causes it to spew big clouds of smoke, but otherwise no major worries. However, cheaper Boxster imports from the US have significantly eroded its value, the quality is nothing special, and he will probably not replace it with another Porsche.

WHAT TO LOOK FOR

STRUCTURE

Ill-fitting roof structures and wind noise (can usually be adjusted out), inaccurate speedo and fuel gauges. Check tyre condition, replacements are expensive. Remember that delaminating tyre carcasses can sound exactly like tired wheel bearings. Look for sloppy or squeaky ball joints. Worn ball joints can sound exactly like squeaky bushes.

ENGINE

Erratic idle, oil leaks from oil feed tubes at top and back of engine. Rear crankcase oil seal leaks. Rarely, porous crankcases on early cars. Spark plug tubes leak. Leaking radiator caps.

TRANSMISSION

Slipping or juddering clutch, wheel bearing noise. Transmission diff bearings and gears are starting to fail. Tiptronic gearbox should change smoothly: bear in mind that repairs are expensive.

MAINTENANCE AND REPAIRS

STRUCTURE

Door pull cables tend to break, window electrics can fail, rain in door jambs can cause a short-circuit that will fry much of the electrical system. Keep A/C drain tubes clear to avoid wet carpets. Convertible top drain tubes must be also kept clear or flooding and electrical disaster looms, starting with shorted-out alarm and door lock control units. A rattle from behind is often a stretched convertible-top control cable. Be sure to get all spare keys with a car, as replacements are expensive. Key remotes also fail, £175 for replacement. Airbag sensor is unreliable,

airbag light comes on. (This can be related to seat belt buckle connections.) Pre-2000 cars are prone to convertible motor transmission failure, a £1,500 repair.

ENGINE

Access to mechanicals is quite difficult, and only from beneath, which means you'll need a pit, a hoist or substantial ramps and jacks for self-servicing or checking garages' work. This will also add to repair and service bills. Mass airflow sensors fail. Coolant tanks have been known to burst (expensive). Oil separators fail, causing massive smoke from exhaust, looks like engine failure. Frightening the first time, then just embarrassing.

TRANSMISSION

Clutch has a relatively short life, wheel bearings sometimes also have a short life, ball joints likewise. The G86/00 manual box runs with fluid intended to be replaced at 100,000 miles, so change it before that figure unless you're confident somebody else has.

IMPROVEMENTS AND MODIFICATIONS

Boxsters as of early 2010 still tend to have non-technical owners and are still too expensive to have been hacked about much. Mods will tend to be updates/upgrades to later parts, with complications due to facelift changes and electronics compatibility.

PRICES

Values are dropping year by year, but an Internet trawl reveals that in early 2010 early British examples had sunk well below £10,000. LHD drops the value a little, which helps. Generally '97-'99s are £8–12,000 and '98–2000 are at £9–14,000.

Over the Atlantic, prices run rather randomly from $16,000 to $27,000 for 1997s, and '99–2001 from $23–24,000. £10,000 for an early left-hand drive car plus shipping is really not worth the bother, as you'd finish up spending the same in Birmingham, England, as you would in Birmingham, Alabama.

Germany also offers no bargains, except a 2001 for £4,000 which looks way too good to be true and therefore almost certainly is too good to be true, as is a '97 in the USA for $7,000. It would be worth an HPI check and a mechanical check on a UK Boxster at this price, or a Carfax check on a USA car – it may be a cheap Porsche you're buying, but it's not a cheap £10,000 you're spending.

BEST BUYS

The only Boxsters within reach for around £10,000 are early ones with high miles: we don't have the luxury of choosing a best buy, we're just trying to avoid a write-off or a lemon. Having said that, a well-repaired write-off can still be a good deal.

▲ The proportions say mid-rear-engined, which is what the first Porsches would have been if they hadn't got stuck with Beetle floorpans. Mid-rear is still a top position for a performance car's engine.

Chapter 14

The inside track

smart moves and fast moves

Each chapter of this book, generally based on information from Porsche owners and hands-on specialists, has given you their rather partisan but hopefully realistic look at the specific problems and benefits of each of the affordable models of Porsche.

However, there's a certain amount of information collected in this final chapter that applies to all Porsches: you don't want to read it nine times in nine chapters, and I certainly don't want to write it nine times. It's time for me to get on with other books, and time for you to massage your finances and go on the hunt for your affordable Porsche.

In this chapter there's advice on buying Porsches generally, some of which applies to any car – but you may be new to the old-car game, and you may not be familiar with some of the basic rules for buying old cars. There's a section on importing, which gives you an idea of the costs involved and makes what is really quite an adventure as easy as possible. There's an introduction to the bigger Porsche clubs, although you may find other smaller clubs as you get more involved. Racing is briefly mentioned, but only a very few of us will ever go further than watching it. Still, there are people you should talk to if you're thinking about it. Track days are a lot more relevant, and if you're moving up to what is after all a high-performance car, and in the case of rear-engined Porsches, potentially unstable, you really do need some track time where you can overcook it and slide off and merely have people taking the mickey rather than taking your organs for transplant.

Spares – there's not much point in going into that in any depth, as availability and pricing changes every week. For example, people who made OE (original equipment) parts for old Porsches are now sometimes selling them direct at good prices – when you know what you're looking for you can hunt it down at the best price. 911 enthusiast Kent Verderico says if

◄ **Enthusiasts discussing Porsche minutiae. Their considerable experience and knowledge are there for the asking.**

possible use OEM (original equipment manufacturer) stuff, because of unexpected manufacturing short-cuts and wear rates on budget parts: his cheap Turbo tie-rod upgrades lasted six months and had to be replaced with Porsche parts in the end anyway. Not a bargain.

BUYING SECOND-HAND

These rules apply to all Porsche models, and in fact most second-hand cars. There are more specific items in the relevant chapters, but here are some universal basics that are worth reviewing again even if you know them already:

- Top affordability is offered by left-hand drive – 20 to 30 per cent off. Nowadays the only real problem with LHD is car park ticket machines: you will have to either ask a passenger to pull the ticket or get out of the car yourself, a few times a month. Do you want to save an extra £3,000 by climbing out of your car a couple of dozen times a year? It's a no-brainer.
- My personal advice is also to buy a car with no service history, but complain like hell about its relative worthlessness and demand a really big cut in the price, because you may have to sell it later, still with no history. Most people would disagree with this approach, but it's based on pure logic. Car servicing in the UK is historically and endemically dishonest. The British consumer magazine *Which?* regularly secretly sends cars for servicing in all levels of British garages, and only one in 30 carries out the full servicing that's been paid for. I see no reason why Porsche dealers would all be completely different from any other garages, so an FPSH – Full Porsche Service History – is not worth much to me. Without any history, all you really have to go on is what you can find out by examining and driving the car, which is there in front of you. For example, check the amount, colour and consistency of the oil on the dipstick. If it's low, runny and black, the oil probably hasn't been changed for 10,000 miles: trust the dipstick in the engine rather than the dipstick who wrote the invoices.
- *Don't ever buy a car at night*. They look much better than they are, but like an intemperate dance-floor decision about a night-time companion, dawn can reveal some unpleasant surprises. Ten minutes' embarrassment while making a farewell coffee is one thing, but if you've traded your entire wad for a dodgy Porker you're going to have to live with it for rather longer than ten minutes.

- If you can back a car into a garage or a covered car park while examining it, squat down right at the back and look along the sides towards the daylight. This is a top way to see any ripples or dents. If there *are* any ripples, find out why. If there are any suspect areas, run a magnet along the body (wrapped in a soft cloth to avoid scratching the paint). If the magnet falls off, there's filler rather than steel under the paint. It might seem weird, but ask the seller if you can hand-wash the car. It's remarkable how many faults you'll see and feel while running your hands over the whole body.
- Previous accident damage is a worse problem the faster the car. A slightly squint 356 used for summer tootling is one thing, but hard cornering in a bent 911SC could be unwise. A straight Porsche should be able to drive hands-off in a straight line on a flat surface, bearing in mind that roads are cambered.
- Tyre wear patterns can tell you quite a lot. If the inside or outside edges of the front tyre tread are worn much more than the middle and the other side, the wheels are pointing in at the front or splayed out. This can simply be maladjustment, but a full alignment check would be wise before buying the car. If tyres are bald in the middle or bald on the outside edges, that means poor maintenance and a careless owner. If just one tyre (of a matched pair on either axle) is worn on the outside or inside, that suggests the suspension on that corner is bent. That tyre and wheel are at the wrong angle compared to the rest. If the rear tyres are worn unevenly, the suspension is either worn, damaged or modified. If the owner claims no mods, be careful.
- A stolen and recovered car can be an excellent buy, if it's a model that is well catered for by the second-hand spares market. You also get to see rather more of the structure of a stripped car than you do of a complete one.
- The same applies to abandoned restoration projects, as long as there isn't too much missing and as long as you have time to hunt down the missing parts at acceptable prices. Many people get a project 90 per cent finished, with the bodywork all restored to solid metal and the engine rebuilt, and then it all gets too much, they get sick of the sight of it and they abandon the project and sell it for a very small percentage of what's gone into it.
- Once you've decided which Porsche you're going for, *try at least three of your chosen model* to get a feel for what's a good one. I wouldn't say don't buy the first one you see,

because you might luck into a total bargain – but definitely go and see two others before you go back and buy the first one you saw.

- Check the engine for oil seepage with a torch and a mirror. Check the exhausts visually as well, and the heat exchangers on air-cooled models. While you're on the ground anyway, check the inside surfaces of the tyres and wheels for damage and sidewall cuts or swellings.
- Listen to the engine warming up from cold, and listen for any noises developing as it does warm up.
- If any oil hoses show signs of swelling at the connections, they will need replacing, so knock some money off.
- Poor tyre condition and mixed brands of tyres can indicate a cheapskate owner. If the tyres are bald, the chances are that he hasn't been changing the engine oil either.
- Check the brake discs for wear and condition. You can't check for warping by looking, but pulsing at the pedal in time with wheel rotation can mean warped discs. Not a big deal, but more money off the price, please.
- Look to see if the claimed mileage – worth about the same as a full service history, by the way – tallies with the wear on the steering wheel, seats and pedal rubbers. American cars generally tend to do much higher mileages than European cars, but it's mostly medium-speed highway cruising. That doesn't really wear cars out, it just makes them run more smoothly. A London car is probably getting quite tired at 100,000 miles, but a California car can have 200,000 on it and still be quite fresh.
- *Run an HPI check on the car's sales and theft history* – it may well still belong to somebody else even after you think you've bought it, and a frighteningly large proportion of UK cars have something dodgy in their past. Carfax is the American equivalent.
- Bring a tape or a CD to check the sound system.
- Make use of MOT test centres by taking a prospective Porsche buy for an MOT whether it already has one or not. Bear in mind also that the MOT certificate that comes with the car may have been bought in a pub. Quite a lot of the points covered by an expensive inspection are checked during a much cheaper MOT test, particularly if you ask the tester to give it a really good going over. You can often also get to look underneath quite thoroughly with a lead-light, which saves a lot of jacking up and grovelling underneath, and an MOT inspector will usually be happy to show you exactly what he's checking for. However, an inspection by a genuine Porsche repair specialist can also pay off big time, as they will be able to check for Porsche-specific problems such as a clutch cable about to pull through the bulkhead on a 911, or repaired damage on the inner front wings.

- You need to be sure you have insurance to test-drive a car, particularly a performance car. Check out with your broker what cover you have, and also check what a Porsche is going to cost to insure if you can't get it on a classic car policy: if you fancy a turbo 911 but you're 20 and live in Ladbroke Grove, think about a nice little 356 replica instead.
- *Don't take any risks when examining a car.* In particular, don't rely on a jack to hold it up. You don't know how good the jack's single rubber hydraulic sealing ring is, and you don't know how strong the sills and floor are on the car you're looking at: that's precisely why you're getting underneath it. Don't *ever* put anything you want to use again under a jacked-up car, such as your head. Get the car up on a pair of ramps, wheels chocked and in gear before even thinking about getting under it.
- Checking the underside of the radiator cap for white water-in-oil goo is a top idea, but do it while the engine is cold. If you take the rad cap off when the engine's hot, the steam will boil your head.
- Overspray on the window rubbers indicates a respray or partial respray. Why? In America resprays due to faded paint are relatively common, but in the UK they tend to suggest damage.

IMPORTING

Talk to Kingstown Shipping in Hull, originally recommended to me by somebody who ships cars regularly, and who are indeed helpful and efficient. Talk to them when you've decided what you want to go and get from the US, and in what condition you're thinking about importing it. You may opt to use your budget to get a really good 356 shell by buying a non-running project, but if you're going for a 911 you can expect to buy a solid and drivable one in the States for your £10,000.

Kingstown have good contacts in the major North American ports, from LA to New Jersey and Miami, and will liaise to get you a good deal on shipping. Among other things, they will try to consolidate your car with other cars to fill a container, and that way everybody saves. A ball-park figure for the physical shipping of a car from the dockside in the California ports (Long Beach for LA and southern California, Oakland for San

Francisco and northern California) – to a UK port in early 2010 was between £1,100 and £1,500, not including taxes and official bumf. (Shared container shipping from New Jersey costs around $1,000.) This was rising with fuel price surcharges, so shop around for plenty of quotes and recommendations – my only personal shipping experience is with Kingstown. It will also reduce on the down side of the boom/bust cycle as fuel costs deflate.

It can be slightly cheaper to ship a car on a Ro-Ro (roll on, roll off ferry), but it has to be either drivable, in which case you're looking at under a grand, or towable, in which case you have to attach a towbar or tow hook to the front end and pay another £200 or so. Ro-Ro is generally only available from ports on the eastern seaboard, from New York down to New Orleans. It's also less secure, and you can't stuff the car with cheap spares, which you can do if you ship it by container.

Customs rates change – as of 2010 a privately re-imported German EC-built car costs a flat duty fee of £50 plus VAT. If a company rather than an individual imports the car it's 10 per cent of the value plus VAT. This is all partly down to luck and timing, as officials have to keep changing rules in order to look busy. I'm not clear why they're allowed to impose any duty in a free trade zone, but there you go.

More duty rules and charges will probably reappear sooner or later on top of the £50 fee, so check what rules apply when it comes to seriously thinking about importing.

If you're importing from America, different rules and taxes apply. Duty is assessed on the value of non-EC-built cars, and is 10 per cent of the assessed value. The duty rate is less for a rolling shell or a spares donor at 3.5 per cent, although that's probably not much help for most of us. The smaller the amount of money on your receipt for the car – which could well just be hand-written on a piece of paper from the previous owner – the less duty you're likely to pay.

Make sure you have a legal title to a US car or you can't export it from the States. The TV show *Pinks* refers to racing for pink slips: these, or a similar document, are the formal legal title to American cars.

Importing from California is relatively simple, but in some of the other useful dry states such as Texas there are complications: getting title documents for exporting a Texas car can take weeks, so check the local bumf regime carefully.

Carfax, mentioned above, is a useful American company that can source a car's legal status and crash history.

It's galling but unavoidable that you pay Value Added Tax on the Customs duty, which is paying tax on paying tax, but there's nothing to be done about that rule.

More bumf – if you import a car to the UK that is less than ten years old, it will require an SVA (Single Vehicle Approval) test. This test is the familiar UK government shambles and the rules are frequently silly, but essentially the tester will visually inspect the car, but not its structural condition, to decide mostly whether the design and construction of the projections inside and outside the cabin look as though they would meet European TUV regulations. Lack of chassis triangulation is not an issue, but an insufficiently smooth radius on the edge of a sidelight is a fail. The whole thing was an ill-conceived, badly executed mess, but is now slightly less of a mess. In reality, most SVA issues are trivial and cheap to sort out. The test costs £600 and rising. *Kit-Car* magazine sells a useful guide to the weird world of SVA. Porsches less than ten years old are unlikely to fail the test on these issues. SVA complications and alterations are likely to include headlight beam dipping direction, the fitting of a rear fog lamp, a speedo marked in MPH, a catalytic converter for cars built after 1992, the radio frequencies of the alarm system remote control, indicator repeaters, and dealing with projections such as dangerously long exhaust tailpipes, which might injure a pedestrian were you to reverse over one. Yes, I'm serious.

Cars more than ten years old simply require an MOT, a rear red fog light, redirected headlights and amber indicators. The smart move would be simply to avoid buying a car less than ten years old: if your budget stretches to a nine-year old Porsche, just buy one a year older and with better specs and lower claimed mileage.

Without going too far, make a duty-liable car look bad rather than good when shipping it in, as customs duty is based on the car's value. Just don't risk taking the mickey and annoying them. If you've bought something in rough condition, cut or bash out the visible rust before customs valuation, and take any suspect areas back to bare metal with sandpaper. To go on a Ro-Ro ferry the vehicle has to *be* drivable but it doesn't have to *look* drivable. In any case, to be fair to yourself, you can't see the actual state of the car until you've opened up any rust holes. If its condition is a bit nasty, let's pay the right amount of duty for a nasty car. Don't import it as spares, though, as you may have trouble registering it if you plan to restore it instead of scrapping it. A car imported as a car should have a Customs & Excise form 386. You will also have to take the car home from the UK docks by trailer, because it has no British registration documents or number plates. It's technically legal to insure it on its chassis number and drive it 'to a destination' from the docks, but it depends how much you enjoy arguing with junior traffic cops who don't know that. DVLA in Swansea will issue it with an age-related British registration number.

Insurance for cars during shipping can usually be better and cheaper organised through your own broker than through shippers, based on the car's chassis number as its identity. Shippers' insurance tends to be more expensive and will sometimes only pay out on a total loss basis, such as if the container ship gurgles to the bottom with your Porker on board. Kingstown can organise comprehensive loss and damage insurance for two per cent of the car's value, so check that out against your broker's offer.

The exchange rate for dollars is volatile at the moment, and you may get an even better rate in Canadian dollars. It's odd, but old cars in damp Vancouver don't seem to rust much at all, and it's another optional port to ship from.

Talk to your bank about the best currency exchange rate they can get you, making sure you get the rate for larger amounts if there is one. Also check banks' rates against what's offered by the British post office, who used to be consistently good on exchange rates. It's legal to carry a large sum of cash into the US, but it must be declared to US Customs. If possible, avoid looking Arabic while doing this.

The concept of going across to California to buy and bring back a Porsche may leave you thinking 'Okay, good idea, but how do I actually go about it?'

I'll make it easy for you. First, hunt about for a cheap flight to Los Angeles on the Internet. Allow a couple of weeks for the trip, and if you have a family, make it the annual holiday and take them to Disney, Universal Studios, Hollywood and so on. In that case, a package holiday based on a hotel in Anaheim is a good idea. If you're just going there to find a Porsche, fly to Los Angeles (LAX) airport. Take the free courtesy shuttle bus (they sometimes call it a limo) to the Howard Johnson hotel, which costs about $85 a night. If you land after about 11:00pm, use the free hotel courtesy phone in the arrivals terminal to call the HoJo and ask for the shuttle to be sent. Get a room as high up in the building as you can, because the view is nice. If you like steak, beer and burgers go to the Sizzler on Manchester Avenue, which you can see from the HoJo's windows. If you feel like trying a very good Persian restaurant instead, go just past the Sizzler to a little mall and follow your nose. The restaurant's called Pars. A takeaway Fesendjan, which is chicken in a delicious super-rich pomegranate and walnut

sauce, will be too big for a Brit to eat, but you'll enjoy trying.

Don't drive on the first day, because you're jetlagged. On the second day, get a tatty Toyota from Tommy Lu in the Howard Johnson's foyer for $25 a day, and go west on Manchester Avenue (the hotel is on the junction of Manchester and Airport Boulevard) until you find a bigger mall with an office superstore, where you can buy a Thomas Guide to Orange County and LA county, which is more or less an A-Z of the LA basin. This is assuming you don't have a laptop or a GPS with a US maps program. When you look at a map you'll find that the Howard Johnson is conveniently located, as they say, just a few blocks from the Interstate 405 freeway, which is one of the big north–south highways across LA and Orange County.

Next job is to contact the local Porsche clubs, say you're a British Porsche Club member – which you will be by then, of course – and tell them you're looking for a good 911SC, 356A, whatever. You can rely on American hospitality and a genuine welcome. There are also free newspapers full of cars for sale, there are magazines, there are dealers, and there are even Internet cafes where you can surf for cars for an hour or so for just a few bucks.

Florida is another option for a Porsche hunt, although it's like a steam bath compared to California.

SERVICING

I've already alarmed you with *Which?* magazine's statistic that in the UK only one garage in 30 carries out correct servicing. Many Porsche specialists will do better than this, but some won't. So servicing your own car is not only the affordable way to run a Porsche, it's the best way to protect it from garage servicing.

Sadly, the advent of computer diagnostics in recent years has removed that option to a great extent for newer cars, so all you can do is check what service items should be changed and mark

◀ **This is a bit of a worry – you're not expected to get any closer to the engine than these filler caps. I've never actually seen a Boxster engine – there's not enough room to get underneath without a ramp, and underneath is the only access. I imagine you're just supposed to take it to a Porsche dealer if anything goes wrong… the 'affordable' concept is evaporating in front of our very eyes.**

► **This is what we like. Eveything visible here can be rebuilt for the cost of a decent sushi dinner.**

them visibly with red paint. That should encourage your garage to be the one in 30 that does the job properly – at least on your particular car.

With the more affordable Porsches, home servicing is increasingly possible the older the car. Each model is different and has additional items that need attention, so get a Haynes manual for your particular model of Porsche. The service schedule for a 1965–85 911 gives you a good idea of what's involved (as 911s are air-cooled, that saves you having to look after the cooling system):

Every weekend
- ☐ Check tyres and tyre pressures
- ☐ Check oil
- ☐ Check brake fluid reservoir
- ☐ Check brake and handbrake performance
- ☐ Check lights and warning lights
- ☐ Check instruments and gauges
- ☐ Check screen washers, top up fluid
- ☐ Check wipers, horn
- ☐ Check engine oil, top up
- ☐ Check battery electrolyte level (unless battery is maintenance-free)

Every 6,000 miles
- ☐ Check suspension ball joints and linkages for slop
- ☐ Check rubber boots
- ☐ Check brake pad wear
- ☐ Check master cylinder pushrod free play
- ☐ Check and adjust valve clearances
- ☐ Replace engine oil and filter

- ☐ Clean magnetic drain plug, check for steel fragments
- ☐ Replace contact points if applicable
- ☐ Gap spark plugs
- ☐ Check drive belt tension
- ☐ Lubricate distributor
- ☐ Check dwell and ignition timing
- ☐ Check condition of heat exchangers, exhaust system
- ☐ Lubricate engine linkages
- ☐ Check fuel system hoses
- ☐ Lubricate door locks, all body hinges

Every 12,000 miles
As 6,000-mile service, plus:
- ☐ Clean or replace fuel filter
- ☐ Replace spark plugs
- ☐ Clean or replace air filter
- ☐ Replace transmission oil
- ☐ Check magnetic drain plug for steel fragments
- ☐ Check rubber seals on doors, bonnets, hatches etc
- ☐ Clean out rain drainage holes
- ☐ Replace oil supply line on mechanical injector pump
- ☐ Replace brake fluid

Every 30,000 miles
As above, plus:
- ☐ Replace air pump drive belt
- ☐ Clean or replace EGR (Exhaust Gas Recirculating) valve

CLUBS

Porsche Club GB is the biggest UK club. It was formed in 1961 and is now a large organisation, with visibly close connections to the Porsche factory. It's probably more aimed at people buying new or newer Porsches, but that just means a good set of social activities rather than a more black-fingernailed orientation. There will be some snobs and show-offs, but they can always be avoided. I'm told on good authority that most PCGB members are top people who just like fast cars and good engineering.

The *Porsche Post* magazine has a good mix of events, profiles, techy bits and advice, and a lot of useful classifieds – so before you go charging off to LA you can find out what the real cash price is for your chosen model in the UK. There are also trade ads, which can to some extent be regarded as being endorsed by the club. Anybody seriously dishonest is likely to get complained about often enough to be binned and banned as an advertiser.

Club activities are to some extent chopped up by region, and activities are a mixed bag of local and national options. The main club organises Porsche factory visits, racing and some major trips. Mixed national and local activities include rallies, runs to all sort of places such as air museums for display days, weekends away and an annual run to

Le Mans for the June 24-hour race – the one with modern Audi diesels rather than Bugattis.

There's also classification by Porsche model types into different registries, so once you're narrowed down by region and by model, you could be joining quite a small group with a lot in common. One notably useful thing the PCGB does is to organise a track day calendar through the year with a total of 1,000 opportunities to get out on the track. Using half a dozen of those track day places would be very useful and very good fun.

For the Porsche Club GB, contact the membership secretary, PCGB, Cornbury House, Cotswold Business Village, Moreton in Marsh, Glos, GL56 0JQ, fax no 01608 652944. Websites are www.porscheclubgb.com and www.msdpcgb. co.uk for motorsport information.

The Independent Porsche Enthusiasts' Club is smaller and tends to cater more for hands-on enthusiasts, although again it will welcome all comers. When I say smaller, it still has 20 regions covering the country, so there's some action near you. The calendar for the main club features trips to Le Mans, Goodwood and Le Mans again, for the bi-annual Classic event: strongly recommended, as the place is just thundering with vintage Bentleys, Bugattis, Le Mans Porsches, in fact every car you ever liked from 1924 to 1978. There are no crowds

▼ **Targas-R-Us. A Targa top knocks a useful chunk off the price of a Porsche, at the cost of only a small chunk knocked off its shell rigidity.**

for the Classic, so you can get a beer and a *steack frites* in Le Mans centre without a scrum.

The Independent club scene is great for racing, at many levels. The regions of the club race each other as well, which adds some amusing regional needle to the game. Many a Yorkshireman would enjoy an extra little frisson on beating a Lancastrian, and vice versa. Our featured 928 owner John Oakes is active in the Porsche Club of GB, the Independent Porsche Enthusiasts' Club and the more general 200+ Club, for people with cars punching more than 200bhp. His favourite club outing so far was a trip to the Nürburgring, including some lap time on the Old Circuit. This is now way too dangerous for Formula One racing, but is still open to clubs and the public at their own risk. It takes out a couple of dozen overconfident bikers every year, and has been responsible for more underwear changes than most circuits.

Less dramatic and demanding Independent Club events in the UK, randomly picked, include a Chinese meal, karting, a visit to an aviation museum, a Rolling Road dyno test day, and a trip on the North York Moors Railway. Everything from Chow Mein to choo-choos, in fact.

Underlining the sort of prices I've been talking about in other chapters, a sample from the classified ads in the club's *All Torque* magazine at the time of writing includes a 1986 left-hand-drive 911 Carrera at £9,000 and a 924S at £2,500. There's a very useful forum for on-line questions and answers, and although the club doesn't organise track days, it recommends where to go for good ones – www.bookatrack.com.

The club's postal address is 36 St Margaret's Drive, Chesterfield, S40 4SX. The website is www.tipec.org.uk.

The Porsche Club of America is a biggie. This one has 140 regions, including some in Canada and even in Germany. As you can imagine, there are plenty of regions in California, and a good few just around the LA basin. From personal experience, I can tell you that the Orange Coast region alone is jammed full of friendly and helpful people, and I see no reason why the other California regions wouldn't be the same.

The PCA organises lots of races every year and is into all sorts of hands-on restoring and upgrading. The tech section has a forum that's called 'Up-fixin' Der Porsches', so they don't take themselves too seriously. They run autocrosses, which involve lots of charging around with smoking tyres between rows of cones; they have rallies, runs, concours contests and 30 races altogether including club racing series and vintage racing series for (more or less) road cars – so there's bound to be some fun

Porsche action in between hunting down cars if you're over there.

The address is PO Box 5900, Springfield, VA 22150, the daytime telephone (daytime being Eastern US time) is 703 451 9000, and the club's website is www.pca.org.

www.356porsche.co.uk is a forum and website rather than a club, and a brief surfing session recently yielded a 1958 356A coupé for £13,500 in London. It was right-hand drive, red, looked nice and clean, and if it was as good as it looked it could have been worth stretching the budget for. The site also grades the 356B as the cheapest of the 356 parade, which could be useful info if you're not too specific about the exact model you want. There's a useful booklist too.

www.356-911.com is another on-line community, and checking it out revealed what looked like another good car in the UK – a 1972 right-hand-drive RS replica, with a rebuilt 2.4-litre engine complete with new oil-fed tensioners, which suggests somebody knew what they were doing. The car was K registered, tax exempt, and the owner was asking £12,000. Again, if it was as good as it looked and would run for a long while without major hassle, it was becoming affordable. Also typical of the price levels we've been looking at was a clean-looking German 928 on sale at £2,900.

www.thesamba.com is an excellent source of cheap Porsches and spares, although it's primarily a VW site.

There are many model-specific Internet sites, some the work of a solo geek and others large, organised and useful. They appear, disappear and change all the time, so a web-surf around the model number of your choice will be worthwhile and may unearth the bargain you're looking for. Again, bear in mind that information on the Internet comes with the full authority and expertise of a bloke in the pub.

TRACK DAYS

Preparing yourself and your car will help to get the best out of both. Car preparation advice from the Porsche Club GB has a lot of good points in it.

Their members are sorted into novice, intermediate, and experienced drivers, and on Club track days they all go out separately. This is a good idea – on mixed track days, some people don't understand even the basics of straightening out corners and cheerfully pootle around right in the centre of the track, ambling across the racing line twice on each corner without looking in their mirrors. Others are seriously quick, and are experimenting with fine-tuning their late braking

◀ Entering the proper June 24-hour race at Le Mans is slightly out of reach for those with affordable Porsches, although your affordable will be a top companion for driving down there as a spectator.

▼ You can definitely think about running a budget Porsche 911 in the Classic Le Mans, which in some ways is more fun anyway. To get sponsorship, tell business people that apart from the marketing benefits, it's huge fun, team-building and fully tax deductible.

on the limit, and you can find yourself trying to steer between them without either hitting one or getting hit by the other.

On most track days you would hope for one to two hours of actual circuit action on the cheaper tracks, which is probably enough. Don't rush to get out on the track, though: by the time the afternoon session gets going, there usually isn't a queue, because everybody's knackered. Track driving is and should be exhausting, so let the others wear themselves out first and then get all the track time you want later. That applies to airfields and smaller circuits. You tend to get something like 40 minutes at Brands, which isn't enough, but it is a good circuit and worth driving a few times. The Porsche Club's top track day is at Silverstone.

▲ **You can also race a 356 at Le Mans and other classic races and hillclimbs, and enjoy the agility of the car once you've got the hang of the rear end.**

Track-day prices vary quite a lot – being a club member helps, but it's not a cheap day out. Passengers cost around £5 now because of increased insurance costs, apparently as a result of al-Qaeda's attack on the World Trade Centre. Porsche clubs don't generally make a profit on track days, but the circuits and insurance companies do.

Track days on the proper circuits in the UK, and particularly on the posh ones like Brands and Silverstone, are usually expensive. Cheaper venues such as Bruntingthorpe airfield are almost as much fun and have the advantage of hundreds of reassuring yards of runoff if you misjudge the balance of tyre friction and centrifugal force. You can also get out to circuits in France, Belgium and Germany. Spa (and the drive to Spa) is gorgeous, and the Nürburgring Old Circuit is quite often open to the public. You just hand over a few Euros for tickets and pop one in the ticket machine (unless you have a right-hand-drive car, in which case you have to get out and run around the car to get to the machine). Check the availability of the Nürburgring before you go, as the owners close the circuit to the public quite often in order to run more lucrative corporate business jollies.

Porsches make pretty good track cars, as there is a lot of racing in their history. Their success has not been based on being either the fastest or the best-handling cars, but by hanging together until the end of races and by being consistent. Lotus visionary Colin Chapman thought a Lotus racing car was a success if it won a race and then fell to bits a hundred yards later, but the Porsche approach is the opposite. Most Porsches will not find hard track day use to be a problem. However, any weak spots will be found out – if your layshaft or big ends are past it, they might be okay for road use for a while yet, but a track day is likely to finish them off.

Check the brake pads and discs – worn pads and thin discs won't last the day. Also, change the brake fluid, ideally to a better spec, because your ordinary fluid is probably full of hygroscopically attracted water and probably hasn't been changed in years. It will boil after a few laps of serious use.

Make sure you have the same brand of tyre on each end of your axles, although you don't necessarily need them to be the same brand front and back. Some people keep a set of wheels with bald tyres for track use. These work like slicks and are grippy in the dry but hopeless in the wet, and bear in mind that the carcass of a bald tyre can be as knackered as the tread.

Tape up your glass lights just in case, and stow whatever you've got in the car securely so that it can't get loose and roll around under your feet.

Fill the tank up with super unleaded, but don't get any on your hands, as it's carcinogenic. (In a lab, it would be kept in a chemical cabinet rather than being open to the atmosphere.) Filling the tank fully on a 911 will also help the handling. Bring some spare oil, as a thrashed engine even in good condition burns a lot more oil on the track than during road use. Buy your own crash helmet, as you otherwise have to share a spare one with everybody else, which is not ideal: firstly, commonly shared helmets get unpleasantly sweaty, and secondly, there may not be enough to go around, and you won't be allowed out on the circuit without one. I use a cheap open-face race-legal bike helmet on the track, because I don't like the claustrophobic feeling of full-face helmets. Your arms and legs must also be covered, but not necessarily with fireproof Nomex overalls, gloves and bootees – you only need that level of kit for actual racing.

You should be able to get track day cover for your car from your insurance broker – if not, check with club members and find another broker. You should be paying classic car rates on most affordable Porsches anyway.

When you're out on a track day, come off the circuit every few laps to let the engine cool down and to check your oil, water, tyre pressures and whether or not your wheels are falling off. I'm not joking – wheels do bend during hard cornering and the nuts can come loose, so tighten them up regularly to make sure. Be aware that while sliding sideways off the circuit on to either the grass or the kitty litter, it's possible that your wheels can dig in and roll you over. This is rare, but it does happen. If you've bought a 924 or 944 with the intention of racing it, you will obviously be pushing it harder than most in order to learn quickly, so get the rollcage fitted now rather than waiting until you start racing. Have a chat with Safety Devices (www.

safetydevices.com), who sell ready-made bolt-in and weld-in rollover bars and cages, and who as far as I can remember on my last visit were actually working on a cage for a 944.

Don't go too mad during a track day, even if you do have a cage. I've noticed that my own driving becomes much more dashing and adventurous when I'm strapped inside a nice big rollcage. You're not supposed to be racing on a track day, and you're not supposed to spend the

▲ An early 911 is not only eligible for some quite high-level classic competition, it will also do very well indeed against its contemporaries. It's as good as a large Mercedes isn't.

◀ Porsche clubs offer some good opportunities to race 911s. There's a lot to learn when driving them on the edge.

▲ **Mission Raceway near Vancouver is tight and twisty, and offers a challenge to this tidily driven 944.**

day spinning like a government spokesman. The track boss on the day is the boss of the circuit, and you can get black-flagged and permanently chucked off if you're considered dangerous.

RACING

Much of the Porsche racing in the UK is organised by the Porsche Club GB. They run the Speed Championships, the Porsche Cup, the Porsche Classic Championship and the Porsche Open Series. Details are on their website at the Motor Sport Division section on www.msdpcgb.com. The Porsche Open is deliberately open to any Porsche, and is split into four classes to make sure you've got people at the same sort of level to race with.

Class 1 in the Porsche Classic is genuinely open to all, but Class 2 seems to be rather dominated by the 911SC – which is fine if you've got one and the money to race it.

The Northern Sports and Saloon Car Championship is based at Croft circuit and is very open racing. It's generally run to a budget, and doesn't require expensive preparation of cars. A 924/944 could do well in this, and could be competitive without monster funding.

The Welsh Sports and Saloon Car Championship is the same sort of thing – lots of different cars and varied levels of skill, with reasonable budgets.

Lodge Sports (www.lodgesports.org.uk) sponsor the 924 Series as well as competing in it. 924s race at Oulton Park, Mallory Park, Croft, Donington, Lydden, Anglesey, Brands Hatch and Snetterton, so you get a pretty good tour of the UK racing circuits if nothing else.

The Autofarm also sponsors series. They report capacity grids for the 924s, and they support keeping the regulations very tight to keep the racing fair and to make sure that drivers win rather than chequebooks.

In California, The Porsche Racing Club of San Francisco runs some good racing – check out www.porscheracingclub.com.

Many older Porsches are eligible for the Classic Le Mans 24-hour event, which is tremendous fun. More on www.lemansclassic.com.

RACING 924s AND 944s

I can see why people race these – they're fast, the handling is forgiving enough to let you learn by your mistakes as you push on to gradually better lap times, and if you do make a big mistake in the

wrong place and stuff one into the Armco, it's only a £2,000 car and not the end of the world.

There are a good many opportunities to race a 924, many of which are organised by the Porsche Club GB. The Porsche Club series is well stocked with these cars, and because of their sensible cost there will always be lots of action at the back of the grid as well as at the front. As always, there will be people whose serious budgets or talent will put them permanently in front of you, but there will also be plenty of beginners in cheap 924s at the back, squabbling over who's not going to be last. That's where your racing career starts and where much excitement and fun is to be had.

The Porsche Classic series seems to be mostly for 911s, with the odd 924 among them. The posh Porsche Club Championship has a rolling year-of-eligibility system, so newer cars become eligible year by year: the 944S2 is now allowed to join in, and with this series you get to race at Brands Hatch, which is a good circuit and great fun apart from the stomach-wrenching drop after Paddock Bend. Think about some preparatory sit-ups if your stomach currently looks more like a pint pot than a six-pack.

There are other series open to 924s as well – racing in the Northern Sports and Saloon Car Championship based at Croft circuit isn't going to break the bank, and the handling and power of a 924, and maybe later a 944, will give you a crack at some reasonable placings once you've got the hang of the whole thing and got rid of your first-year novice's yellow-and-black cross sticker on the back of the car. You don't even have to use a special track-only car covered in sponsor stickers, because much of this sort of racing requires a valid MOT, and a rollcage is actually a good idea anyway for a fast road car. It's slightly naff driving around the roads in a seriously stickered race car, but you do get to know the car better driving it for a few thousand miles a year on the road than just driving it for 50 miles on the track. In the UK, it's illegal to drive around with numbers on your doors in case you're road-racing. You have to stick a taped cross over racing numbers: as we all know, it's impossible to race if your numbers are taped over.

Most of the information above regarding the 924 still applies to the 944. However, there was also a specific 944 available for racing called the Club Sport, with rollcage provision and much excess weight stripped out. However, if it's already been raced quite a lot you're probably better off with a road-going shell that hasn't; a

▲ A 928 makes an unusual track car, but the budget's right: with a manual gearbox it would provide much fun per quid.

USEFUL CONTACTS

Replica Speedsters and Spyders – Pilgrim Cars, 01273 493860, www.pilgrimcars.com; Chesil Speedsters, 01308 897072, www.chesil.co.uk; GP Spyders, 01326 573646; Vintage Spyders, 001 714 538 6550, www.VintageSpyders.com; Spyder club, www.spyderclub.com.

Kit-Car magazine, www.kit-cars.com.

Fast Beetle engines – www.JustVeeDubs.com and www.volkszone.com/914.

Red Line Tuning, Langley, Bucks, 01753 655522: rolling road, expert tuning of carbs, considerable Porsche experience.

www.continentalcartours.co.uk – Budget Continental car rallies and trips, well organised and great fun.

www.912registry.org

www.912bbs.org – Dave Hillman's nightmare 912 stories and chat site.

www.shastadesign.com – replacement parts for 356 engines.

Chaters Bookshop, Isleworth, London, 0208 568 9750, www.chaters.co.uk.

www.pelicanparts.com – spares, Brembo brake deals, discussion forums, 911 engine rebuilding, 356 questions. Also www.101projects.com/rebuild/htm.

www.lodgesports.org.uk – Manchester garage, service, repairs, sales, race prep.

www.douglasvalley.co.uk – breakers of prestige cars including Porsches of all ages.

www.pro9.com – spares by mail, racing body panels, breakers.

www.design911.com – £60 for 911SC service kit at time of writing: oil/fuel/air filters, plugs, sump drain gasket and rocker cover gaskets.

Dansk Porsche Parts – exhausts, body parts. Currently off line through geek problems, but worth hunting down via www.google.com.

www.kingstown-shipping.co.uk – Kingstown Shipping, Hull, 01482 374116. Car import/export specialists.

Club Sport is quite likely to be more expensive; and stripping out the interior from an ordinary 944 doesn't take long anyway.

As usual with Porsche, there was continuous development throughout the life of the 924 and 944, so later versions can offer more car for the same sort of money. The 924 began with its 2-litre four and became the 924S with a 2.5-litre Porsche-built engine, and then evolved into the 944.

Porsche themselves raced the 944 with some success in the 1980s: when up against Corvettes, Camaros, Saab Turbos and Mazda RX-7s, it usually walked away with a win. There were also one-make 944 races which were popular, with new Porsche Cup 944s sold by the factory specifically for racing, in relatively standard trim. Twenty years later, and basically the same 944 can be bought and raced against other 944s in pretty much the same way, except that the budget for a successful season is now going to be in the low thousands rather than the high tens of thousands.

CLASSIC RALLYING

I would recommend starting out in the company of the estimable Jonathan Bowles of Continental Car Tours, who runs a lot of low-budget weekend rallies and trips and likes to keep the price down to get lots of people involved. I don't recommend going out for an evening's pub-crawling with him, though – it's unlikely that you'll be able to keep up, and if you're driving in a rally the following day, you'll regret having tried.

Continental Car Tours runs both casual and semi-serious classic car rallies in the UK and in France and Belgium, and this is an excellent way of tasting classic rallying to see if you're going to enjoy it. For a fun weekend rally, the eligibility rules as to the age of a car are somewhat elastic, so you really just need to find a friend with an old car and persuade them to give it a go.

The rallies are usually in timed stages, and legally the average speed has to be below the local legal speed limit. However, miss a turn and you have to do three times the correct speed to catch up again. The route maps are of the 'tulip' type, which means you get a diagram of the next junction looking vaguely like a bunch of three or so tulips, with an exact distance to the junction. A standard odometer (mileometer) is okay for a fun weekend rally, but if you get serious you'll need proper rally timing and distance devices to be competitive. You also have to collect and write down letters and numerals from little signboards stuck into the verge along the route to prove that you didn't cheat and take a short cut, and cutting off little triangles of road to make a short cut and save a hundred yards is a bad move, as there is almost certainly a board to miss on most of these short cuts.

Even on the weekend fun rallies the competition is fierce, as it all gets taken much more seriously than it should, car enthusiasts being what they are. There are no prizes, as that would make the rally an illegal road race, but during the post-rally dinner there is much piss-taking of the less successful and much smugness from the more successful entrants. A Porsche of almost any type will do very well in this sort of rallying, except possibly a 928 which would have trouble getting down narrow Belgian tracks.

Commander Eoin Sloan is a Porsche enthusiast whose advice on 911s we have already read. He gets a lot out fun out of rallying his 911, and he spent some time hunting down what he regards as the perfect rally Porsche. It's a 911TR, which is a 911T with 911S mechanicals, one of a rare and obscure breed (200 were made) which not many people know about. They do now, obviously, but they didn't before they read this book. Porsche's customers realised the competition potential of the 911 before Porsche did, and they tended to apply all the delete options to get rid of as much weight as possible, combined with the strongest engines.

The old rally rules said 1967 was the cut-off for eligibility, largely to avoid grubby lower-class oiks with twin-cam Ford Escorts wiping the floor with all the Healeys. That made an early 911 a top rallying tool. However, the cut-off date is now 1978, which lets in much more powerful Porsches: but Eoin says he still prefers the older, lighter and more nimble 911s, and in fact continues to drive the same car. In tight, twisty rally routes the lightness and balance of an earlier car could still give it the edge, depending on the driver.

BEETLING AROUND FOR SAVINGS

There is a little crossover between the worlds of VW and Porsche on some models. The 914 and the later reintroduced 912 use the VW flat four, and if your budget runs to a 356 project with a blown or missing engine you can also use a Beetle engine – just don't open your engine lid in public. Lots of VW air-cooled enthusiasts like to liven up Beetles with bits of Porsche, but they trade these parts at VW rather than Porsche prices – a trawl through the classified ads of a random issue of *Ultra VW* gets us a typically useful haul of Porsche parts. For example, a pair of freshly retrimmed highback 911 seats was on offer for £230, with second-hand tan leather ones for £150. A set of freshly refurbished cookie-cutter Porsche alloys,

refinished but not used, was £300, and new pair of replica teardrop rear lights for early Beetle and 356 was £38 a pair. There was even a 356 Speedster replica, which came with a full MOT, 13,000 miles, a new 1,776 twin-carb engine and an Empi shift, and was creamy yellow with a blue interior and hood. The price was £11,750. While you're thinking about trading originality for affordability in terms of performance, you can get a brand new turnkey Beetle engine for a relatively sensible price. The tuning is taken much further than a period Porsche engine, with featherweight flywheels, I-beam or H-beam rods, forged steel cranks and rockers, and Weber and Bosch fuel and sparks. The same applies to brake kits which fit Beetles and early Porsches up to the 356B – I bet VW high-performance vented disc upgrades cost a lot less than Porsche equivalents, simply on the basis of whom they're being sold to.

When it comes to body restoration, it could also save you a lot of money to use a VW restorer rather than a Porsche specialist – the body structure is similar and the skills are the same, but the hourly rate may not be.

Fuchs alloys are expensive, and fake Fuchs wheels can be of unclear origin and quality, but five-spoke Empi wheels in polished alloy have a good name and some have similar styling. (Old 'real' period Empi and new Empi are not the same thing, though.) For a 356 that needs slightly more rubber on the road without a year-long hunt for a set of the appropriate original wheels to be crack-tested, prepped and finished, how about a set of four chromed OE 5.5J x 15 five-stud Beetle wheels at £399.95 including VAT and new tyres, with hub caps for another six quid each? Bargain.

So… is there such a thing as an affordable Porsche? Yes, there certainly is. At the less desirable end of the Porsche market it can be cheaper and more cost-effective to buy and run a Porsche than a Morris Minor. Even if you head for the top of the £10,000 budget and go for the best 911 you can achieve, you could still get a good car for a good price. It's also rather fun that 99 per cent of the general public will think you have spent serious money, and that you are a thrusting and successful executive. The Porsche name is still prestigious, and people, if they know the difference, will assume that you're driving a classic 1972 911 rather than a modern 1994 911 because you want to, not because you're on a budget. Drive an older BMW and you're likely to get stopped at night and searched for burglary tools: prestigious is not the first word that comes to mind.

Affordable? Absolutely. Go and buy one.

Chapter 15

Number crunching

A frighteningly large percentage of UK-registered cars have something nasty in their history, and even with a 924 costing a couple of thousand pounds, you don't want to find yourself driving a stolen car or a bodged cut-and-shut write-off. If a car's worth buying it has to be worth an HPI check in the UK, or a Carfax check in the US. A US-bought car is much less likely to be repossessed or held as evidence by the police once it's crossed the Atlantic, but even so make sure not just that the VIN is right for the car, but that the VIN plates themselves have not been tampered with. A common stunt is to weld in a chunk of bodywork with the plate attached to it, so look around the plate as well as at the plate itself.

You also want to be able to choose whether you buy something that's not what it seems – such as a later 3-litre car that's been fitted with a dodgy 2.7-litre engine. You may well still go ahead and buy it, but certainly not at anywhere near the same price.

Even if you buy a 912 to convert into a 911, the wrong engine will still knock a chunk off the price, as the seller doesn't need to know that you don't actually want the engine at all. So it's always worth crunching the numbers.

When you go to look at a Porsche, take a copy of the Haynes *Porsche Data Book* with you to consult: you can then spend some time genuinely checking the numbers, and then a little more time looking doubtful and lowering the expectations of the seller.

You may quite reasonably think it's just an old Porker, I don't care whether it's got the right engine or not as long as it works. However, if you then buy expensive spare parts for the engine you thought you had but actually don't, you will definitely be cross.

Don't make the mistake of researching Porsches on the Internet, as much of the information there is pure garbage. This seems odd as Porsche enthusiasts enjoy accuracy, but is nevertheless the case. The Haynes *Data Book* was written from direct factory information, which is the most reliable available.

◀ **When these Porsches were new, they were pretty expensive, with the luxury bahnstormer 928 at the top of the tree and the top of the picture. Thirty years later, a 928 is worth about the same as a set of wheels for a 911. Alas, how are the mighty fallen. On the other hand, if you fancy a V8 Porker in 2010 you can buy one for the price of a dirty weekend in Paris!** [Porsche AG]

TRANSLATING VIN NUMBERS

Internal Porsche numerical chassis numbers were used until 1981, when the international VIN number system began.

'WP0' is the international Porsche code.

Fourth, fifth and sixth characters are fill-in characters for European and Rest of World cars, but for North American cars the fourth digit represents body style; A/B or C- Coupé/Targa or Cabrio.

Seventh, eighth and twelfth digits represent model code. Therefore a 911 will be WP0XXX**91**XXX**1**XXXXX and a Turbo (930) will be WP0XXX**93**XXX**0**XXXXX. Similarly, WP0XXX**96**XXX**4**XXXXX is a 964, WP0XXX**99**XXX**3**XXXXX is a 993, WP0XXX**99**XXX**6**XXXXX is a 996 and WP0XXX**98**XXX**6**XXXXX is a 986 (Boxster).

Tenth digit is the model year or series. A=1980, B=1981, C=1982, D=1983, E=1984, F=1985, G=1986, H=1987, J=1988, K=1989, L=1990, M=1991, N=1992, P=1993, R=1994, S=1995, T=1996, V=1997, W=1998, X=1999, Y=2000; then it changes to numerals, 1=2001, 2=2002 etc.

Eleventh digit is place of manufacture: S= Stuttgart.

Thirteenth digit onwards is the production number.

911

To 1970

Chassis numbers are numerical on earlier 911s. Engine numbers are stamped on the casting by the cooling fan, and there is also a second designation number with more details stamped nearby. Early USA 130bhp 911 engines run from 900001–903550, ending in 1965. 903551–909000 means 1966, 909001–912050 means 1967, and all those are 130bhp engines. 960001–962178 are 160bhp 911S engines from 1967. From 1968 they used codes rather than plain numbers. 3280001 breaks down into 3=130bhp, 2=911 manual, 8=1968, and the rest is serial number. From 1969–71, 6200001 breaks down into 6=cylinders, 2=911E (1=911T, 3=911S), 0=1970 (9=1969, 1=1971), and so on.

▼A typical 'nomenclature' plate, fitted on the luggage compartment floor on an early 911T.

1971–80

Engine numbers are stamped on the casting by the cooling fan, and there is also a second designation number with more details stamped nearby. From 1969–71, 6200001 breaks down into 6=cylinders, 2=911E (1=911T, 3=911S), 0=1970 (9=1969, 1=1971), and so on. The year numbers are consistent from 2=1972 through to 0=1980.

1981–90

VIN numbers follow the 17-digit system from 1981. Engine number letters for years continue as before: 1982 becomes C, 1983 becomes D and so on up to 1993, which is P.

1991–6

As before. R=1994, S=1995, T=1996.

924

VIN numbers.

1976–9

Ten characters. First three characters, model type (924). Fourth character, model year (6, 7, 8 or 9). Fifth character, version (1 is Europe 125bhp, 2 is US/California/Canada 90bhp, 3 is Japan 90bhp, 4 is Turbo). Sixth to tenth characters, serial number.

1980

First two characters, model type. Third character, model year. Fourth character void (0). Fifth character, vehicle type. Sixth character, engine type (3 is US/Japanese 110bhp, 1 is European 125bhp). Seventh to tenth characters, serial number.

From 1981

Standard VIN codes. First three characters, manufacturer code (WP0). Fourth to sixth characters, US vehicle codes. Body type (A is coupé), engine type (A is US 2-litre), safety system type (0 is seat belts only, 1 is driver airbag, 2 is driver and passenger airbag). Seventh and eighth characters, vehicle type (92). Ninth character is void or a test code Z. Tenth character is model year code (B for 1981, C for 1982 etc). Eleventh character is build location (N is Neckarsulm). Twelfth is vehicle type. Thirteenth is body/engine code. Fourteenth to eighteenth characters are serial numbers from 0001.

Engine numbers from 1976 on

125bhp non-USA engines, XK + 6-fig number. RHD non-USA engines, XJ + 6 figs.
1977 US/Canada 90bhp engines: XH + 6 figs. California/Japan 90bhp engines, XF + 6 figs.
1978 California/Japan emissions engines: XE + 6 figs.
1980 on, US/California/Japan engines: VC + 6 figs.
Turbo engines to 1981: M31/01. 1981: M31/60 and M31/70. 1982, 1983: M31/03 and M31/04.

▼A typical paint code plate fitted to the door pillar of an early 911.

944

VIN numbers. WP0=Porsche; AA2=coupé, 2-litre, 2 x airbags; 95=944 Turbo; X=test code; N=Neckarsulm built; I=extra digit from code (951 is 944 Turbo); 123456 serial number.

Engine numbers

First digit, 4=944 engine. Second digit, 1 or 3 or 6=2.5-litre 944 or 944S (6 in 1989 means 2.7-litre, 2 in 1990 means 3-litre). Third digit, F=1984, F=1985 (and so on).

968

VIN numbers. W=World vehicle ID code. P0=Porsche. ZZZ=non-USA. 96=Vehicle type. Z=Test code. P=Model code (1993). S=Stuttgart made. 8=Vehicle type. 00000=Sequential shell number.

356

For a fee, Porsche will consult factory records and tell you what engine was originally fitted to a particular chassis. If you do finish up with the correct engine in or with a car, it's worth hanging on to it even if you don't want to use it.

An earlier engine with a five-digit number starting with 6 or 7 is a Normal, and starting with a 6 means it's a 1958–61 Super. Six-digit numbers starting with a 6 are 1960–3 Normal, those starting with a 7 are 1961–3 Super, those beginning with a 7 and over 710,000 are 356C engines, and those starting with an 8 are Super 90 or SC engines.

Boxster

VIN number WP0CA2989VS622882 translated:

Digits		
1–3	Maker and destination WP0 = Porsche	
4	Series	C
5	Engine type	A=2.5-litre
6	Restraint system	2=Dual airbags
7–8	Model	98 = Boxster
9	Check digit	9
10	Model year	V = 1997
11	Plant	S = Stuttgart (U= Uusikaupunki)
12	Model	6 = Boxster
13–17	Sequential production number	22882

Porsche technical specifications

Porsche 911/911T/911S
1964–68/1967–68/1966–68
ENGINE
Six-cylinder horizontally opposed, air-cooled; aluminium-alloy crankcase and cylinders; rear-mounted*

Bore x stroke	80.0 x 66.0mm
Capacity	1,991cc
Valve actuation	sohc per bank
Compression ratio	9.0:1/9.8:1
Induction	two triple-choke Weber**
Power	110bhp at 5,800rpm
	130bhp at 6,100rpm
	160bhp at 6,600rpm
Maximum torque	115lb ft at 4,200rpm
	130lb ft at 4,300rpm
	133lb ft at 5,200rpm

*cast-iron cylinders on 911T
**Until February 1966, six Solex single-choke carbs on 911

BRAKES
Front: Disc (11.1in), ventilated on 911S
Rear: Disc (11.2in), ventilated on 911S

PERFORMANCE
(Source: Motor/Porsche)

Max speed	129.8mph/124mph/140mph
0–60mph	8.3sec/10.0sec*/7.6sec*
Standing ¼-mile	16.1sec/not quoted/ not quoted

*0–62mph

Porsche 911T/911E/911S (2-litre)
1968–69
As earlier 911 except:
ENGINE
Magnesium-alloy crankcase on all models; 911T retains cast-iron cylinders
Compression ratio 8.6:1/9.1:1/9.9:1

Induction	two Weber triple-choke carburettors/ Bosch injection/idem
Power	110bhp at 5,800rpm
	140bhp at 6,500rpm
	170bhp at 6,800rpm
Maximum torque	115lb ft at 4,200rpm
	130lb ft at 4,500rpm
	135lb ft at 5,500rpm

BRAKES
Ventilated discs on 911T Targa and 911E/911S

PERFORMANCE
(Source: Porsche/Autocar/Motor)

Max speed	124mph/130mph/136.5mph
0–60mph	10.0sec*/9.8sec/7.3sec
Standing ¼-mile	not quoted/17.0sec/15.8sec

* 0–62mph
911E figures are for Sport-o-matic

Porsche 911L
1967–68
The 911L was almost identical to the early 911, except for altered cam profiles. Power unchanged.
As for early 911 except:
PERFORMANCE
(Source: Motor.)

Max speed	124mph
0–62mph	10.0sec

(Source: Porsche Cars)
Sport-o-matic 911L

Max speed	127.0mph*
0–60mph	9.8sec
Standing ¼-mile	17.1sec

*Note: Porsche Cars only claimed a modest 121mph for this model

Porsche 911T/911E/911S (2.2-litre)
1969–71
As 911 2-litre except:

ENGINE

Bore x stroke	84.0 x 66.0mm
Capacity	2,195cc
Compression ratio	unchanged/9.1:1/9.8:1
Induction	two Solex carburettors/ Bosch injection/idem
Power	125bhp at 5,800rpm
	155bhp at 6,200rpm
	180bhp at 6,500rpm
Maximum torque	131lb ft at 4,200rpm
	141lb ft at 4,500rpm
	147lb ft at 5,500rpm

BRAKES
Front: Disc, ventilated (11.1in)
Rear: Disc, ventilated (11.4in)

PERFORMANCE
(Source: Autocar/Motor/Porsche)

Max speed	129mph/137mph/143mph
0–60mph	8.1sec/7.0sec/7.5sec
Standing ¼-mile	16.0sec/15.4sec/not quoted

Porsche 911T/911E/911S (2.4-litre)
1971–73
As 911 2.2-litre except:
ENGINE

Bore x stroke	84.0 x 70.4mm
Capacity	2,341cc
Compression ratio	7.5:1/8.0:1/8.5:1
Power	130bhp at 5,600rpm
	165bhp at 6,200rpm
	190bhp at 6,500rpm
Maximum torque	145lb ft at 4,000rpm
	152lb ft at 4,500rpm
	159lb ft at 5,200rpm

(From 1972 model year onwards, US versions of 911T 2.4 produced 140bhp at 5,600rpm)

(Source: Porsche/Autocar/Motor)

Max speed	127mph/139mph/145.3mph
0–60mph	7.6sec/6.4sec/6.2sec
Standing ¼-mile	15.7sec/14.4sec/14.7sec

Porsche 911/911N/911S
1973–75/1975–77/1973–77

(These were British names for selected models on sale in these periods)

ENGINE

Six-cylinder horizontally opposed, air-cooled; light alloy crankcase and cylinder heads with cast-iron cylinder liners; rear-mounted

Bore x stroke	90.0 x 70.4mm
Capacity	2,687cc
Valve actuation	sohc per bank
Compression ratio	8.0:1/8.5:1/8.5:1
Induction	Bosch K-Jetronic fuel injection
Power	150bhp at 5,700rpm
	165bhp at 5,800rpm
	175bhp at 5,800rpm
Maximum torque	174lb ft at 3,800rpm
	195lb ft at 4,000rpm
	174lb ft at 4,000rpm

BRAKES

Front: Disc, ventilated (11.1in)
Rear: Disc, ventilated (11.4in)

PERFORMANCE

(Source: Autocar)

Models quoted: 911 Coupé and 911S Coupé

Max speed	130mph*/142mph
0–60mph	7.8sec/6.1sec
Standing ¼-mile	15.8sec/15.0sec

* Porsche figure

Porsche 911SC
1977–83

As 2.7-litre 911S except:

ENGINE

Crankcase aluminium-alloy instead of magnesium-alloy

Bore x stroke	95.0 x 70.4mm
Capacity	2,994cc
Power	180bhp at 5,500rpm*
Maximum torque	188lb ft at 4,200rpm

*Power raised to 188bhp in 1979 and 204bhp in 1981

BRAKES

Front: Disc, ventilated (11.3in)
Rear: Disc, ventilated (11.6in)
Servo assistance

PERFORMANCE

(Source: Autocar)

Max speed	141mph est/146mph
0–60mph	6.5sec/5.8sec
Standing ¼-mile	15.1sec/14.2sec

(Coupé, 1977/1981)

Porsche 911 Turbo (930) 3-litre/3.3-litre
1974–77/1977–90

ENGINE

Six-cylinder horizontally opposed, air-cooled, turbocharged, aluminium alloy crankcase and Nikasil-coated bores; rear-mounted

Bore x stroke	95.0mm x 70.4mm
	97.0mm x 74.4mm
Capacity	2,994cc/3,299cc
Valve actuation	sohc per bank
Compression ratio	6.5:1/7.0:1
Induction	Bosch K-Jetronic injection; KKK turbocharger; intercooler (3.3)
Power	260bhp at 5,500rpm
	300bhp at 5,500rpm
Maximum torque	253lb ft at 4,000rpm
	303lb ft at 4,000rpm
	(318lb ft from 1983)

BRAKES

Front: Disc, ventilated (11.1in/12in)
Rear: Disc, ventilated (11.4in/12in)
No assistance (3-litre)
Cross-drilled discs, four-pot callipers and servo-assistance (3.3-litre)

PERFORMANCE

(Source: Autocar/Motor)

Max speed	155mph (min)/156mph*
0–60mph	6.0sec/4.9sec*
Standing ¼-mile	14.1sec/13.1sec*

*1989 3.3 five-speed, capable of 160mph; 156mph was recorded on Millbrook bowl

911: 1981-90

Porsche 911 Carrera
1983–89

As 911SC except:

ENGINE

Bore x stroke	95.0 x 74.4mm
Capacity	3,164cc
Compression ratio	10.3:1
Induction	Bosch DME injection

Power	231bhp at 5,900rpm*
Maximum torque	209lb ft at 4,800rpm

*Power reduced to 217bhp if fitted with catalytic converter (from late 1986)

PERFORMANCE

(Source: Motor)

Max speed	151mph
0–60mph	5.3sec
Standing ¼-mile	14.0sec

Porsche 911 Carrera 2 & Carrera 4 (964)
1988–93

ENGINE

Six-cylinder horizontally opposed, air-cooled; aluminium-alloy crankcase, cylinders and heads; rear-mounted

Bore x stroke	100.0 x 76.4mm
Capacity	3,600cc
Valve actuation	sohc per bank
Compression ratio	11.3:1
Induction	Bosch DME
Power	248bhp (DIN) at 6,100rpm
Maximum torque	228lb ft at 4,800rpm

BRAKES

Front: Disc, ventilated (11.7in)
Rear: Disc, ventilated (11.8in)
Four-pot callipers; servo assistance
ABS standard from 1990 model year

PERFORMANCE

(Source: Autocar & Motor)

Max speed	158mph/156mph
0–60mph	5.1sec/5.2sec
Standing ¼-mile	13.6sec/13.9sec

(manual Coupé)

911: 1991-96

Porsche 911 Turbo (964) 3.3-litre/3.6-litre
1991–92/1992–93

As 930-series 3.3-litre except for power and capacity increases indicated:

ENGINE

Bore x stroke	100.0mm x 76.4mm (3.6-litre)
Capacity	3,600cc (3.6-litre)
Compression ratio	7.5:1 (3.6-litre)
Power	320bhp at 5,750rpm*
	360bhp at 5,500rpm

Maximum torque   332lb ft at 4,500rpm
                  383lb ft at 4,200rpm
*355bhp was available with the 3.3-litre
Cabriolet with performance kit for the 1992
model year

BRAKES

Front: Disc, ventilated and cross-drilled (12.7in)
Rear: Disc, ventilated and cross-drilled (11.8in),
with ABS

PERFORMANCE

(Source: Porsche/Autocar & Motor)
Max speed   167mph/174mph
0–62mph/0–60mph   5.0sec/4.6sec

Porsche 911 Carrera/ Carrera 4 (993)
1993–97/1994–97
ENGINE

Six-cylinder horizontally opposed, air-cooled;
aluminium-alloy crankcase, cylinders and heads;
rear-mounted
Bore x stroke   100.0 x 76.4mm
Capacity   3,600cc
Valve actuation   sohc per bank
Compression ratio 11.3:1
Induction   Bosch DME with sequential
                   multi-point injection
Power   272bhp at 6,100rpm*
Maximum torque   252lb ft at 5,000rpm**
*Raised to 285bhp with variable cam timing for
1996 model year; from late 1994 285bhp or
299bhp performance kits available
** UK market figure; 243lb ft in certain other
markets

BRAKES

Front: Disc, ventilated (12.0in)
Rear: Disc, ventilated (11.8in)
ABS; servo assistance

PERFORMANCE

(Source: Autocar & Motor/ Porsche)
Max speed   160mph/167mph
0–60mph/0–62mph   5.2sec/5.6sec
Standing ¼-mile   13.8sec/not quoted

Porsche 911 Carrera/ Carrera 4 (996)
1997–2001
ENGINE

Six-cylinder horizontally opposed, water-cooled;

aluminium-alloy crankcase, cylinders and heads;
rear-mounted
Bore x stroke   96.0mm x 78.0mm
Capacity   3,387cc
Valve actuation   dohc per bank, four valves
                   per cylinder, VarioCam
Compression ratio 11.3:1
Induction   DME engine management
Power   300bhp at 6,800rpm
Maximum torque   258lb ft at 4,600rpm
Performance kit gave 320bhp at 6,800rpm and
258lb ft of torque at 4,600rpm

BRAKES:

Front: Disc, ventilated (12.5in)
Rear: Disc, ventilated (11.8in)
Cross-drilled discs with four-pot callipers; servo
assistance; ABS

PERFORMANCE

(Source: Autocar)
Max speed   173mph/164mph
0–60mph   4.6sec/4.8sec
Standing ¼-mile   13.0sec/13.3sec

924

Porsche 924/924 turbo/924 Carrera GT
1976–85/1978–82/1980–81
ENGINE

Four cylinders in line, cast-iron block, light alloy
head
Bore x stroke   86.5mm x 84.4mm
Capacity   1,984cc
Valve actuation   sohc, two valves per cylinder
Compression ratio 9.3:1/7.5:1/8.5:1
Induction   Bosch K-Jetronic injection/
                   idem plus KKK
                   turbocharger, intercooled on
                   Carrera GT
Power   125bhp at 5,800rpm
                   170bhp at 5,500rpm*
                   210bhp at 6,000rpm
Maximum torque   121.5lb ft at 3,500rpm
                   181lb ft at 3,500rpm*
                   203lb ft at 3,500rpm
*Series 2 turbo engine, for 1981 model
year, uprated to 177bhp (and 184lb ft at
3,500rpm) thanks to digital ignition and
8.5:1 compression ratio. Performance little
changed but fuel economy improved by
claimed 13 per cent

BRAKES

Front: Disc (9.4in) on 924;
          ventilated disc (11.5in) on
          turbo/Carrera
Rear: Drum (7in) on 924; disc (7in)
          on turbo/Carrera
Servo assistance

PERFORMANCE

(Source: Motor)
Max speed   121.3mph/140mph
                  est/150mph est
0–60mph   8.2sec/7.0sec/6.5sec
Standing ¼mile   17.0sec/15.4sec/not quoted
(924 figures for 4-speed manual car)

Porsche 924S
1985–88
As 924 except:
ENGINE

Four cylinders in line, alloy block and head
Bore x stroke   100.0mm x 78.9mm
Capacity   2,479cc
Compression ratio 9.7:1/10.2:1
Power   150bhp at 5,800rpm
                   160bhp at 5,900rpm
                   (1988 model year)
Maximum torque   144lb ft at 3,000rpm
                   155lb ft at 4,500rpm
                   (1988 model year)

BRAKES

Front: Disc, ventilated (11.1in)
Rear: Disc, ventilated (11.4in)

PERFORMANCE

(Source: Motor)
Max speed   135.1mph 137.1mph (1988)
0–60mph   7.8sec/7.4sec (1988)
Standing ¼-mile   16.1sec/15.7sec (1988)

944/968

Porsche 944 (944 Lux in UK)
1982–89
ENGINE

Four cylinders in line, alloy block and head,
counter-balance shafts, water-cooled
Bore x stroke   100.0mm x 78.9mm
                   104.0mm x 78.9mm
Capacity   2,479cc/2,681cc

Valve actuation   sohc, two valves per cylinder
Compression ratio   10.6:1/10.9:1
Induction   Bosch injection
Power   163bhp at 5,800rpm
165bhp at 5,800rpm
Maximum torque   151lb ft at 3,500rpm
166lb ft at 4,200rpm

BRAKES
Front: Disc, ventilated (11.1in)
Rear: Disc, ventilated (11.4in)
Servo assistance
ABS standard on 2.7-litre

PERFORMANCE
(Source: Motor/Autocar & Motor)
Max speed   137mph*/136mph
0–60mph   7.2sec/7.0sec
Standing ¼-mile   15.1sec/15.7sec
*Porsche figure

Porsche 944 S/S2
1986–93
As 944 except:
ENGINE
Bore x stroke   104.0mm x 88.0mm (S2)
Capacity   2,990cc (S2)
Valve actuation   dohc, four valves per cylinder
Compression ratio   10.9:1
Power   190bhp at 6,000rpm
211bhp at 5,800rpm
Maximum torque   170lb ft at 4,300rpm
207lb ft at 4,000rpm

BRAKES
Front: Disc, ventilated (12.0in) (S2)
Rear: Disc, ventilated (11.8in) (S2)
ABS optional; standard on S2

PERFORMANCE
(Source: Motor/Autocar & Motor)
Max speed   138.1mph/146mph
0–60mph   7.5sec/6.0sec
Standing ¼-mile   15.7sec/14.4sec

Porsche 944 turbo /turbo SE
1985–88
As 944 except:
ENGINE
Compression ratio   8.0:1
Induction   KKK turbocharger, intercooler

Power   220bhp at 5,800rpm*
250bhp at 6,500rpm
Maximum Torque   243lb ft at 3,500rpm
258lb ft at 4,000rpm
* There was a special series of 1000 944 turbo S 250bhp models in 1988, based on the Turbo Cup racing specification

BRAKES
Front and rear: Disc, ventilated (11.8in)
ABS standard from 1987
Uprated to four-pot with larger callipers for turbo SE

PERFORMANCE
(Source: Motor/Porsche)
Max speed   157.9mph/161mph
0–60mph   5.9sec/5.7sec
Standing ¼-mile   14.5sec/13.9sec

Porsche 968/968 Club Sport
1991–95
As 944 S2 except:
ENGINE
Valve actuation   VarioCam variable valve timing
Compression ratio   11.0:1
Induction   Bosch DME injection
Power   240bhp at 6,200rpm
Maximum torque   225lb ft at 4,100rpm

PERFORMANCE
(Source: *Porsche Cars, Autocar & Motor)
Max speed   153mph/157mph*
0–60mph   6.1sec/6.1sec

Porsche 968 Turbo S
1993–95
As 968 except:
ENGINE
Valve actuation   sohc, two valves per cylinder
Compression ratio   8.0:1
Induction   Turbocharged, with intercooler
Power   305bhp at 5,400rpm
Maximum torque   369lb ft at 3,000rpm

BRAKES
Front: Disc, ventilated (11.7in)

PERFORMANCE
(Source: Porsche)
Max speed   174mph
0–62mph   5.0sec

912

Porsche 912
1964–68
As original 911 except:
ENGINE
Four-cylinder horizontally opposed, air-cooled; rear-mounted
Bore x stroke   82.5mm x 74.0mm
Capacity   1,582cc
Valve actuation   pushrod ohv
Compression ratio   9.3:1
Induction   Two Solex 40 PJJ-4 carburettors
Power   90bhp at 5,800rpm
Maximum torque   90lb ft at 3,500rpm

BRAKES
Front: Disc (10.6in)
Rear: Disc (11.0in)

PERFORMANCE
(Source: Motor)
Max speed   116.6mph
0–60mph   11.7sec
Standing ¼-mile   18.2sec

928

Porsche 928
1977–82
ENGINE
V8, aluminium block and heads, water-cooled; front-mounted
Bore x stroke   95.0mm x 78.9mm
Capacity   4,474cc
Valve actuation   sohc per bank, two valves per cylinder
Compression ratio   8.5:1
Induction   Bosch K-Jetronic injection
Power   240bhp (DIN) at 5,000rpm (from late 1981 5,250rpm)
Maximum torque   257lb ft (DIN) at 3,600rpm (from late 1981 280lb ft)

BRAKES

Front: Discs, ventilated (11.1in)
Rear: Discs, ventilated (11.4in)
Servo assistance

PERFORMANCE

(Source: Motor*)*
Max speed   140mph
0–60mph   7.0sec
Standing ¼-mile   15.2sec
(manual car)
\

Porsche 928S/928 S2
1979–1983/1983–86

As 928 except:

ENGINE

Bore x stroke   97.0mm x 78.9mm
Capacity   4,664cc
Compression ratio   10.1:1/10.4:1
Power   300bhp (DIN) at 5,500rpm
                    310bhp at 5,900rpm
Maximum torque   283.5lb ft (DIN) at 4,500rpm
                    295lb ft at 4,500rpm

PERFORMANCE

(Source: Motor/Autocar*)*
Max speed   155mph/158mph
0–60mph   6.2sec/6.2sec
Standing ¼-mile   14.2sec/14.5sec (manual car)

Porsche 928S4/GT
1986–91/1989–91

As 928 except:

ENGINE

Bore x stroke   100.0mm x 78.9mm
Capacity   4,957cc
Valve actuation   dohc per bank, four valves
                    per cylinder
Compression ratio   10.0:1
Power   320bhp (DIN) at 6,000rpm
                    330bhp at 6,200rpm
Maximum torque   317lb ft (DIN) at 3,000rpm
                    317lb ft at 4,100rpm

BRAKES

Rear: Discs, ventilated (11.8in)
ABS standard

PERFORMANCE

(Source: Motor/Autocar*)*
Max speed   164mph (S4 auto)*
                    168mph (S4 manual)*
                    165mph (GT)

0–60mph   6.4sec (S4 auto)
                    5.6sec (GT)
Standing ¼-mile   14.9sec (S4 auto)
                    13.8sec (GT)

*Porsche figures

Porsche 928 GTS
1992–95

As 928GT except:

ENGINE

Bore x stroke   100.0mm x 85.9mm
Capacity   5,397cc
Compression ratio   10.4:1
Power   350bhp at 5,700rpm
Maximum torque   362lb ft at 4,250rpm

BRAKES

Front: Disc, ventilated (12.7in)

PERFORMANCE

(Source: Autocar*)*
Max speed   168mph
0–60mph   5.4sec
Standing ¼-mile   14.1sec

914

Porsche 914/6
1969–72

ENGINE

Six-cylinder horizontally opposed, air-cooled;
magnesium-alloy crankcase with cast-iron cylinders,
alloy jackets and alloy heads; mid-mounted
Bore x stroke   80.0mm x 66mm
Capacity   1,991cc
Valve actuation   sohc per bank
Compression ratio   8.6:1
Induction   Twin Weber 40 IDTPI
                    carburettors
Power   110bhp at 5,800rpm
Maximum torque   115.5lb ft at 4,200rpm

BRAKES

Front: Disc, ventilated (11.12in)
Rear: Disc, solid (11.26in)

PERFORMANCE

(Source: Motor*)*
Max speed   120mph*
0–60mph   8.8sec
Standing ¼-mile   16.1sec
*Banked track: Porsche's claimed 125mph is
realistic

Porsche 914/S
1969–73

(This was the UK name for the original 914)
As 914/6 except:
ENGINE

Four-cylinder horizontally opposed, air-cooled;
cast-iron cylinders, alloy heads
Bore x stroke   90.0mm x 66.0mm
Capacity   1,679cc
Compression ratio   8.2:1
Induction   Fuel injection
Power   80bhp at 4,900rpm*
Maximum torque   98.3lb ft at 2,700rpm
*By 1973, Californian version was down to
69bhp

BRAKES

Front: Disc (11.0in)
Rear: Disc (11.1in)

PERFORMANCE

(Source: Motor*)*
Car tested: Crayford rhd conversion
Max speed   106.5mph
0–60mph   12.3sec
Standing ¼-mile   18.7sec

Porsche 914/4
1973–75

As 914/S except:
ENGINE

Bore x stroke   93.0mm x 66.0mm
Capacity   1,795cc
Compression ratio   7.3:1
Induction   Fuel injection
Power   73bhp (SAE) at 4,800rpm*
Maximum torque   89lb ft (SAE) at 4,000rpm*
*US specification (85bhp/102lb ft in German
                    market)

PERFORMANCE

(Source: Porsche*)*
Top speed   110mph
0–62mph   12.0sec
(German-market model)

Porsche 914 2.0-litre (inc SC)
1973–76

As 914/S except:
ENGINE

Bore x stroke   94.0mm x 71.0mm
Capacity   1,971cc

Compression ratio 7.6:1
Induction   Fuel injection
Power   100bhp (DIN)
                  at 5,000rpm/91bhp (SAE)
                  at 4,900rpm/84bhp
                  (SAE) at 4,900rpm
Maximum torque   116lb ft (SAE) at
                  3,500rpm/109lb ft (SAE)
                  at 3,000rpm/
                  108lb ft(SAE) at 3,500rpm

PERFORMANCE
(Source: Motor*)*
Max speed   115.5mph
0–60mph   9.1sec
Standing ¼-mile   17.1sec

356

Porsche 356
(Stuttgart-built Pre-A)
1950–54
ENGINE
Four-cylinder horizontally opposed, air-cooled;
rear-mounted
Bore x stroke   73.5mm x 64.0mm
Capacity   1,086cc
Valve actuation   pushrod ohv
Compression ratio 7:1
Induction   Twin Solex 32 PBI
Power   40bhp at 4,200rpm
Maximum torque   52lb ft at 2,800rpm

1.3-litre (from 1951)
As 1.1-litre except:
Bore x stroke   80.0mm x 64.0mm
Capacity   1,286cc
Compression ratio 6.5:1
Power   44bhp at 4,200rpm
Maximum torque   60lb ft at 2,800rpm

1500 (1952)
As 1.3-litre except:
Bore x stroke   80.0mm x 74.0mm
Capacity   1,488cc
Compression ratio 7:1
Induction   Twin Solex 40 PBIC (1953–
                   55: Twin Solex 32 PBI)
Power   60bhp at 5,000rpm (1953–
                   55: 55bhp at
                   4,200rpm)
Maximum torque   75lb ft at 3,000rpm (1953–
                   55: 78lb ft at 2,800rpm)

1500 Super (1953–55)
As 1500 except:
Compression ratio 8.2:1
Induction   Twin Solex 40 PBIC
Power   70bhp at 5,000rpm
Maximum torque   80lb ft at 3,600rpm

1300 Super (1954–55)
As 1.3-litre except:
Bore x stroke   74.5mm x 74.0mm
Capacity   1,290cc
Compression ratio 8.2:1
Induction   1955: Twin Solex 32 PBIC or
                   40PBIC
Power   60bhp at 5,500rpm
Maximum torque   65lb ft at 3,600rpm

BRAKES
Hydraulic; light-alloy drums with cast-iron inserts
Front: Drum (11in), twin-leading-shoe
Rear: Drum (11in)
Earliest models have 9in drums all round
No servo

PERFORMANCE
(Source: The Autocar*)*
(1500 Coupé)
Max speed   87mph
0–60mph   17.0sec
Standing ¼-mile   20.1sec
Figures for other models can be found but are
not regarded as reliable

Porsche 356A
1956–59
As earlier 356s except:
ENGINE
1300 (1956–57)
Bore x stroke   74.5mm x 74.0mm
Capacity   1,290cc
Compression ratio 6.5:1
Power   44bhp at 4,200rpm
Maximum torque   60lb ft at 2,800rpm

1300 Super (1956–57)
As 1300 except:
Compression ratio 7.5:1
Power   60bhp at 5,500rpm
Maximum torque   65lb ft at 3,600rpm

1600
As 1300 except:
Bore x stroke   82.5mm x 74.0mm
Capacity   1,582cc

Compression ratio 7.5:1
Power   60bhp at 4,500rpm
Maximum torque   81lb ft at 2,800rpm

1600 Super
As 1600 except:
Compression ratio 8.5:1
Induction   Twin Solex 40 PBIC (1958–
                   59: Zenith 32 NDIX)
Power   75bhp at 5,000rpm
Maximum torque   86lb ft at 3,700rpm

1500 GS Carrera (1956–58)
As 1600 except:
Porsche Type 547 engine with aluminium blocks
and heads, crankshaft roller bearings, dry sump –
all-new, designed in-house by Dr Ernst Fuhrmann
Bore x stroke   85.0mm x 66.0mm
Capacity   1,498cc
Valve actuation   dohc per bank
Compression ratio 9.0:1
Induction   Twin Solex 40 PII
Power   100bhp at 6,200rpm
Maximum torque   88lb ft at 5,200rpm

1500 GS Carrera GT (1957–58)
As 1956–57 GS Carrera except:
Induction   Twin Solex 40 PII-4
Power   110bhp at 6,400rpm
Maximum torque   91lb ft at 5,200rpm

PERFORMANCE
(Source: Porsche)
1600 Coupé/1500 GS Carrera GT Coupé
Max speed   99mph/124mph
0–62mph   16.5sec/11.0sec

Porsche 356B
1959–63
As 356A except:
1962 Super 75
ENGINE
Four-cylinder horizontally-opposed, air-cooled;
rear-mounted
Bore x stroke   82.5mm x 74.0mm
Capacity   1,582cc
Valve actuation   Pushrod
Compression ratio 8.5:1
Induction   Twin Zenith 32 NDIX double-
                   choke downdraught
Power   75bhp at 5,000rpm*
Maximum torque   Not quoted
*Also available in standard (60bhp) and
Super 90 (90bhp) form

BRAKES

As 356A except for new cooling fins; a few late 356Bs had 356C disc brakes

PERFORMANCE

(Source: The Motor)

Max speed	106.6mph
0–60mph	13.5sec
Standing ¼-mile	18.8sec

Porsche 356C 1600/1600SC
1964–65

As 356B except:

ENGINE

Power	75bhp at 5,200rpm/
	95bhp at 5,800rpm
Maximum torque	91lb ft at 3,600rpm/
	91lb ft at 4,200rpm

The 1600SC had aluminium cylinders with a ferrous coating

BRAKES

Front: 10.8in discs
Rear: 11.2in discs

PERFORMANCE

(Source: Porsche/Motor)

Max speed	108.5mph/
	112.5mph
0–62mph	14.0sec/13.2sec
Standing ¼-mile	18.8sec/18.7sec

Boxster

Porsche Boxster 2.5/2.7/S
1996–2002
ENGINE

Six-cylinder horizontally opposed, alloy heads and blocks, water-cooled; mid-mounted

Bore x stroke	85.5mm x 72.0mm
	85.5mm x 78.0mm
	93.0mm x 78.0mm
Capacity	2,480cc/2,687cc/3,179cc
Valve actuation	Variable timing, dohc per bank, four valves per cylinder
Compression ratio	11.0:1/10.8:1
Induction	Bosch Motronic
Power	204bhp at 6,000rpm
	220bhp at 6,400rpm
	252bhp at 6,250rpm
Maximum torque	181lb ft at 4,500rpm
	192lb ft at 4,750rpm
	225lb ft at 4,500rpm

BRAKES

Front: Disc, ventilated (11.7in on 2.5/2.7 and cross-drilled 12.5in on S)
Rear: Disc, ventilated (11.5in on 2.5/2.7 and cross-drilled 11.8in on S)
Four-pot callipers; ABS; servo assistance

PERFORMANCE

(Source: Autocar)

Max speed	139mph
	(136mph Tiptronic)/
	149mph/161mph
0–60mph	6.5sec (7.3sec Tiptronic)/
	6.4sec/6.0sec
Standing ¼-mile	15.6sec
	(15.5sec Tiptronic)/
	14.9sec/14.3sec

Porsche Boxster/Boxster S
2002–2005

As 1999 2.7 except:

ENGINE

Compression ratio	11.0:1
Power	228bhp at 6,300rpm
	260bhp at 6,200rpm
	236bhp at 6,400rpm*
	266bhp at 6,200rpm*
Maximum torque	192lb ft at 4,700rpm
	229lb ft at 4,600rpm
	199lb ft at 4,700–
	6,000rpm*
	229lb ft at 4,600rpm*

* From late 2003

PERFORMANCE

(228bhp Boxster/260bhp Boxster S):
(Source: Autocar/Porsche)

Max speed	155mph/164mph (165mph with 266bhp)
0–60mph/0–62mph	6.3sec/5.7sec
Standing ¼-mile	14.8sec/not quoted